Created and Directed by Hans Höfer

200

INSIGHT GUIDES

Vancouver

Edited by John Wilcock
Photography by Stuart Dee
Managing Editor: Martha Ellen Zenfell

Editorial Director: Brian Bell

HOUGHTON MIFFLIN COMPANY

APA PUBLICATIONS

Vancouver

First Edition (Reprint)
© **1993 APA PUBLICATIONS (HK) LTD**
All Rights Reserved
Printed in Singapore by Höfer Press Pte. Ltd

Distributed in the United States by:	Distributed in Canada by:	Distributed in the UK & Ireland by:	Worldwide distribution enquiries:
Houghton Mifflin Company	**Thomas Allen & Son**	**GeoCenter International UK Ltd**	**Höfer Communications Pte Ltd**
2 Park Street	390 Steelcase Road East	The Viables Center, Harrow Way	38 Joo Koon Road
Boston, Massachusetts 02108	Markham, Ontario L3R 1G2	Basingstoke, Hampshire RG22 4BJ	Singapore 2262
ISSN: 1064-7929	ISSN: 1064-7929		
ISBN: 0-395-65990-6	ISBN: 0-395-65990-6	ISBN: 9-62421-167-1	ISBN: 9-62421-167-1

ABOUT THIS BOOK

Like its coastal counterparts south of the Canadian/US border, Vancouver is one of the last stops on the continent for West-bound adventurers. "Without seeming to try very hard, [it] lures people from all over the world because it has beauty, thrust and vitality," writes Seattle columnist Emmet Watson, an ardent admirer of this city that, he says, "thrives on life's juices."

Vancouver's unusual blend of raw pioneer spirit and Pacific Rim sophistication proved enough to lure Apa Publications into adding the city to its expanding list of Insight Guide destinations. With more than 160 titles spanning the globe, and a formula that combines frank writing with bold photojournalism, the Insight series has the scope to do justice to Vancouver's energetic urbanity as well as the surrounding scenic splendour.

The books also rely heavily on teamwork, and the expert team that assembled this guide seems to bear out the truth of Watson's words: they were drawn to Vancouver from all over. This provides evidence for the theory shared by many travel editors that, to write about a place with true insight, it's better to have come first from somewhere else.

Putting The Pieces Together

Fittingly perhaps, project editor **John Wilcock** long ago mastered transatlantic spelling by exchanging a Fleet Street reporter's job in Britain for one on Toronto's *Saturday Night* magazine and then moving south to work on the travel desk of the *New York Times*. His 14 books cover something like 30 countries, and he now lives (much of the time, anyway) in Los Angeles, from which he edited *Insight CityGuide: Los Angeles.*

"Apart from the magnificent harbour," Wilcock says, "the thing I notice most about Vancouver is the inevitable rain. But when I started work on this book I came to appreciate how important rain is to an understanding of the place. I abhor rain and, like everyone else, love those mountains, but can you have one without the other?"

Inclement weather is something **Martha Ellen Zenfell**, editor-in-chief of Apa's North American books, knows about. A native of the American south who now works in Apa's often rain-shrouded London editorial office, Zenfell steered Wilcock through the pitfalls and pleasures of putting together an Insight guide. One of her first tasks was to hire photographer **Stuart Dee**, and, later, to sift through countless slides to put together the visual look of the book. Dee, who specialises in travel, people and location photography, spends four months each year working abroad, so a chance "to shoot my home town was a welcome assignment." He worked in all areas and, yes, all weathers, from blazing sun to freezing temperatures, to produce the year-round visual portrait presented on these pages.

Stanley Young also has an English connection, having been born in London before moving to Los Angeles and co-writing the history sections of *Insight CityGuide: Los Angeles.* Young continued his exploration of the origins of the West Coast by writing the history chapters of this book as well as researching the pictures that accompany it.

Scottish-born contributor **Melanie Chandler** (who wrote the "Water on My Mind" chapter) has an explanation for her attachment to Vancouver's moody mists. "Water is like the blues," she suggests. "In the form of

Wilcock

Zenfell

Dee

Young

ocean or rain, its moods externalise your own, so you are left feeling peaceful. Maybe this is why to other Canadians Vancouverites seem so irritatingly laid back."

For preference, Montreal-born **Michel Beaudry** ("The Vancouver Character") would choose snow, having been a champion skier and a member of the country's National Telemark Team. An editor of various sports magazines, he once won a silver medal as a swimmer at the Canada Games, and also carried off an award as "athlete of the year".

Another fan of the outdoors is **Dan Hilborn** ("Spirit of the Forest"), a writer for the publication *Burnaby Now,* who was born at Nelson, BC, in the Kootenay region of the Rocky Mountains. Growing up in the forest-covered district of Port Moody, he spent his youthful summers exploring old logging roads and digging around in abandoned camps.

Toronto-born **Annie Boulanger**, who claims to enjoy meeting both people and deadlines, wrote the essay on the Pacific Rim as well as "Way Out West", a piece she felt supremely equipped to handle because of her own offbeat career. "I love Vancouver," she says, "because it accepts everybody, no matter how different or weird." This willingness to tolerate the unusual has excellent financial, as well as social, advantages. Read all about it in the essay "Hollywood Northwest", written by **Angela Murrills**.

Author and poet **Sue Nevill** ("West Side Story"), was born in England but has lived for 30 years on and off in Vancouver, which she describes as a city that meets at least "three quarters of her emotional, intellectual and physical needs." **Dianne McGuire** ("An Artist's Life"), was raised in Jamaica, and lived in three countries before returning "home" to Vancouver, while Saskatchewan-born **Alex Gabrie**l headed west after completing her journalism training in Calgary, Alberta. Given to wandering in the nearby mountains, Gabriel was the perfect person to write the chapters on the grandeur of the landscape that surrounds the city.

The city is something **Chuck Davis,** local writer and broadcaster, knows all about, having written several books on the subject. He shares his personal view and favourite places on pages 78–81.

W. Ruth Kozak ("Travel Tips") says her love affair with Vancouver began at 13 after a long, cross-country journey across Canada, a trip that inspired her to write about the early pioneers. "I love the accessibility to the forest and the sea, as well as the city's multiculturalism," she says. Beginning as a copy girl at the *Vancouver Sun*, Kozak became a news librarian and later used her research skills to start work on a historical novel.

Credit Where It's Due

In Vancouver, **Laurel Yates** helped with research, transportation and editing. In Victoria, the **Empress Hotel** offered genteel hospitality to both the editor and the photographer of this book, while, high up in the mountains, the **Chateau Whistler** did the same, ensuring that our photographic coverage of the Canadian Northwest was as comprehensive as possible. **J. Kingston Pierce** commuted and contributed from Seattle.

Across the sea in Insight Guides' London editorial office, **Jill Anderson** attacked hundreds of scrawled red-pencil marks and turned them into readable corrections on her Macintosh computer. **Carole Mansur** proofread the final manuscript and indexed the book.

Boulanger   *Nevill*   *Gabriel*   *Kozak*

History

Features

Places

Maps

TRAVEL TIPS

Compiled by W. Ruth Kozak

**For detailed information
see page 217**

A City Poised for Success

Vancouver, squeezed between Burrard Inlet and False Creek, bordered on the east by the sharp-shouldered Cascade Mountains, and positioned about as far west as you can go in southern (i.e., urban) Canada without having to don a wetsuit, has always seemed to be poised just on the sharp edge of success. It's a linguistic irony that the city's original centre, the historic district now called Gastown, was known by the native Indian population as *Luck-Lucky*. Luck had much to do with Vancouver's very existence, if not its present fortunes.

Despite explorer George Vancouver's exclamation, on his initial visit in 1792, that this area required only the trappings of civilisation "to render it the most lovely country that can be imagined," early settlers had little use for it. Even the British naval authorities preferred to create an anchorage to the south at New Westminster, the town that in 1859 was named as capital of the new British Columbia colony. When a decade later the capital shifted across the Georgia Strait to Victoria, on Vancouver Island, most of the colony's population, not to mention its prestige and trade, went packing with it. In fact, had it not been for the fiscal shrewdness of the Canadian Pacific Railway, which in the 1880s selected Burrard Inlet over Victoria as its western terminus, there might never have been a Vancouver at all; certainly not the prosperous city it subsequently became. (Of course, the fact that CPR owned most of the land that now forms the city's downtown undoubtedly encouraged their decision.)

The railroad brought money here. It also invited some famous tourists. British author Rudyard Kipling, seduced by the area's natural beauty, proclaimed in his *Letters of Travel* that "such a land is good for an energetic man," and added, "It is also not so bad for the loafer." Even the Queen Mother, during her first excursion to Vancouver in 1939, described this city as "the place to live".

Nobody has ever questioned its natural beauty. "A clean, prosperous, lively city in the most magnificent natural setting," raved London's *Sunday Times*. "Once a setting in search of a city [that] has blossomed into one of the most attractive places in North America," opined *Saturday Night* magazine. "A city that turns on life's juices... [with] beauty, thrust, vitality," wrote Seattle columnist Emmett Watson.

Of course, it wouldn't be fair not to mention the rain. The natives are used to it – *Rain As a Way of Life* was the title of a widely quoted essay – and some even claim they can distinguish between the different kinds. One local guide defined showers as "the original Vancouver euphemism used by forecasters to mean anything from light cloudbursts to torrential downpours." What they have in common, usually, is that they last a long time.

Once you get used to the showers, though, they don't seem so bad and if you're well prepared, a rainstorm can even be fun if only to see the greyness punctuated by brightly coloured plastic coats, umbrellas and scarves that bloom all around. And if one colour really predominates in the environs of this lovely city, it's green. All because of the rain.

In an unusual turnabout, US city planners from south of the border have come north to see what they can learn from Canada. A recent delegation from nearby Seattle, for example, found themselves impressed by the night-time vitality of Vancouver's Robson Street. This was made possible, it was explained, by the Canadian city's penchant for high-density housing – much of it discreetly sighted and attractively designed – in the downtown area itself.

Vancouver's growth has astonished everyone, not least its own citizens. The air here literally vibrates with the clatter-bang of accelerated construction. Even critics in Washington State – where Vancouver was long thought to be a rather loopy neighbour, one that must be tolerated, if not exactly embraced – have lately been lumping plaudits on this city for its sane development.

Sane? That's the way outsiders talk, anyway. Locally, the outlook is rather more cautious. So quickly and thickly is Vancouver's skyline filling out that the local press now regularly wrings its hands over whether city administrators can encourage growth and, at the same time, preserve some character of the older, more architecturally diverse, less Americanised metropolis that Vancouver used to be.

It may now be the third largest city in Canada (after Montreal and Toronto), but Vancouver still sounds like an outpost on some brighter frontier. "The best thing about downtown Vancouver is that you can catch a glimpse of freedom at the end of the street," wrote Allan Fotheringham, a former columnist for the *Vancouver Sun.* "Stand at Georgia and Burrard [streets], or Georgia and Granville, and there, at the end of the canyon, is a slice of blue water and green mountain. It's the tiny visual escape-hatch that Toronto or New York would trade a pack of skyscrapers for; a touch of soothing sanity for asphalt-bound office-workers. It's evidence that out there somewhere, beyond the IBM machines and inter-office memos and diesel buses, there is a better piece of living."

"The city hasn't decided what it wants to be when it grows up," concluded local social critic Sean Rossiter. "Think of this beautiful town as raw talent."

Right, sliding smoothly into the future.

Like Columbus three centuries before them, the first Europeans to sail into Canada's Gulf of Georgia flew the flag of Spain and were looking for a northwest passage to the Orient. Under the command of Captain José Maria Narvaez, the crew of the *Santa Saturnina* charted the area in 1791 and named its principal headlands. The following year, two more Spanish ships, continuing the work of exploration, crossed paths with the *Discovery* and *Chatham*, ships of the British Navy under the command of Captain George Vancouver. The 35-year-old Vancouver, a veteran explorer who had accompanied Captain Cook to the South Pacific, had just finished charting a large sound to the south, which he had named "Puget" in honour of one of his fellow naval officers.

Fearing treacherous waters, Vancouver chose to explore this more northerly "Gulph" in a longboat and just past First Narrows came across the inhabitants of the village of Whoi-Whoi. "These good people," he wrote of the Squamish Indians, "finding we were inclined to make some return for their hospitality, showed much understanding in preferring iron to copper" and had an "ardent desire for commercial transactions." Vancouver named the long inlet "Burrard", after yet another of his navy colleagues, and proceeded up the coast.

For nearly 70 years after Vancouver and the Spaniards first charted their waters, the indigenous people continued to live as they had for centuries. Ancestors of the Eskimo, they were descendants of Mongolian tribes who crossed the Bering Strait in antediluvian times and gradually spread down the coast living with the rhythms of the ocean.

Indian ancestors: There were an estimated 20,000 native peoples living along the shores of Burrard Inlet, for the sea was their source of the salmon. We know they also enjoyed clambakes in their cedar plank longhouses because many of their villages, including

Whoi-Whoi, were built on a moraine of mollusc shells up to 5 metres (15 ft) deep. In fact, the first road around Stanley Park was surfaced with some of these shells.

We know more, perhaps, about the Squamish, Kwakiutl and other peoples of the area thanks to the writings of Franz Boas, who for over 50 years lived with his subjects and wrote a series of ethnographic studies of the area that now serve as the basis of anthropology. The Indians of this part of the West Coast are noted for their distinctive artistic designs, including elaborate wood carving. While most visitors equate this skill with the prominent totem poles, their masks, canoes and many other artefacts bear the same identifiable style and the unique graphic sensibility seen nowhere else on the continent.

Much of this elaborate artwork was devoted to the wealth of ceremonial crests and costumes that were so much a part of their intricate organisation of social ranking. At the bottom were slaves: women stolen in raids on villages to the south and enemy warriors who were hamstrung to prevent their escape. The social zenith was occupied by the wealthiest individuals whose position was assured through the unique "potlatch", a ceremony as unique as their artwork. Potlatch guests were feted royally on shellfish, smelt, sturgeon and smoked salmon, with much dancing, drumming and singing.

The high point of the celebration was the presentation to the guests, depending on their status, of canoes, carved chests, slaves or, at the other end of the social scale, small strips of blanket to commemorate their attendance. A careful account of all exchanges was kept by paid witnesses so that the giver could be paid back with interest at an agreed-upon time. Sometimes the increase in value was as much as 100 percent.

Failure to reciprocate was taboo. If a man died, credit or debit fell on his heirs. Reasons for holding a potlatch varied from celebrating experiences as important as marriage, to events seemingly as trivial as the first time a baby's hair was accidentally singed. Saving

Preceding pages: the *Beaver*, first West Coast vessel to trade for furs. <u>Left</u>, Haida totem pole.

face was often a crucial motive for a potlatch, for example when a man fell into the water in full public view. Tribal artisans vied with each other to produce the finest canoes, the brightest blankets, the most elaborate songs and dances. Eventually, the potlatch was banned by the British after most of the local tribes had been granted reservations and, in many cases, hunting and fishing rights.

Attraction of furs: It was the fur trade, not the Indians' cultural life, that drew the first Europeans to the area. Simon Fraser, whose name was given to the major river of what is now the Greater Vancouver area, found the local population hostile when he arrived by

canoe in 1808 to search for new fur-trade routes, although he quickly adopted their custom of carrying tightly packed bales of dried salmon for sustenance on his lengthy journeys. The Russians were also wandering down the coast in search of the prized sea-otter pelts, competing with enterprising Yankee skippers sailing out of Boston trading pelts for rum and ironware. It was, however, the impassive and redoubtable Hudson's Bay Company that came to dominate the fur trade on the West Coast.

In 1827 the HBC established Fort Langley, 49 km (30 miles) from the coast on the Fraser River, as their outpost in the area. Eight years later the company was running the pioneer steamship on the West Coast, the *SS Beaver*, a smoke-belching paddle-wheeler whose purpose, as one HBC official put it, was as much to "overawe the natives" as it was to beat the competition to the furs. American captains in their four-masters watched helplessly at sea as the *Beaver* easily headed into the wind to make the first bid in a village's supply of pelts. The *Beaver* was *the* symbol of the ubiquitous Hudson's Bay Company on the West Coast for over half a century, until the good ship went aground off Prospect Point in what is now Stanley Park.

The clerks and factors who oversaw the HBC's operations in out-of-the way forts might easily have been mistaken for fastidious law clerks straight out of a Dickens novel set in London. Not so the fur traders who moved among the Indians.

A mixed bunch of mountain men, adventurers and scallywags, these first European residents of the Northwest were "the very scum of the earth," according to the dour Sir George Simpson, who was sent out to reorganise the company's Northwest division in the 1820s. "They are," he declared, "the most unruly and troublesome gang to deal with in this, or perhaps any other part of the world." These colourful fur traders developed the trading jargon known as "Chinook" to the Northwest and introduced the pleasures of rum to the local populations. British Columbia was, as one historian pointed out, little more than a "savage fur farm".

The discovery of gold on the banks of the Fraser River in 1858 brought a new band of adventurers to the area. Within a year 25,000 miners had arrived on the mainland, and the Hudson's Bay Company, the only form of authority in the wilderness, lost no time in extracting as much as possible from the gold seekers. James Douglas, the local Chief Factor, or superintendent, of the HBC and governor of Vancouver Island, established monthly land fees and set up a monopoly on mining supplies for miners. Unwilling to lose these potential revenues on the mainland to the Hudson's Bay Company, the British Parliament created the crown colony of British Columbia and extended Douglas's control to the vast area of land from the coast to the highest peaks of the Rocky Mountains.

"He turned parsimony into an art form," said one historian of Douglas, the offspring born out of wedlock to a Glasgow merchant and a black freewoman from Barbados. Raised in Scotland, Douglas was an able apprentice in the fur-trading business at the age of 17 and moved steadily through the ranks of the Hudson's Bay Company. Married to a "mixed breed" wife, as the nomenclature then went, Douglas was fully able to deal with the cultural subtleties of the indigenous peoples. The whites of the area were less enamoured of his governing abilities.

River – to protect the colony against an American invasion. Besides naming Lulu Island after a comely lass in a dancing troupe sent to entertain the British soldiers, Moody also persuaded a private company to cut a road due north to the shores of the Burrard Inlet. Within two winters his foresight paid off when the Fraser froze over and freight had to be hauled down this "North Road" from the ice-free Burrard Inlet.

Call of the Cariboo: Later that same year rumours of highly concentrated deposits of gold came out of the Cariboo Country, far in the British Columbia interior. After J. C. Bryant washed out eight pounds of gold from

"The Governor is a wonderfully clever man among the Indians," said one visiting Royal Navy officer, "but he does not seem to be governing a white population at all."

As part of the new colony's development, a team of 25 sappers under Colonel Richard Moody arrived in British Columbia from England in 1858 and set about surveying what would later become Greater Vancouver. He laid out the limits of the town of New Westminster on the north bank of the Fraser

Left, Europeans and Indians trade for furs. **Above**, miners of the Cariboo gold rush, 1858.

a single pan, miners left the played-out Fraser River deposits and headed north, along with another rush of reckless gold seekers from all corners of the world. The timing was perfect for the California "49ers" who by then were coming up empty. "Hundreds too impatient to wait for the steamers mounted horses," wrote historian H. H. Bancroft. "In May, June and July, 23,000 persons went from San Francisco by sea and about 8,000 overland."

Few were successful. One such unlucky Englishman, John Morton, spotted a chunk of coal in a window in New Westminster. Having worked as a potter in his Yorkshire home, Morton knew that coal often lay mixed with clay, so he hired a Squamish guide in the summer of 1862 to take him by canoe around what is now Stanley Park and Coal Harbour. He found his coal, but it was embedded in sandstone, not clay. His hopes were dashed for a pottery, but his canoe trip filled him with admiration for this small section of British Columbia. He convinced two of his prospecting countrymen, Sam Brighouse and William Hailstone, to "squat" on land that would later become Vancouver.

The "three greenhorns", taken for fools by their gold-panning colleagues, chose lot 185 – some 225 hectares (550 acres) – cleared a

1911, "and when they learned to use it they were overjoyed. In return for the privilege of using it, the grateful natives kept the shack well supplied with fish and *mowich* – deer, elk or any wild animal suitable for eating."

When, in 1884, the Canadian Pacific Railway began negotiating with the colony regarding a site for their terminal, the three greenhorns donated part of their parcel toward the venture. But they held on to the greater part, expecting a boom, and called the West End "Liverpool City". Two were rewarded handsomely for their foresight, but as an old man John Morton was living on Denman Street, his house representing the

small patch of land and constructed a shack on a bluff overlooking the inlet (just west of the present site of the Marine Building) in the winter of 1863. Their first task was to cut a trail south to False Creek which would link up with the military trail to New Westminster, a task that entailed hacking their way through more than a mile of freezing and intimidating rainforest.

The three pioneers then built a brickyard and planted a vegetable garden, but it was their grindstone that proved to be their gold mine: "The Indians had never seen [one]," said a historian who interviewed Morton in

tiniest piece of the original land he and his mates acquired. Far from being embittered by the vagaries of fortune, Morton was full of life and humour. "Ay, lad, ay, I had [a lot of land]," said the old pioneer to an interviewer. "Then I fell among forty thieves… "

Birth of Gastown: Another refugee of the Cariboo gold rush was John "Gassy Jack" Deighton who arrived at Burrard Inlet on 29 September 1867 with his Indian wife and mother-in-law, a yellow dog, two chairs, two chickens, a barrel of whisky and $6 in cash. Deighton embodied the entrepreneurial spirit rampant at the time.

By the mid-1860s, the entire shore was covered with forests of fir and cedar – the Indians called it *Luck-Lucky*, meaning grove of beautiful trees, and apart from a trading-post run by Portuguese Joe the only other business was Captain Edward Stamp's Hastings Mill, started earlier that same year. A good hand-logger could earn as much as $1,000 a month, and with the nearest tavern miles away, Deighton was in the right place at the right time.

Across the inlet was Sewell P. Moody's Pioneer Mill which had gone up on the north shore in 1865 and which soon was to be known as Moodyville. There were still only

Deighton House Hotel, its owner by then nicknamed Gassy Jack because of his lengthy monologues, was a thriving success. A Yorkshireman with the gift of the gab, Deighton set up his dispensary close enough to the nearby mill so that the workers could stop by, but far enough away so that the lumber company had no say in the matter.

Its precise location was in the heart of "Gastown" where, today, Water and Carrall streets meet. Jack wrote to his brother Tom in England: "I can assure you it was a lonesome place when I came here first. Surrounded by Indians, I dare not look outdoors after dark. There was a friend of mine, about a mile

nine buildings grouped in a crescent along the shore when the Royal Engineers surveyed the townsite of Granville in 1870, but the nearby sawmill provided plenty of customers if only because its owner banned liquor on the premises.

After he discovered that the nearest saloon was about half a day's walk away in New Westminster, Gassy Jack built his own within 24 hours of his arrival. The subsequent

Left, city officials met in a tent after Vancouver was destroyed by fire, 1886. **Above**, first trans-continental train, 24 May 1887.

distant, found with his head cut in two." Gassy Jack survived and Gastown was registered as the Granville Townsite. Eleven years later the first census of the future city of Vancouver revealed a thriving population of 44 loggers, 31 millworkers, four butchers, two shoemakers, two ministers, one school teacher, one wine seller and a policeman.

Trans-continental railway: But it was two thin strips of steel – the Canadian Pacific Railway – that would change the fate of Gassy Jack's Granville forever. British Columbia's entry into Canadian confederation in 1871 had been conditional upon completion of this trans-continental lifeline, and six years later Prime Minister Mackenzie announced plans for the construction of the last section along the Fraser River Valley. Unknown as yet, however, was the exact location of the railroad's terminus, the pot at the end of this steel rainbow.

Speculators chose Port Moody at the head of Burrard Inlet as the terminus, but William Van Horne, general manager for the CPR, preferred the deeper waters around the Granville townsite. After receiving a settlement from the government that included most of the acreage that bordered the waterfront there, Van Horne decided that Granville

simply was not a fitting name for Canada's next major metropolis. "This is destined to be a great city in Canada," goes his apocryphal remark to a CPR surveyor. "We must see that it has a name that will designate its place on the map. Vancouver it shall be, if I have the ultimate decision."

Royal approval: Van Horne, as one of the most powerful men in the county, had his way, and after the city of Vancouver was given royal assent, on 6 April 1886, the land rush was on. Within a month 500 buildings had been constructed and the first city elections were held. (Indians, Orientals, lunatics

and women were not allowed to vote.) The city councillors' first resolution was to safeguard the vast military reserve to the west of the new city, and Stanley Park was born.

Two-man saws cut down the hemlocks and firs – some as much as 2.5 metres (8 ft) in diameter – of the primeval forest that covered the new city. Teams of oxen pulled out the stumps to clear the new streets, and the brush was burned. One such fire got out of hand on 13 June 1886 and, although the conflagration lasted less than an hour, 20 people died and every building in Vancouver burned to the ground. But there was no holding back the energy of its inhabitants, for within a day the City Council was meeting in a tent, and hotels were selling liquor before their roofs had been put on.

By the end of the year, the young city was handsomely rebuilt, with 23 hotels, nine saloons, one church, and more than 8,000 pioneering souls who called Vancouver their home. When the first CPR train trundled into its new terminus on the eve of Queen Victoria's birthday, 23 May 1887, in the jubilee year of her coronation, Vancouver's future as the Canadian commercial centre on the West Coast was assured.

Since the city is set amidst some of the largest and sturdiest trees in the world, lumber was bound to become its major industry. Ever since the founding of New Westminster to the south, it was obvious that the evergreen forests of the peninsula would supply wood for the world. The first sawmill, established in 1862 in what is now North Vancouver, exported lumber to Australia.

By the 1880s Hastings Mill, the sawmill on the Vancouver side of Burrard Inlet, was exporting millions of "Vancouver Toothpicks" (knotless timbers 1 metre/3 ft square and 18 metres/60 ft long) worldwide. Churches and buildings around the world sported impeccable beams from the Vancouver environs, and many a clipper ship of the day carried masts and spars hewn from these primeval forests of the Vancouver area by lumberjacks and millworkers who received $1.25 for a 10-hour working day.

Left, a new dance craze hits the city. **Right**, law and order in a frontier town.

A year to the day after Vancouver's disastrous fire, in 1887, the *Abyssinia,* a CPR-chartered passenger ship from Yokohama, was the first to dock in Vancouver's new deep-water port. She carried 22 first-class passengers, a cargo of mail, tea and silk, and 80 Chinese in steerage.

In Vancouver, the products from far-off Cathay were clearly more valued than the people from those far-off shores. Tens of thousands of Chinese, most poor bachelors from Hong Kong, were already in British Columbia, having arrived to build the railroads there for a dollar a day. Once the railroad was finished the "Celestials" competed with the European immigrants for jobs at every millsite, cannery and mine in the province – and they worked for less money.

Gold Mountain: In China the news was widespread about "Gold Mountain" which is what some called Vancouver; how if you came without your family, worked hard clearing the stumps from the land, slaved night and day in the mines, helped to build the railways – how, if you endured all this without complaints, a better life was possible than could ever be found back home.

"My father worked all his life here and when I was four years old he moved back to China and bought land in Canton," recalled Sing Fung who owned a store on Pender Street. "But when the Communists took over he lost everything. I came back to Canada, I worked hard every day – 10 days a week at least. I don't work eight hours a day, I work 16, seven days a week, maybe that's more than 10 days. If you don't work that hard you'll never make anything. But in Canada, if you make it you keep it."

There had already been anti-Chinese riots in 1887 where marauding settlers razed Chinese camps on False Creek and Coal Harbour; Chinese men were tied together by their pigtails and beaten publicly, their shacks

Preceding pages: Haida Indians, *circa* **1910. Left,** the Canadian Pacific Railway linked Vancouver to the rest of Canada.

and tents were burned. In September of that same year the Asiatic Exclusion League demonstrated against the arrival of the *SS Monteagle*: "900 Hindus, 1,100 Chinamen and a bunch of Japs" read the pierside sign which welcomed the ship. Within a month, a general economic boycott, organised by local businessmen, went into effect against firms that traded with the Chinese. Stores which insisted on dealing with the "Asiatic hordes" had black crosses painted on the pavement in front of their doors.

The anti-Chinese sentiment became a fixture of the young province and its largest city: from 1878 to 1913, more than two dozen anti-Chinese statutes were passed in British Columbia and, as late as 1907, as many as 30,000 people showed up on the Cambie Street grounds in Vancouver to cheer the speakers at a parade held by the Asiatic Exclusion League.

Still, Vancouver's Chinatown managed to become well established. Sun-Yat-Sen found sanctuary in the Chinese Freemasons building at One West Pender for a time before returning home in 1911 to establish the modern state of China. Many buildings housed secret gaming rooms where "chuck-a-luck" was played, the participants dodging the frequent police raids or shakedowns. Opium dens were commonplace, and the use of the drug was so widespread that its wholesale consumption offended the delicate sensibilities of those attending the city's first rudimentary opera house on Dupont Street.

"If the disgusting perfume of opium which always hangs in the atmosphere were removed," exhorted a newspaper reporter in 1886, "there would hardly be anything to offend the nostrils in the balmy air." Two years later the City Council passed a law requiring all persons selling or manufacturing opium to pay $500 a year. The object of the law was not so much to diminish the lucrative trade, but shift its profits from the Chinese proprietors to white druggists and chemists – who were, as it happened, exempt from the annual fee.

Vancouver, far from the sedate and live-able metropolis of the present, was in those early days a rough milltown whose hardworking inhabitants lived a rowdy existence. A federal study in 1895 showed Vancouver led the Dominion in per capita consumption of alcohol. Locals, of course, blamed the Indians. The Yukon gold rush brought a new wave of gold seekers and increased the general air of uproariousness in the city. Outfitters made a killing by selling mining aspirants the necessary 455 kg (1,000 lb) of provisions demanded by the Canadian authorities before they allowed the miners to enter the frozen goldfields. Many

not alone in making a fortune from prostitution in Vancouver, which, with its preponderance of single men, was rampant. "They say it doesn't exist," said a visiting police chief from Toronto in 1903, "but the social evil is spread all over the city."

By 1902, Vancouver had a population of 30,000. The railroad had certainly made a city out of Gassy Jack's Granville, but the relationship between the Vancouverites and the CPR was one fraught with tension. Railroad executives established their mansions in the city's West End and set a civilised tone in the rough town whose citizens bridled at the imperious attitude of this company that

of Vancouver's most flourishing businesses owe their origin to those rowdy days.

Other would-be goldminers made their fortunes in different fields of endeavour. Desire Brothier, on his way to the Yukon from Lyon, France, landed in Vancouver, took one look at the demographic imbalance and returned within the year with a shipful of shop girls. He had convinced them they could make better wages as domestics in Canada, but knowing no English, and arriving illegally, the ladies dared not protest when they discovered just what kind of houses they were expected to work in. Brothier was

owned more than half the area's real estate. "With time," wrote author Eric Nicol, "the fairy godmother (CPR) came to look less and less like the matronly goodbody and more and more like the Wicked Witch of the East."

When the notorious American bandit Bill Miner (later immortalised in the film *The Grey Fox*) was captured in 1904 at Kamloops after the first train robbery in Canada's history, the hung jury there acquitted him. "Bill Miner's not so bad," went the joke of the day. "He only robs the CPR once every two years, but the CPR robs us all every day." Miner was eventually sentenced to 25 years in a trial at New Westminster, but escaped from his Canadian jail in 1907 at the age of 67.

Since the turn of the century the world had begun to be changed by the automobile and Canada was no exception. Vancouver's first gasoline station at the corner of Smith and Cambie had been supplying cars with fuel transported from the east in barrels (much of it evaporated en route) since June 1908, and it was not much later that a Mr Annard turned his bicycle repair shop at Hastings and Columbia streets into the city's first garage. Horse-drawn tankers delivered the gasoline which retailed for 20¢ a gallon, and there was no tax to pay. Twelve years later there were

1964 that the last section of the Trans-Canada Highway (the long Port Mann Bridge across the Fraser River) was completed.

Off to war: On 4 August 1914, Britain declared war on Germany and the city fathers claimed that Vancouver sent more soldiers to France than any comparably sized city in Canada or the United States. One of the local regiments, the 72nd Canadian Infantry Battalion, Seaforth Highlanders, was particularly decorated. Far from the scene of battle, the city profited from the war. The Vancouver branch of the Red Cross rolled bandages, the Council of Women raised money to equip a hospital ship and the local lumber mer-

28,000 registered vehicles on the highways of Vancouver.

Before the decade was over, endurance runs were becoming popular. William Ball set a record in 1928, driving from Vancouver to Yreka, California, and back – a distance of around 3,000 km (2,000 miles) – in just over 52 hours, an average speed of almost 60 kph (37 mph). Motorists were soon demanding a cross-country highway but it was not until

Left, the second (of four) Capilano Suspension Bridges, *circa* 1910. **Above**, downtown Vancouver, *circa* 1930.

chants reacted favourably to an increased demand for their products, particularly Sitka spruce. Women were welcomed into the workplace during the war years and soon advanced the dual causes of suffrage and women's rights.

The opening of the Panama Canal in August 1914 also did much to brighten the young port's future. Now Vancouver could ship wheat and wood to Britain and the Continent as well as the Far East. With the journey to Liverpool cut by 5,600 sea miles, as far as a freighter was concerned, Vancouver now lay the same distance from England as the harbours of the Orient, and so began its life as a bona fide world port catering to markets other than those in the Pacific Rim countries. By now, too, Vancouver had developed many of the cultural accoutrements that make for international stature. When the city won the Stanley Cup in the 1915 national hockey championship, it came as no surprise that the team's name was the Vancouver Millionaires.

The year 1918 that marked the end of World War I also seemed to be the city's coming-of-age: movies, radios, motor cars – and an upsurge in propriety – grew by leaps and bounds. "The practice of courting in contraband rum, too. Many a dark ship made the 80-km (50-mile) voyage across the international border to the American San Juan Islands where the liquor was dropped off on lonely beaches for later retrieval.

Boom time: Vancouver was important enough for Warren G. Harding to visit in July 1923. It was the first time an American president had paid a social call to Canada, and it also proved to be Harding's last public appearance: he died of fever one week after his speech in the city. By the end of the Roaring Twenties, Vancouver was booming. Amalgamation with South Vancouver and Point Grey gave the city 79,000 addi-

automobiles in Vancouver has got to cease," reported one lady writer in a local magazine of 1920. "Inspector Hood, who is the moving spirit in the crusade, describes the habit as 'dangerous'."

When the men came home from the front, they were greeted like heroes but most found themselves unemployed. War industries, in particular shipbuilding, dwindled as a worldwide postwar depression affected Vancouver. However, the city's deep-water, ice-free harbour became a convenient port for the export of wheat, and, as four years of Canadian Prohibition came to an end, for

tional inhabitants and much more land.

Vancouver had become a city of middle-class homes, without architectural grandeur or slums like those in Montreal or Toronto. It had accomplished the incredible: turning a pre-war boom town into a 20th-century metropolis in a decade, but at a price. As a historian described it at the time: "In downtown Vancouver… the air was heavy with grime and soot as boats and trains, sawmills and flour-mills, breweries and food-processing plants, shoe factories and clothing factories belched clouds of heavy smoke. The city was now held fast in the toils of industry."

And Vancouver would also soon be held in the grip of the Depression. Following the October 1929 stock market crash, building came to a standstill, lumber sales shrank, sawmills closed, and wheat shipments declined. By December, breadlines stretched outside the City Relief Office. The unemployed streamed in from shut-down mines, logging camps and fish canneries. By the winter of 1932–33, nearly 40,000 men, women and children, about 15 percent of the city's population, were on some form of relief. To prevent the schools from closing, local teachers agreed to work the month of December 1933 without pay.

ployment insurance in Canada conditions deteriorated. In 1938, 1,500 demonstrators occupied the Art Gallery, Hotel Georgia and the main Post Office at Hastings and Granville, demanding a public works programme. The standoff lasted a month before the end came on "Bloody Sunday".

"Fleeing before a barrage of tear gas bombs and the swinging batons of city police officers," wrote a reporter for the *Vancouver News-Herald*, "a swarm of shouting, blood-spattered men... looted stores and for more than an hour created a reign of terror in the city." It is hard to imagine how unusual and traumatic public violence on such a scale is

In April 1935, 2,000 unemployed men advanced on Vancouver, demanding "work and wages". They invaded the Hudson's Bay Store, tangled with police and marched to Victory Square for a mass rally. Although Mayor Gerry McGeer addressed the crowd, demanding that it disperse, a sympathy strike by local workers and a solidarity meeting of 15,000 people urged abolition of the "slave compound" labour camps. With no unem-

for Canadians, especially outside the confines of a professional hockey rink.

As elsewhere in North America, the September 1939 outbreak of World War II in Europe brought few changes to the city. Guns were set up along the coast and the old Hotel Vancouver became first a recruiting centre, then a barracks that housed the headquarters of the army's Pacific Command. However, when the Japanese attacked Pearl Harbor in December 1941, the war came home. A nightly blackout was established and thousands of Japanese citizens were promptly removed to internment camps.

Left, the Depression hits Vancouver, 1934–39. **Above**, Japanese children are rounded up during World War II.

The treatment of the Japanese became yet another case in the litany of Vancouver's strained race relations. By the mid-1930s there were as many as 30,000 Japanese inhabitants of British Columbia. About one quarter of these people lived in Vancouver, most of them in Japantown (the blocks of Powell Street between Gore and Heatley). Most of these were *Nissei* (Canadian-born) and although there had been a "gentleman's agreement" between Canada and the Mikado in 1908 limiting Japanese emigration to 150 a year, many more had smuggled themselves into the province.

Hundreds of Japanese fought valiantly as

by the Custodian of Enemy Property; Japanese were ordered to surrender all motor vehicles, cameras and radios at Hastings Park. The newspapers were full of exceptional bargains on former Japanese property but little of what was seized was ever returned. Within three months, Japantown in Vancouver was wiped out.

Post-war growth: The memory of the hardships of the war was erased by the boom that followed it. Vancouver's population in 1941 was 275,000. Ten years later, the city alone had 345,000 and Greater Vancouver numbered over half a million. Many of these were immigrants from war-ravaged Europe, or

CITY HALL, VANCOUVER, B. C., CANADA.

Canadian troops in the war, but an article in the *Vancouver Province* on 7 April 1937 summed up the feelings of the white majority: "The old Oriental immigrant was objected to because he brought to Canada the low standard of living... of Asia and because he worked for low wages and so tended to undermine the standards of white labourers [*sic*]..."

After Pearl Harbor the fate of the Japanese was sealed: by January 1942, all Japanese males between 18 and 45 were ordered to be removed from the coast. All stock in Japanese-owned stores was seized and liquidated

Canadian servicemen who had been stationed in the area. In 1954 Vancouver made the world's headlines as the venue of the British Empire Games where, for the first time – in a famous one-mile race won by Roger Bannister – the 4-minute record was broken.

The 1950s marked a period of similar speed in the city's economic growth, much of which centred about Vancouver's position as a major port. During the 1960s First Narrows was dredged to a depth of 15 metres (50 ft) to allow for the new bulk carriers, and in 1970 a causeway was opened to export

Canadian coal (from the Crowsnest Pass) to Japan. John Morton's 1862 lump of coal had finally borne anthracite fruit.

The now mostly middle-class and some-what sedate city began to celebrate its gamy past. In 1970, a statue of Gassy Jack Deighton was erected in Maple Tree Square, at the intersection of Carrall and Water streets, and in 1972 Mayor Muni Evers unveiled a head-stone to commemorate the unmarked grave in which his remains had lain for 97 years.

Greenpeace: Given its glorious natural setting, it is no coincidence that Vancouver also spawned one of the most celebrated and effective environmental organisations in the

attention to issues of serious environmental abuse around the world.

Expo 86 was nothing less than a world-wide public celebration of Vancouver's beauty and importance. By this time Canada's third largest and most beautiful city, it had finally come of age. In a world suddenly turned environment-conscious, the city has become something of a landmark. Hollywood film and television producers, attracted by Canada's lower costs and its geographical proximity, have made the city a major location spot.

And in an ironic twist, the newest influx of immigrants is from Hong Kong, whose resi-

world. When 12 activist members of the Vancouver group, "Don't Make a Wave Committee", sailed their small boat out of the Strait of Georgia and into the US atomic test zone off Amchitka Alaska in 1971, Greenpeace was born. Today, although Greenpeace has branches throughout the world (its present headquarters are in Amsterdam), Vancouver will be remembered as the home of the gutsy environmentalists who continue to risk their lives and draw public

dents have chosen Vancouver as their safe haven in preparation for the annexation of their colony home by the People's Republic of China in 1997. These new immigrants, many of them millionaires, have given the imprimatur of international respectability to Vancouver, deeming it a liveable city with a secure future.

Certainly, today's Vancouver has come a long way from the rough and ready frontier town of lumber mill and gold rush days. It has managed to maintain a certain civility and self-respect which, along with its jewel-like setting, distinguish it as a city that works.

Left, the prosperous 1950s. **Above**, Greenpeace sails into world headlines via Alaska in 1971.

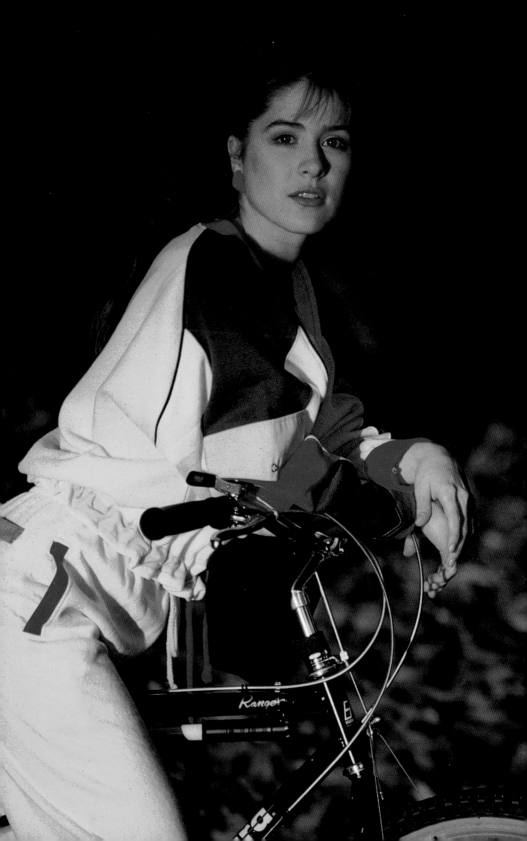

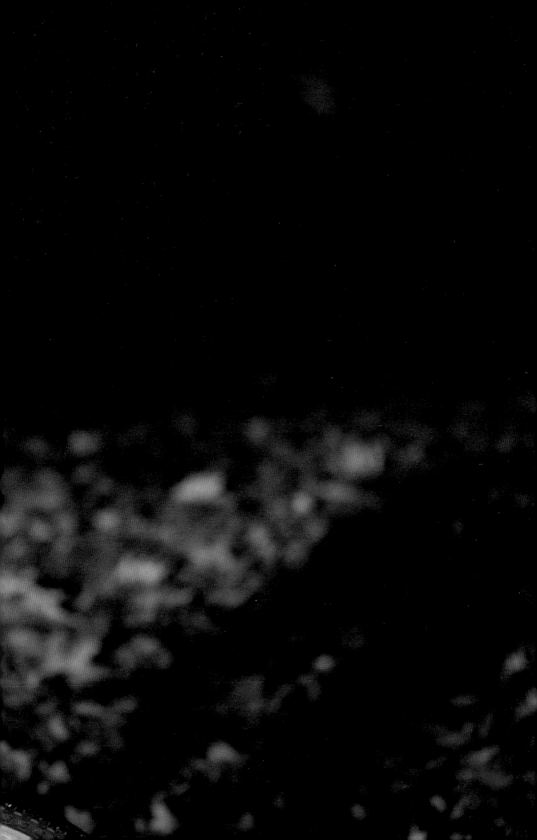

THE VANCOUVER CHARACTER

Vancouver is a young city and, in many ways, an orphan. Cut off from the rest of the country by the Western Cordillera's mountainous barricade, and blessed with a climate that is decidedly un-Canadian, this coastal port has been left to its own devices for much of its 100-year history. The natural bounty of its surroundings and its isolation from the rest of the country have combined to create an intriguing metropolitan area.

An object of desire for most urban Canadians, Vancouver has a character that reflects the still-wild flavour of the Pacific Northwest. Its coat-of-arms says it all: a logger and a fisherman hold the provincial seal over their heads above the legend "By sea, land and air we prosper." And while it still lacks something of an urban soul – the city's music and arts scene suffers when compared to Toronto's or Montreal's – its still-strong ties to its natural habitat are immediately apparent. Huge tracks of forested parkland cut wide swathes of green through prime city real estate; world-class ski-runs rise directly above terraced suburban gardens. Today's Vancouverites are among the biggest outdoor sports *aficionados* in the world.

Little more than a century ago, however, Vancouver was a frontier village, a logging backwater barely afforded a glance by the hordes of gold-maddened prospectors stampeding into the interior of the province in search of fame and fortune. In 1883 there were all of 145 registered (white) residents living here: loggers, mill hands, stevedores, fishermen and merchants. It was nothing like cosmopolitan Victoria across the Strait of Georgia or booming New Westminster up-river on the Fraser.

But already, discerning entrepreneurs were sizing up its awesome potential as a West Coast trading centre. "It is only once in a lifetime that the public have such a chance as the present," wrote a writer for the Portland-based *West Shore Magazine* in 1884, "and

we would recommend to those who have money to investigate the merits of Vancouver... before making other investments."

It has often been said that the finest trees on the entire Canadian west coast once stood in the heart of what is now downtown Vancouver. Blessed with such a seemingly inexhaustible source of wealth, few questioned the early methods of exploitation by the loggers. The land was so vast, the geography so overwhelming, that nobody imagined the

well could ever run dry. Understandably, this led to a carnage of unimaginable proportions that lasted for many years.

Natural harbour: But Vancouver was also blessed with one of the best natural harbours on the west coast – a fact that would soon lead to its rapid expansion. With the arrival of the Canadian Pacific Railway, linking the harbour to the grain belts of western Canada, Vancouver soon became an important cog in the developing Pacific trade routes while also serving as the gateway to the wild – and profitable – interior of British Columbia. Slowly the rough-hewn logging town donned

Preceding pages: Vancouver vehicle; fiddling time away. <u>Left</u> and <u>right</u>, sporting style.

a more gentrified skin. But do what it might, it could never truly lose its rowdy boom-town roots.

Casual chic: And therein lie its charms. For if Vancouverites have something of the entrepreneurial Californian in them, they also have the unabashed play ethic of the coastal Australian. The operative word in this town is casual. Cotton slacks and open-necked shirts are far more popular than suits. And being fit is simply understood. Tight muscles and a well-sunned skin are not only highly appreciated, they are *de rigueur*. You don't do lunch here, you meet for a run or a swim or a ride. Tennis, golf, skiing, scuba

diving, windsurfing, kayaking, climbing, cycling – they're all available within the city limits. In Vancouver, it's not so much what you do at the office that's important, it's what you do during your leisure time.

Eastern Canadians refer to the country's third largest metropolitan area as Lotus Land – Canada's capital of hedonism. To them, Vancouver is a sub-tropical paradise peopled by dreamers, schemers and eccentric New-Agers. Wrapped in the chill of winter, they wince every time they see news clips of Vancouverites playing tennis or golf in January. They shake their heads despairingly

when they hear Vancouverites enthuse about snowboarding or bungee jumping and sigh in exasperation when their western colleagues arrive for board meetings dressed in jeans and sandals.

It is when the drums beat loudly at night, though, when the spirit dancers weave their magic from within their longhouse on the shores of the Fraser River, that Vancouver's wild soul seems most apparent. Hidden behind the sumptuous golf courses of Vancouver's posh Point Grey district, the modest wooden homes of Musqueam village sprawl across the coarse marsh grass that lent its name to this native tribe.

But make no mistake. Despite the encroachment of modern Canadian society, the Musqueam culture is still very much alive. Hunters and gatherers still, the Musqueam are consummate watermen who look to the sea for the source of their wealth. Salmon, prawns, clams, oysters, crab: these are just some of the bounty found in the oxygen-rich waters of the Fraser estuary around the western headlands of Vancouver.

The Musqueam are only one of a handful of native bands who still inhabit their ancestral lands on the edges of the city's boundaries. Almost annihilated during the 19th century by smallpox and other European diseases, the Musqueam and Burrards, the Kwantlen and the Squamish have experienced a strong resurgence in recent years and their voices can be heard increasingly in the day-to-day affairs of modern Vancouver. The Musqueam, for example, run a successful shipbuilding firm on the Fraser River, while the North Shore Squamish control great chunks of very desirable real estate just below Lions Gate Bridge.

Of even greater promise to the bands' future, however, is the curiosity and interest shown among the young for the old ways. Once-forbidden rituals like the potlatch and the spirit dance are now practised openly. "It is a way of reinforcing our own identity," says Wendy Grant, tribal chief of the Musqueam and herself an initiated dancer. "It is a way of finding within ourselves the power to resist the wholesale destruction of our culture."

A very private ceremony, the spirit dance

is one of the most sacred rituals of the Coast Salish people. Today, it is often used by the Musqueam to reset the life course of a troubled youth or adult. Inititiates do not choose to become dancers. Rather, they are chosen by the other dancers and are often taken against their will. "It can be a very traumatic experience," says Grant of the week-long initiation which employs fasting, meditation, exercise and sweat baths to reveal an individual's personal spirit guide (usually an animal: a bear, a wolf or even an eagle). "But," she adds, "it most always turns out to be a positive experience."

Salish spirits: The cultural fabric of the

ibly on the city that was born under its spell.

"How can a resident of this region ignore an art form so obviously in tune with its environment?" asks Vincent Massey, a third-generation Vancouverite (and the grandson of actor Raymond Massey). A successful potter and a passionate outdoorsman, Massey lives in the popular alpine resort/suburb of Whistler, only 115 km (70 miles) north of Vancouver. "It is obvious from their art that the Coast Salish had a very deep kinship with their natural surroundings before the coming of the whites. For them, it wasn't a question of man against nature but of man existing within nature. Everything was in balance –

region's first people infuses the spirit of Vancouver like no other city in North America. And it is in its artistic incarnation that this native power is most accessible. An obstreperous raven or a leaping killer whale; a soaring bald eagle or a playful otter – the haunting geometric renderings of the Salish spirits carved on wood, stone and precious metal are coveted by collectors from all over America, Asia and Europe. It is a potent vision of the world that imprints itself indel-

Left and **above**, Vancouver is Canada's capital of hedonism.

everything had to be treated with respect."

In many ways, Massey embodies that balance. He grew up on the far edges of West Vancouver, in a cliffside house designed by his architect father, Geoff Massey, overlooking the Straits of Georgia. The view to the west, north and south was stupendous. Behind the house, rising in one solid wave of granite and fir, were the imposing North Shore mountains. It was an idyllic spot in which to grow up.

"The ocean was our playground," says Vincent. "Each summer my dad would pack us all in his boat and we'd take off for some destination up the coast. We'd fish and crab and dig for clams; camp on the beach and cook over big ol' driftwood fires. It was coastal adventuring at its best." In the winters, Massey Sr would lead his family into the mountains on skiing trips. "Dad wasn't into skiing the runs at the local ski hills," adds Vincent. "More often than not, he'd take us deep into the mountains for some backcountry exploring."

By the time he was a teenager, Massey was as comfortable taking an outboard engine apart as he was leading a party of skiers through a mountain blizzard. But that was only half of his education. His mother, a

between work and play. Mornings will often find him at his wheel or mixing a new batch of clay; afternoons are most often spent snowboarding at Blackcomb or mountain biking in the hills behind his house or windsurfing down on the waters of Howe Sound. And all at full-tilt boogie. "I like to have fun," he says without regret. "Both at work and at play. For me, that's what life on the coast is all about."

Massey is not alone in voicing these sentiments. Vancouverites are almost rabid in their pursuit of the good life. Which is not surprising: Vancouver's charms have always revolved around its physical attributes. The

painter, encouraged her four children to develop their artistic talents early. While his brothers were drawn to film-making and his sister took up photography, Vincent chose to work with his hands. "Pottery just felt natural to me," he says of his chosen profession. "It is a very physical activity. Yet there are subtle sensibilities involved, too."

Coastal life: Like the English potters with whom he studied, Massey works at home in a studio he built adjoining his house. Despite the growth in popularity of his pots – and consequently, the drain on his free time – Massey still manages to maintain a balance

Coast Salish migrated here because of the abundance of food and the mildness of the climate. The first white settlers came here because of its seemingly inexhaustible supply of timber, game and fish. Today, tourists travel here to bask in its breathtaking and ever-changing scenery.

From the impossibly steep slopes of the North Shore mountains to the great sandy beaches of English Bay and Kitsilano, from Point Grey's spectacular Pacific Spirit Park to clothing-optional Wreck Beach, the city offers up a variety of outdoor settings. The denizens of Vancouver are quick to take advantage. After all, in what other major metropolitan area is it possible to fish for a 14-kg (30-lb) salmon right in the harbour of the city itself?

Interestingly enough, the importance of protecting Vancouver's natural beauty was well appreciated by its founding fathers. The primordial forest of Stanley Park – its 400 hectares (1,000 acres) within a short walk of downtown – is one of Vancouver's oldest features. The decision to acquire the peninsula of land and turn it into a park dates back to 1886; indeed, it was the first resolution of the city's first council, which was meeting only for the second time in its existence.

Pedestrian priorities: For that great thumb of green at Vancouver's northwestern gate – interspersed with walking trails, beaches and playing fields – has always set the tone for the city's sporting style. Walking is so respected that pedestrians are given the right of way over all vehicles. Step off the curb at many major intersections in Vancouver and cars will stop immediately and let you pass; otherwise they risk a hefty fine.

Nowhere is Vancouver's outdoor flair more apparent than at Kitsilano Beach in summer. Minutes away from downtown, Kits Beach offers a microcosmic view of the city's hedonistic culture – along with a slough of

Despite being surrounded by wild, impenetrable rainforest to the south, east and north – and despite having to deal with the ravages of a massive fire that had destroyed the town completely only two weeks earlier – Vancouver's fledgling council considered preserving this tidal island of still-unlogged forest as its most important order of business. It was an act of radical foresight. And one that would provide the young city with a strong and impressive signature.

Left and above, Vancouverites are energetic in their pursuit of the good life.

bronzed bodies that belies Vancouver's reputation for grey skies and rainy days. From muscled-knotted body builders and sleek ocean swimmers to rangy basketball players; from lean beach volleyballers to sculpted triathletes; from hackey-sackers to jugglers and acrobats: the extensive grass-and-sand area of Kits seems to display almost every kind of outdoor leisure activity.

And they all have their own turf, guarding it jealously like tribal warriors. "It's a scene," says Joelle Smith, a longtime frequenter of Kits Beach. "There's no doubt about it. People come down here to be part of a group.

Each has its own hierarchy and if they don't want you around, they'll let you know."

Fitness obession: Tribal or not, places like Kits Beach have created a sporting ethos that has few urban peers in North America. Where other towns have developed a café culture, Vancouver has developed an obsession with physical fitness. Packs of well-toned joggers in $200 running shoes churn up the paths of city parks; smooth-legged cyclists in racing jerseys and $2,000 bikes hammer through the streets of town. When the ski season begins, the action shifts to the mountains. One of the top ski resorts in North America, Vancouver's much-vaunted Whistler Moun-

tain is as hip as they come. Former Prime Minister Pierre Trudeau takes a vacation here regularly, as do a bevy of Hollywood stars including John Travolta, Darryl Hannah and Mel Gibson.

But that doesn't diminish the attraction of the three North Shore ski mountains – Cypress, Grouse and Seymour – from providing near-perfect skiing conditions. Only minutes from downtown, all three offer day and night skiing from November until April. Which means that on a good powder-snow day many Vancouverites will *not* be found slogging away in stuffy, overheated offices.

Vancouver's love affair with outdoor sports goes back a long way. The city's most cherished sports figure was Seraphim "Black Joe" Fortes, who arrived here as an able-bodied seaman in 1885. A tireless promoter of the outdoor lifestyle, Fortes soon took on the responsibility of policing the popular beach at English Bay. "He taught nearly all the boys and girls to swim," wrote novelist Ethel Wilson. "I can still hear Joe Fortes saying in his rotund rich voice, 'Jump! I tell you, jump! If you don't jump off that raft, I'll throw you in.' So we jumped. Joe was a heroic figure."

Fortes's legacy lives on. The city's obsession with fitness and sports has nurtured a number of fine athletes over the years. Sprinter Percy Williams started the whole thing rolling in 1928 at the Olympic Games in Amsterdam when he captured two gold medals. Although no other Vancouverite has managed to match Percy's feat, athletes from the Lower Mainland have always provided a disproportionately large contingent to Canada's national team.

Vancouver's environment has also inspired visitors to amazing feats of athletic excellence. It was here, at Empire Stadium during the 1954 British Empire Games, that Britain's Roger Bannister nipped Australian John Landry at the wire to win what was to become known as the Miracle Mile. For the first time in history, two men had managed to complete the gruelling run in under four minutes.

From Vancouver's international triathlon to its annual marathon and dragon boat races; from the World Cup ski races hosted at North Vancouver's Grouse Mountain and the prestigious Indy NASCAR race held in the city's downtown streets to the world-championship sailing regattas at Jericho Sailing Centre – the range of high-calibre sports events held here are wide-ranging. "It's one of my favourite places to compete in the world," says superstar triathlete Mark Allen. "Vancouver fairly oozes with vitality."

If watching team sports is your favourite pastime, fear not: Vancouver boasts a major league hockey team (the Canucks), football team (the BC Lions), soccer team (the 86ers) and a triple A baseball team (the Canadians).

All are strongly suppported by local fans.

Vancouver's most fitting – and offbeat – event, however, is one that few people have heard about. It is called the Knee Knackering North Shore trail run and involves negotiating 48 km (30 miles) and nearly 6,000 metres (20,000 ft) of vertical change along a very narrow path in the dense rainforest of West Vancouver's North Shore mountains. The fastest runners complete the course (a journey that takes most backpackers two or three days) in just under five hours; the maximum time allotted to finish is 10 hours.

Different style: The event was conceived in 1988 by Enzo Federico and Shane Collins,

backcountry adventure. "It's the kind of race," explains perennial champion Peter Findlay, "where you need a wide range of skills: balance, agility, flexibility – not to mention endurance and strength. Besides, there is something really special to running alone in the mountains. At times you reach this incredibly peaceful state of mind. It is," he pauses for a moment, then smiles broadly, "pure bliss."

Vancouver – Canada's orphan metropolis. Youthful, hedonistic and showing the self-confidence of a major new world capital, this west coast burg is a blend of very diverse influences, shaped on the one hand by the

who were looking for a way to combine their love of the outdoors and their obsession with running. "Racing on pavement and breathing car exhaust was not our idea of a good time," explains Collins. "So we went for something a little different." Only six other racers chose to accompany the pair on their first trial run in 1989, but two years later that figure had swelled to 102 (89 finished).

Far from knackered, though, most participants seem surprisingly rejuvenated by their

Left and **above**, Vancouver has the self-confidence of a major, new world capital.

mystic visions of the Coast Salish who first inhabited its shores, and on the other by the entrepreneurial spirit of the wild-eyed fortune-seekers who were drawn here during the 19th century.

Health-conscious, sports-crazy, liberal-minded and teeming with energy, Vancouverites live in one of the most beautiful natural settings on the planet. And that too shapes their world view. "I've travelled all over the world," says Vincent Massey, "and I wouldn't live anywhere else but here. Why should I? I've got everything I want right in my own backyard."

With the mountains at its back, Vancouver has always looked for distant horizons towards the West and the Orient. Here, on the coast, the Pacific is both the familiar ocean lapping at the beaches, and the doorway to fabulous and exotic lands – and, lately, even more fabulous entrepreneurs and profits.

Vancouver has woken up to the fact that, with over a quarter of the world's population bordering on the rim of this great ocean, that it is a part of that reality and that the Pacific is where its main trading future lies. The BC government has recently established trade offices in Taipei, Hong Kong, Singapore, Tokyo and Seoul, and has set up the BC Trade Development Corporation specifically for BC manufacturers looking to the export trade. (The local futurist, Frank "Dr Tomorrow" Ogden, says that by the first decade of the 21st century, Vancouver will be an Asian city. "Local business people will be getting plastic surgery on their eyes to look more Oriental, to fit in," he claims.)

Asian influences are, of course, nothing new to BC. The first Chinese workers arrived on the coast in 1779, and ever since, from China, Japan, Hawaii, the US western coast, Mexico, India, Taiwan, Korea, Australia, New Zealand, the Philippines, and from all the other countries around the Pacific Rim, immigrants have come to "Saltwater City", as the Chinese called this land of gentle climate and spectacular scenery, to try their fortunes and sink their roots.

The Pacific is all important to Vancouver. It brings the Japanese current which helps to create the mild climate, a big attraction. It brought the first Europeans, and has always been the most reliable and cheapest carrier of Vancouver's trade goods. More than 200 years ago, trading on the west coast started with sea otter pelts to satisfy the sartorial demands of mandarins in far-off China. Now, it's once again a valuable trade item as posh

Preceding pages: two-thirds of recent immigration has been from Asia. **Left,** Vancouver's trading future lies with the East.

Vancouver hotel boutiques advertise popular Canadian furs (in both English and Japanese) to lure some of the 250,000 Japanese tourists who visit each year.

The gift shops around fashionable hotels all have Japanese signs inviting tourists to buy Canadiana, furs and local salmon; over 20 stores cater to the Japanese gift trade in an area sometimes called "Little Ginza". Vancouver has 33 foreign banks, and in 1990, for the first time, exported more to the Pacific Rim than to the US, the province's former major trading partner.

Now the tourist industry is reacting to the realities of being a Pacific Rim country, and hotels give their employees courses in Oriental customs and etiquette, and what various cultural groups expect of them. Young Canadians have caught the touring fever; tours to Thailand, India and other Asian destinations are popular, as are language courses at colleges and night schools. The traffic, of course, is in both directions.

Planeloads of Japanese tourists arrive in summer embarking on tours to enjoy Canadian scenery, national parks and forests. Tourism from Japan increased by 105 percent between 1980 and 1988. Cruise ships dock 362 times a year, bringing the city 420,000 passengers.

Immigrants welcomed: Canada needed and welcomed the first immigrants from the Pacific Rim. Kanakas from Hawaii jumped ship at Vancouver to settle and make homes, others came to work for the Hudson's Bay Company. The gold rush and the railway boom lured Chinese, many of whom sent money home, but as many stayed on to found Canadian dynasties.

Across the Pacific at the turn of the century came Japanese and East Indians, mostly single men, to work at fishing and logging. Despite being highly visible targets, useful scapegoats for the dissatisfied, their diligence and good business acumen brought many of them prosperity. Sikhs made fortunes exporting BC lumber to Asia, the Japanese were expert fishermen and gardeners.

Chinese started small businesses and bountiful market gardens.

All around the city, their contributions and culture can be seen. In Stanley Park, a stone memorial under the cherry trees commemorates the Japanese Canadians who died for Canada in World War I. In World War II, a highly decorated special contingent composed of second-generation Japanese-Canadians fought with the Canadian Forces in Italy. Near the park's shoreline, the figurehead from *The Empress of Japan* (actually a replica), one of the first of a whole fleet of elegant Empresses that made Vancouver a major Asian tourist port, extends a silent

authentic copy of a scholar's peaceful retreat, part of the Chinese Cultural Centre, where numerous displays and events celebrate the city's Chinese heritage.

At the University of British Columbia out on Point Grey, the beautiful Nitobe Gardens, created by architect Kannosuki Mori as a memorial to the Japanese humanist Inazo Nitobe, provide a tranquil escape for students and citizens alike. Alongside is UBC's Asian Centre for Oriental Studies, and there are plans for a new Arts Centre, partly funded by Tom and Caleb Chan, expatriates from Hong Kong, who after prospering in land development here wanted to put something

greeting to vessels entering Vancouver's huge and beautiful harbour.

Bilingual street signs and recessed second-floor balconies on the buildings in Chinatown are an echo of home to visitors from Hong Kong, and on Pender Street the charming Sun-Yat-Sen Garden is a testimonial to the Chinese leader who visited Vancouver many times while raising funds for the revolution that eventually created modern China. The Chinese who settled in this new land sent their savings back across the Pacific to help their families, and they in turn sent their artists and artisans to build this

back into their new homeland. On the terrace of the Student Union Building a replica of "The Goddess of Democracy" holds her light of freedom high, erected by the students in honour of those who died at Tiananmen Square in 1987.

Exposed to Expo: Over 22 million visitors visited Vancouver's Expo 86. Many liked what they saw and immigrated. From the Philippines came nurses to work in Vancouver hospitals, and families who despised the Marcos regime. Immigrants and refugees came after the Korean and Vietnamese conflicts and East Indians from the Fiji Islands.

As Asian immigration increased, so did their investment. The Japanese trading companies, the "sogo shosha", started the trend in the 1960s by investing in BC's resources. Hong Kong investment, first in real estate, then into high-tech and the garment industries, grew 44 percent annually from 1983 to 1987, until in the early 1990s it was estimated to exceed $6 billion.

Two-thirds of recent immigration to Vancouver has been from Asia, much of it highly-skilled, with both capital and experience. By the start of this decade almost one quarter of Vancouver's residents were of Asian descent, and the same percentage of children

significant from a business as well as a cultural standpoint. Provincial Minister of Multiculturalism Elwood Veitch says: "It fosters a greater willingness to deal with the people you went to school with, so is a great facilitator for trade in the future."

Asian investment is a major one in Vancouver's downtown, including the ultramodern office tower of the Hong Kong Bank of Canada (the country's seventh largest bank) with its fabulous pendulum sweeping back and forth endlessly in the lobby. Vancouver is now the headquarters for this world-wide British banking firm's data bank. Cathedral Place across from the Vancouver Hotel, to-

starting school had Chinese as their first language. By the year 2000 it is expected that at least 75 percent of the children in Vancouver schools will not have English as their first language.

Young Canadians are actively wooed to teach in English schools in Japan, which cater to Japanese who want to equip themselves for world trade and travel.

The student exchange programme is very

gether with adjacent Cathedral Park, is owned by Hong Kong film tycoons Ronnie Shon and Sir Runrun Shaw. The Ramada Renaissance Hotel (New World Developments, Cheng Yu-tung, Hong Kong) has been upgraded to the degree of luxury expected by affluent Asians. Also on the waterfront is the Tokyo Corporation's aptly named Pan Pacific hotel, topped with a glowing multicoloured dome. About 28 percent of Vancouver's hotel rooms are Asian-owned.

Most of these newer hotels and public buildings have, as a matter of course, Oriental ideograms on signs in elevators or wash-

Left, Japanese Festival; Chinese New Year. **Above**, celebrations reflect Vancouver's Pacific Rim heritage.

rooms. The Vancouver suburb of Richmond also has the Aberdeen Centre, North America's largest Asian Mall, owned by the Sun Hun Kai group, Hong Kong's major business dynasty. They are represented here by family member Thomas Fung, who feels that of all Canadian cities, it is Vancouver that is the most friendly to Asians.

Major utilities such as BC Hydro employ multicultural consultants which Hydro says enables them to communicate with their customers in 24 languages. At the Vancouver General Hospital a psychiatrist specialises in the cross-cultural problems of young people. Courses in English as a Second Language

Japanese diners like fast, quiet, efficient service, while Chinese customers like more leisurely, convivial dining. They are told to avoid the numbers 4, 14 and 24 – all of which have linguistic connections with death for the Chinese.

When a prominent Japanese artist, Noburi Toko from Kushiro, came to visit its sister city Burnaby, a Vancouver suburb, he was impressed enough by Canadian hospitality and scenery to create an Ainu work, *The Garden of the Gods*, in gratitude. The Ainu peoples of northern Japan, possibly derived from the same stock as Canada's Eskimos and native Indians, also include carved

(ESL) are now standard in public schools, and in day and night courses for adults.

Slower pace: There is also a proliferation of courses in Oriental business etiquette for the travelling executive, and Canadians are learning that business with the Chinese, in particular, proceeds at a much slower rate than here at home. Vancouver realtors quickly learned what's necessary in a house is for it to have good *feng shui* – that is, a lucky and harmonious aspect, essential if you're trying to sell to Asians. The provincial government runs seminars on how to cater to customers from the Orient, passing on tips such as that

wooden poles as part of their culture. So overlooking Vancouver are a cluster of Ainu totems with bears, whales, owls and ravens, mutual symbols for both Ainu and BC native peoples. A pointer faces out over Burrard Inlet, indicating the direction to Kushiro.

On this same mountain, seminars in Indonesian music and dance are sponsored by Simon Fraser University each summer. Featured are performances on the *gamelan*, the percussion and wind instruments donated to the university by the government of Indonesia after Expo 86.

Throughout the city, there are exotic exclamation points that reflect Vancouver's Pacific Rim heritage: the five golden domes of the Alkali Singh Sikh temple beside the freeway, or the brightly coloured 10-metre (30-ft) dancing statue of Lord Chaitanya, a Hare Krishna saint, in the industrial area on Stewardson Way near Burnaby. On South Vancouver's Marine Drive is a white Sikh temple, its silver filigree onion dome designed by Vancouver architect Arthur Erickson, and on the Steveston Highway in Richmond an ancient-style Chinese Buddhist temple, brightly decorated in red and gold with porcelain tiled roof, sits among western suburban houses near a traditional Shinto shrine. Off Canada Way in the nearby area of Burnaby, behind the trees and shrubs of its Taj Mahal-like forecourt, is the $10 million Ismaili Jamatkhana temple.

The Chinese expression, *Gung Hay Fat Choy*, is heard as often in certain boardrooms in Vancouver as is "Happy New Year" the month before. The Canadian International Dragon Boat Festival on False Creek draws over 100,000 Vancouverites a year.

Grocery treats: In Vancouver supermarkets, Chinese vegetables like *bok choy* and *lo bak,* are staples beside lettuce and carrots and other, once-exotic foods. Sauces and condiments from the Philippines, Malaysia, Taiwan, and Vietnam sit alongside more familiar North American standards on the shelves. Asian visitors enjoy going to shopping centres just to see the wide variety in the grocery superstores, and marvel at the high quality and variety of Oriental foods available in Vancouver's many ethnic restaurants.

The annual Pacific National Exhibition has for the past decade featured Pacific Rim countries and their arts and products, and the semi-annual food trade fair, Food-Pacific, counts about one-third of its exhibitors from Asian Rim countries, including South American countries such as Chile.

Vancouver has at least three full-time ethnic television stations, so at any time you can switch your TV control and see an East Indian movie, an episode in a Chinese historical series, or a Japanese or Korean vari-

ety show. By law, cable companies must dedicate at least one of their channels as a local multicultural community channel. Vancouver also has ethnic radio stations and numerous non-English local publications.

Cathay TV's president, Lucy Roschap, born in Hong Kong of celebrated moviemaker parents, managed the family's chain of Chinese cinemas in Canada after graduating from the University of British Columbia. Then she was invited by the three Vancouver Chinese families who founded Cathay TV to take over its leadership. The station broadcasts in the Chinese, Vietnamese, East Indian and Thai languages, covering and pub-

licising local and community activities.

"Not many people realise just what sacrifices many immigrants may have made in careers and salaries, to come to Canada for a chance to live under a stable government and get a good education for their children," she says. "These people are coming here to stay. They want to mix and be a part of this country, so a lot of our programming is geared to that need."

General donor: British Columbia's current Lieutenant Governor is David C. Lam, a 71-year-old Hong Kong expatriate who became a millionaire working in real estate, and then

Left, Filipino native dance. **Right**, East/West influence.

started giving away his wealth to various local universities and foundations. Reluctant at first to go back into service after his retirement, he finally decided the governorship would help his efforts to increase inter-racial harmony. Now he follows a schedule that would daunt a much younger man, receiving 1,000 people at Government House every month, with up to a dozen appointments every day. Son of a Baptist minister, he tries to combine the philosophies of Christianity and Confucianism, adding his own brand of quiet humour, as when he told a child who asked about his job, " I am here to deny the government absolute power."

With the imminence of 1997, when Hong Kong is returned to China, immigration and investment are gaining momentum; Vancouver is regarded as the preferred destination for Hong Kong citizens with money to invest. Simultaneously, China has begun actively to encourage and invite Western business and expertise. Both large and small BC firms, servicing the resource industries, such as suppliers of electrical high-voltage connections to mining and construction projects, have found China to be a good market for Canadian-made products. The People's Republic of China now has 40 companies based in, and doing business out of, Vancouver.

Vancouver's setting is excellent from a financial, geographical, and transportation viewpoint, situated as it is right in the middle between Europe and Asia, a plus-point both for travel and communications. "Being in Vancouver is not just a close link back to the Pacific Rim, but also a doorway for trade to the western seaboard of the US," says the Multiculturalism minister. "Now that Vancouver has been accepted as the first International Maritime Centre in Canada, with appropriate tax concessions, we expect to see thousands more jobs created as Vancouver becomes even more attractive as a head office site for many international firms wanting a toehold on the North American continent."

When trading between Canada and Japan was reinstated after World War II, loading of Japanese ships was done at night to avoid reprisals. Today, Japan is the largest Asian investor in BC to the tune of over $3.6 billion in recent years. Included in this is BC's north Mitsubishi/Chogoku's largest chopstick factory in the world, producing 10 million pairs a day, and Toyota's $58 million expansion to its Delta plant that turns out 960,000 automobile wheels every year. The next big local Japanese project is Atsugi Nylon Industrial Corporation's $200 million pantyhose factory in the Lower Mainland.

Influx of funds: This new tide of immigrants is different in that they are immediately able to assume a position of influence in their new country, and they are entering at the rate of 10,000 people each year. Vancouver houses appear on Hong Kong computer screens as soon as they are listed, often being snapped up sight unseen. Since both housing and education are cheaper here than in Hong Kong, many of the well-to-do are bringing both their families and their funds with them.

Asian immigrants pumped $122.9 million into the BC economy in one recent year, and Hong Kong money alone is expected to top $2 billion annually. Tiger Balm heiress Sian (Sally) Aw, from Hong Kong, bought IMPARK, Vancouver's largest parking management company, in the early 1980s and sold it 10 years later for $20 million.

When the Expo 86 site went on the block, Hong Kong billionaire Li Ka-shing paid $125 million for what is considered the bargain of the century. He proposes to build a $2 billion urban development on the site. This will be managed by Concord Pacific, under V. P. Stanley Quok, a Hong Kong architect, with expertise in developing large projects. Ka-shing's son, Victor Li, stays in Vancouver to look after the family's Canadian investments in oil, gas and real estate. Hong Kong movie star Patrick Tse, seeking stability to raise his family, chose Vancouver to start a sportswear enterprise that provides 100 jobs and over $3 million in sales.

operator and, like many of his fellow immigrants, is a generous supporter of institutions such as the University of British Columbia and the Vancouver Children's Hospital.

A new emphasis on manufacturing and processing, rather than reliance on resource industries – combined with its new Pacific Rim focus – is propelling BC's economy to be currently one of the strongest in Canada.

"Vancouver seems destined to become an international city, almost a city-state unto itself," says Professor Jean Barman in her book, *A History of British Columbia*. A city on the Pacific Rim, but still a North American city, Vancouver offers citizens and busi-

Other successes: Some Canadian-born Asians, such as the super-successful former beauty queen Andrea Eng, president of the Hong Kong-Canada Business Association, have adapted faster to the new markets, and routinely handle real estate sales in the millions. Asa Jahal was only 18 months old when his family came to Canada from India and started work in a sawmill at age 14. He is now BC's largest independent sawmill

Left and **above**, Asian entrepreneurs recently pumped nearly $123 million into British Columbia in one year alone.

ness people the best of European, American and Asian cultures and worlds.

Reflecting on Vancouver, famous Canadian opera conductor and impresario Irving Guttman says: "I get the impression that people of the west coast, regardless of ethnic origins, are able freely to be themselves."

Vancouver's beginnings and its future are inexorably locked into the Pacific Ocean and its sister countries around its rim. After spending a century climbing the rows of mountain ranges between itself and the rest of Canada, business Vancouver is turning a welcoming face across the sea.

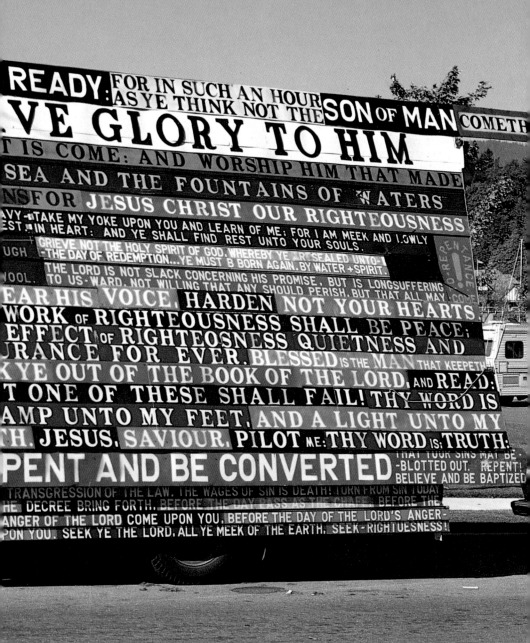

"Go west, young man," newspaperman Horace Greely is supposed to have said in the 1800s to a persistent youth asking for advice on how to get ahead. In North America, as in Europe and Asia, the restless hordes have traditionally migrated west where – stopped by the Pacific and captivated by the mild climate – they stayed. But their energy still bubbles up in various types of west coast looniness. Hyperkinetic types east of the Rockies at times find it difficult to relate to Vancouverites' laid-back, somewhat off-centre lifestyle.

From the very beginning, Vancouver and its citizens didn't bother with very many formalities. Morris Panych, the award-winning playwright and actor, when looking back on his adopted home, says, "Vancouver seems… an idea thrown together quickly, a hodgepodge, precariously teetering on the edge of civilisation, and sort of making itself up as it goes along."

Religious drinkers: The first saloon keeper of this early settlement, Gassy Jack, dispensing words and liquor generously, was a unique host who chased all the drinkers out of his tavern at 10pm, saying he wanted them up bright and early to earn more money for him in the lumber mills. His saloon also doubled as the site for Vancouver's first church service, and many Vancouverites devoutly follow this form of worship to this very day.

(Vancouver, incidentally, is probably the only city that has named a street after an unknown leg. Downtown on False Creek is "Leg in Boot" Square, commemorating all that was found of an unfortunate pioneer hiker who set out to walk the 16 km/10 miles to New Westminster through the bush.)

The young city of Vancouver incorporated itself in April of 1886, and got burned down two months later. Undaunted, the city fathers set up shop in a tent the next day; the first order of business was to have a group

photograph taken of themselves in front of the ruins (*see page 30*) – an early indication, some say, of BC's political priorities.

From the beginning, BC politicians were a special breed. Amor de Cosmos, the first premier, was a displaced photographer from the California gold rush, who started a newspaper in Victoria criticising politicians – until, that is, he became one himself. His name, he claimed, meant "Lover of the Universe", but critics described the premier as a

"waspish man with a venomous pen".

A more recent premier starting as a tulip bulb salesman ended up owning his own Biblical Theme amusement park named Fantasy Gardens, which some say he kept confusing with the entire province. His off-the-cuff pronouncements were considered bizarre enough to have been collected in a little red book, *The Sayings of Chairman Zalm*.

One of his predecessors, nicknamed "Wacky" because of his grandiose building projects and takeovers, included in his cabinet as Minister of Highways a Pentecostal Revivalist nicknamed "Flying Phil" because

Preceding pages: Jesus is coming. Left and right, other Canadians find Vancouver's off-centre lifestyle difficult to understand.

of his extensive collection of speeding tickets. Today he's the septuagenarian mayor of Kamloops, in BC's interior, where one of his recent pronouncements was: "When I tell a lie, it's only because I think it's the truth."

Odd local laws: At one time or another Vancouver's lawmakers have decreed it illegal to sprinkle clothes by spraying water from your mouth, ride a camel down a major street, or run a three-legged race for money.

It must be something about the atmosphere – the air, the climate, maybe the barometric pressure – that seems to attract or produce eccentricity both benign and bizarre. Some say that Vancouver weather is

enough to drive you mad once you get here. Although it's true that you can golf in the morning and ski in the afternoon, it's also true you can watch it mist, drip or pour rain all day for weeks. A popular local postcard shows two identical dripping figures labelled respectively "Vancouver in summer" and "Vancouver in winter". There is, however, no truth to the rumour that 10 years' residence guarantees webbed feet.

Water and Vancouver are synonymous, but its citizens demonstrate their affection for the ocean in unusual ways. The tradition of having a 61-km (38-mile) ocean race

across Georgia Strait from Nanaimo in "bathtubs" seems as normal here as swimming in frigid English Bay on New Year's Day. The ultimate in hang-over cures, beginning the year with a dip in the sea has been a local custom since 1927, the idea being to see who can cavort the longest in the icy water, costumed either in formal dress or crazily attired. Vancouver author and humorist Eric Nicol describes it as "a form of mass dementia, demonstrating the city's penchant for masochism as an outdoor activity".

More uninhibited activities continue all summer at "Wreck Beach" where up to 12,000 bathers bare all on sunny weekends, among hawkers selling hot-dogs, beer, chocolate-covered "magic" mushrooms or English trifle and chocolate mousse. A beach wedding held here recently saw the bride wearing only a veil and the groom a bow tie. Within the past decade, Vancouver has taken enthusiastically to Chinese Dragon boat racings. Local competitors at the last race included a bank president and his tellers and a rival crew, composed of the VP of an airline and his reservation clerks, all rowing as furiously as their up-market rivals.

An even greater splash is generated every year by former football player and local businessman "Butts" Girard running the Great North American "Belly-flop" at one of Vancouver's posh hotel swimming-pools. The only athletic requirement is to have the build of a sumo wrestler, because the winner is decided by the volume and extent of water he manages to displace.

Jumping Jacks: No one should be surprised that the first Canadian to jump from an airplane did it in Vancouver in 1912. The surprising thing is that he used a parachute. Vancouver had its first plane crash just six years later, when a local pilot (probably dissatisfied with the postal service) hit a West End roof while trying to drop a letter on his aunt's lawn. Not only daring but gallant, a Vancouver swain, George McKay, built one of Vancouver's longtime tourist attractions, the swinging Capilano Suspension Bridge, to amuse his girlfriend; it's been amusing generations of thrill-seekers ever since. Another susceptible western male was pioneer Royal Engineer Colonel Moody who named what is now the site of Richmond, a Vancouver suburb, "Lulu Island", after a dance hall performer called Lulu Sweet. What his wife named him when she found out is not recorded.

Flamboyant personalities seem to migrate and settle on the west coast, where they can feel comfortable among their own kind. The 1960s mayor Tom Campbell once said, "Where else could a loudmouth like me win an election except in a crazy city like this?" Other cities had hippie colonies and flower children in the 1960s, but Vancouver was the only one that agreed to hire an official Town Fool. Joachim Foikis, a philosophy graduate

continue his support was not appreciated; his contract was not renewed. A professor of English, Warren Stevenson, said: "Foikis has given Vancouver a unique reputation in a city where uniqueness is routine." In the same era, a citizen who called himself Mr Peanut campaigned in that costume for mayor, even getting some votes. In his alter ego he called himself Dr Brute, appearing in a leopard-spotted costume playing a saxophone, often accompanied by his spotted wife, Lady Brute, and a fellow artist Anna Banana (dressed as a banana, of course).

Colourful street people in Vancouver have a long tradition. In the late 1930s Vancou-

from Berlin and the University of BC, applied and received a $3,500 Canada Council grant in 1967 to be Vancouver's Town Fool, complete with a suit of motley and cap of bells, to create "theatre in the streets". At first outraged, Vancouver city fathers became more tolerant and even gratified when they saw the national attention it brought the then fairly isolated city.

However, Foikis's suggestion that citizens be taxed (1¢ per citizen, 2¢ per politician) to

Left and **above**, Vancouver's eccentrics are both bizzare and benign.

ver's eccentric-about-town was "Professor Francis", a talented former pianist whose regular costume was bare feet in old shoes, a ragged overcoat with overflowing pockets and a dead flower in his buttonhole. He loved concerts and social events, managing to gatecrash all the major ones where he cornered the most important people. One society matron talking to equally prominent friends, was approached at her lawn party with the sad story of the unhappy love that drove Professor Francis to be a derelict. As he talked, the professor rummaged through his pockets looking for his sweetheart's last letter, and kept handing his hostess various papers, unidentified objects wrapped in napkins and finally an old pancake.

The manager of the Orpheum Theatre posted special guards to thwart Francis crashing one concert. But, after getting in and being thrown out twice, the manager told him he could stay, if he revealed how he had stolen in again. "Through the coal chute," said the professor, shedding grime. Eventually, his appearance at a Vancouver socal affair was considered a good omen.

Religious fanatics are legion, of course, but in Vancouver they come in an amazing variety. During the 1950s, Vancouverites

disciples. The building now houses Burnaby's popular Arts Centre.

Maverick mayors: Vancouver has had more than its share of colourful mayors and politicians. In the early years of the century Mayor Louis D. Taylor bought a vacant lot and built a garage on it so it could be assessed at over $1,000 to meet the candidacy residential requirements. But he never lived there and didn't own a car. Somewhat accident-prone, he was nearly killed in 1928 when he backed into an airplane propeller, and had scarcely recovered a year later when he almost drowned on a canoe trip.

His successor, Gerald McGeer, was a

became inured to the sight of acres of bare flesh as large, heavy-set, elderly ladies stripped naked inside and in front of the courthouse at the height of the Doukhobour religious sect demonstrations. They were upholding their inalienable right to set fire to their own and dissenters' homes.

Also in the 1950s, a religious leader who called himself "Pope John" set up the community of the Temple of More Abundant Life on suburban acreage just outside the city. It flourished until he gave a new meaning to the name of their church by running off with the funds and two of his young, nubile

former milkman-turned-lawyer who favoured loud, checked suits, was naturally eloquent but was criticised for having "inflammation of the vowels". His reaction to the Depression was to build an expensive new monolithic City Hall, an illuminated fountain in Lost Lagoon topping things off with lavish Golden Jubilee celebrations.

Mayor Dr Lyle Telford was a reformer who wanted to crack down on bawdy houses, but didn't want to have to throw the girls out on the streets, saying: "It's not fair to send them to Revelstoke, Calgary, Winnipeg and those other places." It's not clear to whom he thought this was unfair. "Tom Terrific" was a mayor in the 1970s who won votes by threatening to "shave all the hippies".

Vancouver even approaches art differently. Tourists wandering Gastown streets and alleyways during a recent summer could see a young actress dressed as a cat burglar scrambling down the side of a building into an outdoor set to take part in an avant-garde production of *#5 Blood Alley*. Locals and a skid row derelict searching the garbage for leftovers scarcely glanced at the travelling cast emoting all around them, or at the audience following them in polite bemusement.

World's worst art: Visual art has survived regularly whipped into a righteous frenzy by the doings of its energetic arts community. BC artist Evelyn Roth gained fame in the 1970s for crocheting Volkswagen covers out of film tape, and creating huge inflatable sculptures of salmon and Santa Claus. She once wrote: "There is certainly a spiritual something hovering on the Pacific Current that affects our lives." Outsiders can sometimes be forgiven if they get the impression that "certain something" may be hallucinogens. But when local artist Rick Gibson announced recently he was staging a public "happening" to kill a pet rat called Sniffy by dropping a heavy weight on him from a

the assaults of a University of British Columbia professor, Dr Norm Watt, who has roamed second-hand shops and garage sales for 14 years collecting the World's Worst Oil Paintings. An annual auction of this artwork has netted the Canadian Paraplegic Association over a quarter of a million dollars. His "Salon de Refusés" has works rejected by the Louvre, the Smithsonian, and almost every prestigious world gallery.

Vancouver's conservative minority are

Left, log-birling competition. Above, lanterns for peace.

considerable height, there was a loud outcry. Vancouver can tolerate eccentricity, but not cruelty to animals.

The monied set also insists on indulging their foibles. Nelson Skalbania, former promoter and hotel owner, donated over a quarter of a million dollars to the YMCA for racquet ball courts on the condition that he get a permanent 5pm playing time daily for the rest of his life. "Chunky" Woodward, heir to a major department store fortune, loves nothing better than to ride herd on his Cariboo ranch or take chances on buying lottery tickets. Jimmy Pattison, auto-salesman turned multi-millionaire, plays the trumpet at his fundamentalist church on Sundays.

Former Torontonian butcher Murray Pezim metamorphosed into a stock promoter in Vancouver and proceeded to win and lose fortunes in mining stocks, while marrying and divorcing a succession of beautiful young women. Pezim recently purchased the local football team, the hapless BC Lions, encouraging them to victory from the owners' box by waving his hands which were encased in oversized orange gloves.

Some signs in Vancouver restaurants raise eyebrows. Café Django advertises that they have "Jeffrey, the Headwaiter from Hell",

and The Elbow Room prides itself on its obnoxious service with the motto, "Abuse is our Game."

A good part of Malcolm Lowry's 1940s novel *Under the Volcano* was written in Vancouver in a ramshackle hut on the shores of Burrard Inlet. Lowry fitted comfortably into the local scene, and his shack became a mecca for many of Vancouver's famous authors, whose recollections of Lowry falling into the inlet from one of its windows while playing a guitar, or floating around the inlet in a drunken haze in a dinghy looking for Port Moody, are legion. Like all writers,

Lowry hated deadlines and once took a hotel room downtown to hide from his New York agent due to collect a promised (and unfinished) manuscript.

Alternative activists: Even eccentricity can become respectable when it comes from the west. When a small dedicated band left Vancouver in a rickety boat to take on the French navy in the Pacific a decade ago in a protest against nuclear testing, the world thought they were crazy. Now they are known worldwide as the environmentalist movement Greenpeace who take on renegade whalers or nuclear vessels anywhere.

Vancouver's Dr Tomorrow, Frank Ogden, the city's pre-eminent futurist, lives in an electronic floating cottage in the shadow of the high-rises overlooking Coal Harbour, serviced by three robots, two satellite dishes bringing in 200 channels, and three computers accessing 40,000 databases worldwide. He runs an information gathering service, is constantly in demand around the world as a speaker, and, though in his 70s, expects to go at the same speed for at least another 15 years, unlike most of the world who are only "using about 1 percent of their brainpower".

Ogden says he gets paid "obscene" amounts of money by national corporations to tell them things like, "by the third millennium, you're going to see humans marrying robots." He is the epitome of the west coast eccentric, his own man, shocking, sometimes outrageous, but like most of Vancouver's free spirits, always entertaining, and sometimes even dead right.

Vancouver's well-mannered motorists still amaze tourists by stopping for pedestrians with a friendly "beep-beep" rather than a blaring horn seeking your attention if you haven't seen the light change. Traffic can be backed up for blocks near the Lions Gate Bridge while a mother goose shepherds her flock of goslings across the road in front of patient motorists. Impatient visitors from other Canadian cities complain that the tempo here is too laid-back, easy-going and tolerant. Sometimes Vancouverites agree when they see how many of those same carping critics later decide to move out here.

Left, street smart. **Right**, personal growth.

Chuck Davis, broadcaster, writer and the man who has often been called "Mr Vancouver," describes his affection for the city.

I love Vancouver. When I arrived with my father in December 1944 there were flowers growing outside the Canadian Pacific Railway Station. We'd just come from my native Winnipeg, where temperatures of 20 below were pretty normal for December. So the climate certainly got my affection for

Vancouver off to an excellent start.

The waterfront was part of the attraction. Nothing quite equals a stroll along this crowded stretch of the inlet's southern shore, watching ships loading and unloading cargo, dodging big trucks as they rumble on to the docks, peeking into fish-processing plants, smelling the sea-wet air, and listening to the eerily beautiful screech of clouds of seagulls. The city's soundscape would be the poorer without them, and watching them fighting and diving for scraps is fun.

Speaking of sound, two unique examples are heard, unforgettably, every day in Vancouver. At noon, huge horns atop the BC Hydro Building startlingly blare out the first four notes of "O Canada", the national anthem; and at 9pm the famous Nine O'Clock Gun in Stanley Park booms out a one-bang time signal that, except for a hiatus during World War II, has been a city tradition for 100 years.

Europeans may be amused by our use of the words "tradition" and "heritage", given that we've been here at most 150 years. The aboriginal people here trace their presence back at least 8,000 years. One famous *midden* (refuse heap), at the time the largest one discovered in North America, is still down there under the parking lot of the Fraser Arms Hotel.

Stunning sculpture: On-site evidence of native life is hard to come by here in Vancouver. To get an idea of what life was like for the earliest residents, visit the Museum of Anthropology on the campus of the University of British Columbia. The building is an airy, lofty marvel, designed by noted architect Arthur Erickson, and dominated at its entrance by gigantic totem poles and the stunning Bill Reid sculpture *Raven and the First Humans*.

Reid's sculpture shows Raven prying open with his beak a gigantic clam, from which, blinking and fearful, the world's first people emerge. (Reid, whose mother was a Haida Indian, is the Vancouver sculptor whose massive and powerful ebony-black sculpture, *The Spirit of Haida Gwai'i*, is set in the reflecting pool in front of the Canadian Embassy in Washington, DC.) If I know friends are going to be visiting the city for just one or two days, this museum is the one location I tell them they must see.

I enjoy showing visiting friends other distinctive buildings in the city, too. The Marine Building at Hastings and Burrard, for example. This gorgeous Art-Deco creation, dwarfed now by taller, glossier neighbours, opened just in time for the Great Depression. Even though it dominated the skyline of the time, for a couple of decades it sat mostly empty; no one could afford the rents. Then prosperity returned. For a great visual buzz, stand before the building's intricately carved main doorway, admiring the birds and planes and ships and seahorses, then afterwards step into the lobby. Wow! The man who designed that lobby eventually went to Hollywood and became a set decorator. The elevators are a glossy symphony of burnished hardwoods. The Marine Building is still the affectionate favourite of most Vancouverites.

in the Bruno Freschi-designed Science World, an Expo 86 legacy, irreverently called the "golf ball", the gleaming spherical giant on Quebec Street to which I frequently point visitors. Lots of ever-changing science shows are held here, with an emphasis on hands-on activities for the kids.

Holy structures: Several of the buildings I like to show visiting friends are churches. There's the little Russian Orthodox church on Campbell Street with its bulbous blue

The Westcoast Building on West Georgia is another eye-popper: the building is suspended from giant steel cables and actually hangs from a central core. Its distinctive look earned it occasional appearances on the TV adventure show *MacGyver*, where it purported to be the headquarters of MacGyver's mysterious operations.

The Vancouver engineer who conceived this building, Bogue Babicki, also had a hand

Preceding pages: two of the city's notable facades. <u>Left</u>, Chuck Davis at the On On Tea Garden. <u>Above</u>, *Raven and the First Humans*.

steeple (the church was built by its own priest, who died while finishing the little tower); St James's Anglican, a spectacularly Byzantine oddity designed by a man who had just finished working in the Middle East; and Holy Rosary Cathedral, a handsome Catholic structure whose placement is one of the great romantic traditions in the city. The bishop of the time, invited to choose the site for the placement of the new church, looked up into the lofty forest that covered most of what would become downtown Vancouver and pointed at the tallest of the trees. "There," he said, "put it there!"

In addition to Glen Brae, the Shaughnessy Heights neighbourhood has dozens of huge and dramatic homes, many originally built for railroad executives. A drive along its curving, quiet, tree-lined streets is an experience to be savoured.

When you visit Chinatown (not, as every city guide seems to have it, the second-largest in North America, but the third, because we're out-stripped by San Francisco *and* New York) you must see the World's Famous Building. That's what owner Jack Chow, a realtor, calls it. The 1912 Sam Kee Building bought, and partly occupied, by the canny Mr Chow is just 2 metres (6 ft) wide,

making it the narrowest commercial structure in the world. At one time, 14 separate companies were located in the building. A Chinese family of five once lived on the tiny top floor.

Unusual facades: The rest of Chinatown is also dotted with unusual facades. In fact, the north side of Pender Street has been called one of the finest groups of historic buildings in Canada. Constructed between 1886 and 1920 they demonstrate, said one admiring architect, a style "reminiscent of the commercial buildings in the proud cities of Shanghai and Beijing and the province of Canton.

Recessed balconies, cornices and pediments crown the facades of brick, often with dates to testify to the year they were built."

Chinatown is always a visually and aurally exciting place to be: barbecued ducks hang in the windows, "hundred-year-old" eggs nestle next to the *bok coi*, other strangely-shaped vegetables share space with more familiar fare on a hundred sidewalk stalls, stores bulge with woks and lanterns, statues of Buddha, lamps, herbs, books and a million other colourful things. Bright neon Chinese characters tempt you inside scores of restaurants where gigantic menus open to page after page of different dishes. Saturday and Sunday are the busiest days, with Vancouver's thousands of Chinese doing their grocery shopping then.

If you've time for just one Chinatown restaurant, I'd recommend the On On Tea Garden, a small and informal gem that's been a favourite with my family for more than 25 years.

Although the building itself is unremarkable, you should set aside half an hour or so to visit the small, but densely packed Museum of Exotic World on Main Street. It's a huge, odd collection of photographs (many from *National Geographic Magazine*) and artefacts from far-flung corners of the world, in Africa, the Far East, South America and beyond, collected on their world travels by a retired gentleman named Harry Morgan and his wife. Harry is delighted to see visitors and tell them about the adventures that he's had and that *they* could have in these distant and exotic worlds. It's fun and free.

The modern trend of gussying up heritage buildings to convert them into glittering retail palaces has been in full flower in Vancouver. Two genuinely attractive examples among many others are the Sinclair Centre and City Square. Vancouver's Gastown area pioneered the concept locally: an entire block-long section of decaying warehouses and crumbling little office blocks was transformed 20 years ago into a busy and hugely popular pocket of small shops, boutiques, bistros and cafés.

Gastown is still a fine place for strolling, with the harbour a few steps away, glimpsed between the old buildings. Art galleries, bookshops – with William Hoffer's big and unique collection of Canadiana worth a visit by the serious, and moneyed, book collector – souvenir stores, antique shops, ethnic emporia… lots to see and no shortage of places to eat an enormous variety of food.

Random photo: One of the town's more well-known sculptures is in Gastown. It purports to show Gassy Jack, the loquacious saloon keeper whose nickname was said to have inspired Gastown's name. I say "purports" because the sculpture, by Vern Simpson, is based on a photograph selected at random 20 years ago to represent old Gassy. A committee was leafing through some archival photos looking for someone who could have been Jack, and liked the look of one portly, bearded gent – name not known – leaning on a chair. Presto! He became Gassy Jack.

We seem to like statues of questionable lineage. A locally famous example is a full-sized Captain George Vancouver, standing on the north side of City Hall nobly pointing at something. That statue was based on a painting that once hung in an obscure corner elsewhere, because the curators decided they couldn't be sure it *was* Vancouver. There's a theory it may be George's brother, Charles Vancouver, a writer on botany. Incidentally, when I show a slide of that statue to Vancouver school kids during talks on the city's history and ask them who it is, they invariably reply: "George Washington".

The Vancouver statue and a great many others in the city were created during the 1930s and '40s by Charles Marega, a Swiss-born artist who fell in love with the city when he and his wife were here en route to somewhere else. They decided not to leave. Marega, over the years, provided us with many of our best statues as well as the dramatic Egyptian-style lions at the south end of the Lions Gate Bridge. His story has a sad ending, however: shortly after the Depression-era commission to do the bridge lions, he died with only $8 in the bank.

Speaking of sculptures, it's been said *The*

Crab, a gleaming and spiky George Norris creation in front of the Vancouver Museum/MacMillan Planetarium complex (*see page 155*), is the single most photographed object in the city. A fountain jets its waters into the innards of this most unusual of Vancouver's outdoor artworks.

Vancouver has been made incomparably more interesting in the nearly 50 years I have known it through successive waves of immigrants. An astonishing variety of peoples has been drawn into the city: Greeks, Germans, Italians, Hungarians, Czechs, Poles, Thai, Chinese, Japanese, Vietnamese, Filipino. Their restaurants and shops have enlivened

almost all of Vancouver's streets, and made it possible to dine and shop around the world at a moment's notice.

There are more than 3,000 restaurants in Greater Vancouver and I hope you'll have time to visit a flock of them. And I hope you'll have time to see a lot of Vancouver itself and environs.

If I were showing you around metropolitan Vancouver I might start or finish by driving you up on to the Upper Levels Highway, just across the inlet and halfway up the mountains. From here, you will be able to see all of the city all at once. The sight is stunning.

Left, horn of plenty. **Right**, the twin domes of Glen Brae, built in 1910, are a landmark in Shaughnessy Heights.

HOLLYWOOD NORTHWEST

When Vancouverites talk casually of a "shoot" on Georgia Street, they're not referring to downtown crime. Familiar with the caravan of trucks and limousines, the cables and sound booms that precede the making of a movie, they're comfortably at home with the jargon of what is one of their biggest and most rapidly expanding industries.

Since 1978, the BC film business has grown from $12 million to – in the early 1990s – $350 million. That's not counting the half billion dollars directly and indirectly generated into the British Columbian economy. It's estimated that 4,000 people are employed in film-making here. The fourth largest film production centre in North America, Vancouver is second only to Los Angeles in producing episodic TV. In one recent year, 332 hours of series, pilots and made-for-TV movies were filmed here. Later, this record was broken, moving the city past Florida into third place. Only in California and New York did more production take place.

Like its counterpart down the Pacific coast, the Vancouver movie industry has generated its own legends. There was the woman in the downtown ice-cream parlour who, finding herself next to Mel Gibson – "or it may have been Paul Newman" – distractedly dropped her double scoop of cherry ripple into her bag, snapped it shut and calmly asked for the star's autograph. There was the couple whose rundown home was completely redecorated top to bottom in a mere 24 hours for a film shoot "and not only that... they got paid for it!" And then there was the hungover commuter who ran whimpering into his office one July morning to announce that he'd just seen Santa Claus.

Lights, camera, action: Proximity to Los Angeles – it's a scant three hours' flying time away – is only one reason why movie crews are drawn to Canada's lower left-hand corner. It's partly, of course, the availability of expert crews, excellent studios and state-of-

<u>**Preceding pages:**</u> long-stemmed roses. <u>**Right**</u>, a location shoot in West Vancouver.

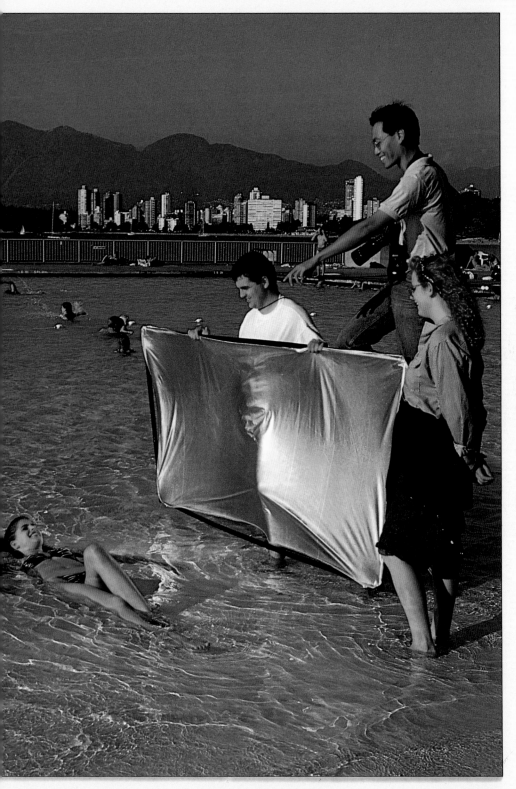

the-art post-production facilities. Directors' and writers' strikes, threatened and actual, together with unpredictably unstable conditions in the rest of the world, have also helped bring business north of the border. But the *numero uno* reason why the city and its surroundings have become the Hollywood of the North is the enormous variety of easily accessible locations. "If you can imagine it, the industry has used it, requested it or blown it up," says Mark Desrochers, former director of the BC Film Commission.

Uncut and unpolished, nature shows off in Vancouver with range upon range of snow-capped mountains, vast sandy beaches and

exchange downtown apartment blocks for a densely wooded canyon complete with a precipitous suspension bridge, or take a crew via cable car and chairlift to the ski slopes of Grouse Mountain. As one heads east, the mountaintop campus of Simon Fraser University is a futuristic glass eyrie tailor-made for sci-fi adventures. Driving another 30 minutes brings movie-makers to Pitt Polder, a stretch of land reclaimed from flood waters some 50 years ago by Dutch immigrants. Today, a flat tidy landscape that Van Dyck or Rembrandt might have painted, it's a *tabula rasa* for set designers.

The producers of the TV show *MacGyver*

sparkling blue waters. For the producer with a crew of 60 lighting experts to move, not to mention art directors, props people, camera-persons, gaffers, best boys and actors – the fact that these locations are mostly within an hour's drive is a distinct financial advantage.

Touting her shamelessly flaunted charms, Vancouverites pimp for their city with engaging enthusiasm. "You can ski in the morning and sail in the afternoon" is a frequent boast, invariably followed by a smug "aren't we lucky" smile. The fact is, you can.

In less time than it takes to sit through a soap opera, a professional movie crew can

built a bunch of huts, spread some empty oil drums around and called it a Cambodian airport. Ted Danson and Isabella Rossellini fell in love here in *Cousins*, a movie that, like the Mel Gibson/Goldie Hawn vehicle *Bird on a Wire*, provides a picture-book look at Vancouver. In recent years, the city was also the location for *This Boy's Life*, starring Robert De Niro and Ellen Barkin, and for the Burt Reynolds-produced *The Man Upstairs*, with Ryan O'Neal and Katharine Hepburn.

Offering magnificent waterfalls, lush meadows, sweeping grasslands, country lanes, lakes and ponds, alpine meadows (just in case they ever make *The Sound of Music 2*) and even genuine savannah grassland, Vancouver and its environs proffers a soup-to-nuts menu of nature *à la carte*. About the only variety of scenery missing is what the Film Commission terms "the big western look, deserts, tumbleweed, sagebrush"; for that, you have to drive half a day into the interior of British Columbia.

Chameleon city: Most shooting is done in and around the Lower Mainland, a loosely defined geographic area that includes the City of Vancouver and its neighbouring suburbs. With its generically North American, architecturally anonymous, downtown tow-

has also appeared on-screen as Munich in *Neverending Story I* and *II*. The thriller *Shoot to Kill* was a rare exception where the city appeared as itself. Transforming Vancouver into a US location is merely a matter of switching the maple leaf for the stars and stripes, adding a few mailboxes and stacking newspaper boxes with copies of the *Philadelphia Star* instead of the *Vancouver Sun*. Covering BC licence plates with magnetic US versions serves to complete the illusion.

Like any seaport, the city has its down and dirty side. Warehouses, factories, docks and oil refineries line part of its waterfront and when, as much of it does, the action on screen

ers side by side with older warehouse areas, Vancouver is a chameleon capable of masquerading as New York, Hong Kong, Los Angeles, turn-of-the-century Boston, Detroit, London or San Francisco.

Yaletown, an enclave of old brick warehouses currently undergoing gentrification, and Gastown, with its flat-iron-shaped Europa Hotel and cobble-stoned streets, have doubled for Baltimore and Philadelphia. Gastown

ends up in an alley, Vancouver has some of the most photogenic ones around, including the evocatively-named Blood Alley in Gastown and what is reputedly the most photographed laneway in North America on the 100 block of East Hastings Street.

Only the grittiest documentary calls for a real alleyway, raw and untouched. In the interests of hygiene, high-pressure hoses wash away the grunge after which "clean" garbage, such as bags full of recycled styrofoam, are artistically spread around. Shooting completed, the alley is cleaned a second time. Compared with most North

Left, easy locations have financial advantages. **Above**, North Shore Studios, Canada's largest, is not open to the public.

American and European cities, Vancouver is unusually pristine. The story goes that an American film crew, dismayed by the every-day cleanliness of an alley, threw down more garbage, left for lunch and returned to discover that an all-too-efficient cleaning crew had made short work of their creativity.

Permanent sets: Most appealing to dollar-conscious producers are those locations that need little or no doctoring. Formerly the provincial courthouse, the neo-classical Vancouver Art Gallery provides a frequently used setting for trials by jury. Burnaby Heritage Museum is a restored period town for both interiors and exteriors: buildings, a

schoolhouse, even a miniature train station. There are two real train stations, the splendidly isolated Canadian National building on Main Street which, up until the late 1980s, offered immigrants from eastern Canada their first view of Vancouver, and the glorious Canadian Pacific station, now the commuter SeaBus terminal and also home to the BC Film Commission. The *Royal Hudson*, Canada's last surviving steam train, and the *Love Boat,* which frequently ties up at the downtown cruiseship terminal, are also familiar sights to audiences glued to the screen.

Although little more than 100 years old,

Vancouver has none the less managed to foster an astonishing variety of residential architecture. Apart from "Vancouver specials" (bland shoebox-shaped duplexes free from any form of ornamentation), there is no such thing as indigenous design. Nineteenth-century timber barons advertised their wealth with massive mansions. Homesick immigrants built English cottages thatched with wood shingles, exuberantly pillared Greek and Italian villas, and stuccoed and tiled Spanish-style houses.

"Monster" homes are an unfortunate mismating of rococo, Olde English and Renaissance influences, an unsightly combination often garnished with wrought-iron gates flanked by stone lions. But Art Deco, Victorian Gothic or ersatz San Francisco, for a film company, it all adds up to more location choices. What is generally termed "west coast architecture", a harmonious melding of timber and glass, clings to the cliffsides and canyons of North and West Vancouver where it often stands in successfully for the Hollywood Hills or, as the BC Film Commission puts it: "Add a few palms and all you see is an exclusive home in an area of exclusive homes."

Movie-making is a high-impact industry. It closes streets, reroutes traffic and takes up parking spaces. For some, the cables snaking across a suburban lawn, the spotlights and cameras are a nuisance; for others, a lucrative income. The BC Film Commission has over 1,000 homes on file and talent scouts constantly knock on doors to find more.

Production companies from around the world can access these files. On any given day, the BC Film Commission's flow chart lists anywhere up to 17 projects being shot by production companies from Canada, the US, Europe and increasingly, Asia. Vancouver has played long-term host to a number of TV series, including *MacGyver, 21 Jump Street* (featuring Johnny Depp before he went on to be Hollywood's Edward Scissorhands) and *Danger Bay* with its action centred on the Vancouver Aquarium and the picturesque village of Deep Cove.

Nude cop show: Catalogued in the BC Film Commission's location files are everything from "airports" to "war memorials" but, even with over 70,000 photos available, resources are occasionally taxed to the fullest. For the forgotten epic *Flesh Gordon Meets the Cosmic Cheerleaders* the producers sought a mountain range that resembled a pair of breasts. The Commission has also been asked where trees can be found with limbs sturdy enough to support dancers dressed as fairies and was once approached by a US cable company eager to discuss the possibility of shooting a nude cop show in Vancouver.

Episodic TV or movies of the week can be shot rain or shine: an average rainfall is rarely torrential enough to register on screen. If the script demands a heavy downpour, rain

crew to Vancouver, whereupon the city went a record 61 days without rain.

Local stars: Over the years, Vancouver has produced its own galaxy of stars. A few have shone brightly, others have shimmered into oblivion, many have headed south at the first possible opportunity in search of Hollywood fame and, in varying degrees, have found it: Yvonne De Carlo, sultry star of *Salome Where She Danced*, *Songs of Scheherazade* and *Slave Girl*; June Havoc, *Dainty Baby Jane*, a vaudevillian from the age of seven, who featured in the movie *My Sister Eileen* but was better known as the sister of stripper Gypsy Rose Lee; Barbara Parkins, who spent

towers are used to boost the more common half-hearted drizzle. Sometimes the weather fails to cooperate. Having scouted Canada coast to coast and rejected most of it because of the severe winter, Paramount constructed a town on the shores of Stave Lake an hour from Vancouver for *We're No Angels*. What followed was the coldest winter ever. Attracted by the area's rainforests, the producers of *Distant Thunder* brought cameras and

a tempestuous five years as Betty Anderson in the TV series *Peyton Place*; Beverley Adams, author, ex-wife of hairdresser Vidal Sassoon and star of *How To Stuff a Wild Bikini*; Katherine DeMille, an orphan adopted by Cecil B. DeMille, who played exotic leads in the 1930s and 1940s. And, most recently – and tragically – Dorothy Stratten's walk down the yellow brick road to Hollywood which led to life as a Playboy bunny, death at the hands of her jealous husband and celluloid immortality as portrayed by Mariel Hemingway in *Star 80*.

Left, Yvonne De Carlo in Stanley Park. **Above**, Mariel Hemingway played pin-up Dorothy Stratten in the movie *Star 80*.

If sensuality has been the common denominator of Vancouver's home-grown female stars, a more solid, stolid but basically unsexy gallery of Vancouver-born male actors would be hard to find. Raymond Burr, *Perry Mason* for nine years, *Ironside* for eight, grew up in Vancouver's oldest suburb, New Westminster. James Doohan is known best for his role as Scotty in the *Star Trek* TV series and subsequent movies. Born on the Burrard Indian Reserve in North Vancouver just before the century turned, Chief Dan George was nominated in 1970 for an Oscar for his performance as the Cheyenne Elder seeking death in *Little Big Man*.

Only when yuppie-incarnate Michael J.

cated here), Bridge Studios opened in its new incarnation in 1987 with North America's largest effects stage and three sound stages. *MacGyver*, the first tenant, was shot here for four years but later switched to Los Angeles. North Shore Studios in North Vancouver is Canada's largest facility. The facades of its seven sound stages and office buildings represent various modern and period buildings, from rowhouses to a small town streetscape, creating a virtual "back-lot on the front-lot".

While tracking down a film shoot demands the investigative skills of a MacGyver, getting into the movies as an "extra" isn't

Fox, of TV's *Family Ties*, came along did a Vancouver actor cause hearts to pound and bosoms to throb. He wasn't the last. "We've had German girls beating down the doors in tears to see MacGyver," says a studio representative, and the prospect of adolescent *sturm und drang* over Richard Dean Anderson, Michael J. Fox or anybody else is the reason why, unlike in Hollywood, Vancouver's movie and TV production facilities are never open to the public.

Pity, because they're among the best in North America. Formerly a bridge-building site (sections of the Golden Gate were fabri-

much harder than picking up the phone. All that some of Vancouver's 40 talent agencies ask is that "you come in and register with a résumé, giving height, weight and body size. We take a picture and then we send you out to work." Over 1,000 would-be stars, aged six to 90, are currently on file.

Extras rarely get rich but no matter, many are happy to work for free; witness the huge crowd that cheerfully donned heavy winter clothing one sizzling summer day to observe the fight between Sylvester Stallone and Dolph Lundgren in *Rocky IV*. While rates can skyrocket to $17 an hour for a "specialty" role such as a cop or a lawyer, the going fee for being part of a nameless throng is five bucks an hour. "That's why we call them extras," says the casting agency. "Because it's only for extra money."

Successful extras know that the one unbreakable rule is never to approach or speak to the stars. In fact, for the movie fan in search of his or her personal god, the trail is a maze of dead-ends. The BC Film Commission has a list of what's being shot around town, but their lips are sealed when it comes to pinpointing exact locations.

Echoes of Expo: In 1986, the world came to Vancouver to marvel at its international ex-

Imax and Omnimax are film formats whose sheer size and scale transcend the usual screen limitations. Each projected frame, 10 times the size of conventional 35mm movie film, displays extraordinary sharpness and clarity while wraparound sound completes the audio-visual experience. Imax socks you with 9,000 watts of sound via four banks of half a dozen speakers. Omnimax cranks up the volume to 12,000 watts.

Movies are changing, and so is Vancouver's film industry. Positioned on the window ledge of Canada, the city increasingly reaches outwards to the Orient for business rather than backwards to eastern Canada.

position. Film, short on dialogue and strong on special effects, was a key component in trans-global communication and, while Expo 86 was razed to the ground, the movie technologies first seen there are still popular tourist attractions today, housed in the futuristic glass golf ball of Science World, a hands-on technology centre at the end of False Creek, and at Canada Place a few minutes' SkyTrain ride away.

Left, still from the TV series *MacGyver*. **Above**, a crew can film both downtown and in a rural setting in the same day.

Already, there are several cinemas in Vancouver that screen only Chinese movies. (The former Vancouver East repertory cinema is now the Far East Theatre.)

One movie, *Black Cat*, has already been shot in Vancouver for the Hong Kong market. A number of Chinese actors resident in Vancouver regularly return to work in Hong Kong. And, as Vancouver's Asian population grows by leaps and bounds, film-makers across the Pacific are sharpening their pencils and looking with new eyes at what may very well turn out to be a major market in the near future.

It laps at their feet and rather too often pours about their ears. Inevitably it seeps into their consciousness: the presence of water can't help but fill the imagination of Vancouver's inhabitants.

In summer, descending from the mistier North Shore, Squamish Indians used to paddle up Burrard Inlet to dig clams. Then as now, the locals had mixed feelings about the water. It was purifying, hypnotic to gaze at; it could also be oppressive. The Indians told stories to each other while in their canoes, shouting across the bewhiskered, bobbing heads of harbour seals.

In one story, a youth plunges endlessly into the ocean to cleanse his body and spirit for impending fatherhood. Impressed, the Indian god Sagalie immortalises the man by turning him into Siwash Rock, ever to stand on the shores of Stanley Park and be dutifully photographed by tourists. A less pleasant myth, reflecting the damper side of a watery clime, has Sagalie in an off-mood. He punishes a greedy native by changing the man into a sea serpent – who systematically thrashes canoes to bits and gulps down their paddlers.

Then as now, attitudes to the water shift. But the fascination never ebbs.

On the boats: *Pacific Yachting* editor John Shinnick, who with his blond hair and beard somewhat resembles popular depictions of Neptune, lives in a Canoe Cove 41 power boat. In the evening he and his wife sit on deck, contemplating the silhouettes of other False Creek Yacht Club boats against the sunset and then the moon. Sometimes Hank the blue heron perches nearby. On occasions they heave anchor and plough off to a more solitary patch. "There's something about looking outside to the clean horizon, the gorgeous water, the boundless pace, that pulls us out to sea," explains Shinnick.

The 35,000 vessels which use the 23-km (14-mile) long Strait of Georgia are divided

Preceding pages: a couple of swells. **Left**, rain has its compensations. **Right**, crab meet.

about equally between sailboats and power boats, but a preference is developing for the latter. This Shinnick attributes to the ageing of the current generation, who want more comfort. Shinnick's colleague George Will, an avid fisherman and editor of *BC Outdoors*, dislikes them all. A lover of the solitary, he deplores the tendency of "high-tech yuppies" to cram boats together in one spot. Huddling in crowds defeats the point of such a meditative sport as fishing, the ex-archae-

ology professor complains. "I don't like tangling my lines in other people's."

Will catches at least a dozen 16-kg (36-lb) salmon during his summer, but respecting the principles of Neptune, he throws most back. "People who think they have to fish to kill are prehistoric."

The pickings are good around the Vancouver waters. Bottomfish include flounder, red snapper, sole, rock cod, the googly-eyed ling cod, halibut and perch, while among the shellfish are crab, shrimp, mussels, clams, oysters, abalone and scallops.

With such reverence toward water, Vancouverites were seriously rattled when a recent government study branded their city the most depressing in Canada. According to the study (produced by the Treasury Board to calculate bonuses for civil servants), the rain and clouds that mist over Vancouver for weeks on end blight the psyche even more than the cold of Winnipeg or Whitehorse.

Reporters scrambled. They hunted out ex-residents of other climes, such as a Whitehorse woman who willingly complained about her former city being "grey, dusty and dark". But Vancouver, she added, was "good for the hair and the complexion". Local climatologists felt personally affronted by the study.

ing the weeping patterns on the window. But be aware that the drops' contents are sadly polluted. Vancouver rain bears ions of sulphate, nitrate, ammonium, sodium, chlorine, magnesium, calcium, carbonate and worse.

On the other hand, the black clouds that disgorge thunderbolts on the prairies further south and the funnel-shaped clouds that frightened Dorothy in the *Wizard of Oz* rarely plague Vancouver, whose clouds are delicate, nimbo-stratus strands.

With the fish: All of the foregoing, however, is scarcely relevant to those attentive to life in the deep. The uniform temperature and salinity of the water off British Columbia's

The weather is "moderated", not depressed, insists Norm Penny, superintendent of climatological data services in the Lower Mainland. As for Ottawa, where he once spent a summer, "It was like walking around in a sauna the whole time."

In the main, Vancouverites seem perfectly able to cope with the 147 cm (58 inches) of water that falls on their downtown area annually. The North Shore receives even more, registering a soggy 173 cm (68 inches) each year.

Some can wax quite romantic about the rain as they sit in cosy coffee houses study-

deeply indented coast have nurtured some of the world's finest fish and fauna extolled by, among others, Jacques Cousteau.

Unaffected by the weather above, oceanographers in the University of Victoria's submersible *Pisces IV* toss gently about under the sea, studying the plantlife and enjoying a rare, subterreanean panorama. They know that what you see is not always what you get. Brought to the surface, the most nondescript dark sponge may turn a stunning crimson. Water absorbs colour and grows inkier in depths away from the light.

The Lower Mainland's 50,000 skindivers

are in a position to spot gangly kelp, whose thick elastic trunks rooted on rocks can withstand the fiercest currents. When parted, the kelp reveals red, white, green and blue cup-like anemones, ridged by dainty tentacles, and transparent moon-like jellyfish. A few lucky divers can catch a glimpse the world's largest seastar, the 24-rayed *Pycnopodia helianthodes*.

Sea-going swimmers may be less enthusiastic to come across one of the 300 to 400 killer whales which thrive off BC's coast. White-bellied and 9 metres (30 ft) long, the whales open their ominous black tops like automobile hoods to reveal rows of sharp,

As society's sympathy for wildlife increased, however, the sight of these wild creatures banging futilely into their pen walls became less entertaining. The aquarium was at the forefront of those concerned: it became the first in the world to decide against capturing more whales, or holding further shows with performing whales.

Water into wine: East and south of the city's Alex Fraser Bridge stretches Burns Bog, 10 times the size of the nearby park, yet barely known to anyone in BC. It is, according to University of Victoria biology professor Richard Hebda, "a 3,000-year-old super-organism, almost a conscious being, a strange

conical teeth – 40 or 50 in all. Swimming along at the pace of a slow-moving car, they whistle and warble to each other both above and below the water.

Despite their name, killer whales have been more harmed than harmful. In less-enlightened times, a host of guidebooks cheerfully suggested visits to the Vancouver Aquarium in Stanley Park, promising that readers would enjoy observing the whales leaping about at the trainers' behest.

Left, ducks' delight. **Above**, around 17,000 sailboats use the Strait of Georgia.

symphony of collaborating life forms."

It is the last major bog on the west coast of North America. Huge, wild orchids grow in its steamy depths. Blue dragonflies which could not survive in the climate of Vancouver itself flit across it. Black bears lumber by; strange mice jump in kangaroo-type arcs.

So mystical has Burns Bog become, with its incongruous alpine and jungle ecology, that people lug away pailfuls of its water in order to make wine. Local legends hold that, the further you venture into the bog, the bigger its wild berries grow; also that at night dead trees turn into monsters.

If you visit Port Moody Inlet, you will see the tidal flats, some of the last in Canada. In 1792, Captain George Vancouver sailed here along the 31-km (19-mile) Burrard Inlet. He met the Squamish Indians – and found himself looking down into the soulful brown eyes of harbour seals, which today still follow canoers, occasionally rearing up out of the water to look around with their plaintive cries and barks. As the Captain chatted to the Indians, the seals little suspected he was discussing fur-buying, their own skins included. Port Moody's tidal flats are also the habitat for sandpipers, geese, eagles, fan-tailed pigeons and tweedy, binocular-clutch-

ing birdwatchers. Until a law banning firearms was passed in 1958, hunting was a popular local sport.

The beaches: When Captain Vancouver's ships poked over the horizon, his men jumped into rowboats and headed to a beach off Point Grey. There the sun and surf lulled them into such comfort one sailor failed to awaken even when rising tide began to carry him away. "I believe he might have been conveyed to some distance had he not been awakened by his companions," Vancouver remarked later.

The sailor's pleasure at sunbathing is shared today by the thousands who plonk themselves down on Vancouver's 16 km (10 miles) of sandy beaches. At Kitsilano, the worshippers are packed shoulder-to-toe with painstakingly aerobicised, mahogany-grilled bodies, all avidly insisting that Vancouver sun isn't strong enough to hurt the skin. Kits Beach is the finishing point of the Nanaimo Bathtub Race, a wild annual free-for-all that takes place every July.

West, Locarno and Spanish Banks Beaches are quieter. Their shallow water is usually a bit warmer than the summer average of 18°C–20°C (64°F–68°F). Beyond these, and invariably snubbed by puritanical tourist board brochures, is the nudist Wreck Beach, discreetly shielded from the University of British Columbia by thick alders and maples. Vendors wearing nothing more than sun visors sashay up and down chanting, "Ice-cold brown, brown, brown cows, white Russians, black Russians."

Across the water, English Bay and several beaches ring Stanley Park. Landing at English Bay in 1862, Yorkshire potter John Morton rhapsodised about its "white sands", and "boulders overhung with branches lapped at high tide". The white glint in the sands probably came from bits of the clamshells the Indians brought back from Port Moody.

Clockwise, North Shore beaches start with Cates Park on Indian Arm, where Malcolm Lowry wrote *Under The Volcano*. The serenity of West Vancouver's Ambleside is deafeningly pierced once daily by the steam locomotive *Royal Hudson*'s whistle, en route to the town of Squamish.

At Christmas, carol ships serenade most beaches. On New Year's Day up to 2,000 of the city's hardy, or perhaps foolhardy, jump into English Bay for the Polar Bear Swim. A few wiry, old souls who still hobble into the freezing water were around for the very first plunge, back in 1927.

In its own eccentric way, another less-publicised event lauds the water more ardently. The Save The Strait Marathon, sponsored by the Save the Georgia Strait Alliance, reminds locals to care for their water now if they want to have anything to celebrate in the future. Of the marathon's participating paddlers, swimmers, cyclists, snorkellers and rowers, one of the most ingenious is shipwright hobbyist Larry Westlake, who once set out in a "bubblegum kayak" constructed from 100 percent recycled materials.

Saving the endangered: There is a growing awareness by Vancouverites that our past behaviour has been very like that of the fabled fisherman's wife who asked and got great treasures from the sea until, in the face of her greed, the plunder ran out. Carcinogenic byproducts of pulp bleaching at Howe Sound mills have already been absorbed into the digestive glands of rock and Dungeness crabs, causing tumours, birth defects and

patched its submersible robot *Scorpio* down to siphon the oil with a hose – but environmentalists shook their heads and compared the increasingly damaged waters with the aftermath of Chernobyl.

As for the region's fabled salmon, University of Idaho scientists have suggested that a fishery sperm bank will soon be needed. The entire Fraser River Basin, they claim, is endangered by a deadly overdose of urban development, logging, grazing, railroad construction, dams and pulp effluent.

One recent year the famed Georgia cohoe, the world's largest salmon run, failed to make its July date for spawning up the Fraser

reproductive failures. These days more and more stark, official signs dot beaches warning people not to catch and eat the local fish. Bob Lyons calculated, in his Greenpeace study *Dire Straits*, that enough waste was being dumped into the Georgia Strait to fill BC Place Stadium 160 times over.

There are frequent oil spills, such as the one from the Japanese fish-processing ship in the Juan de Fuca Strait that killed 10,000 seabirds. The Canadian Coast Guard dis-

Left and **above**, in the Vancouver area you can swim in the morning and ice-skate in the evening.

at Adams River. The fish did eventually turn up, but no one could explain the somewhat ominous delay.

There aren't many rays of light in this ecological scenario but one of them is that what Greenpeace calls North America's worst polluter – the paper pulp industry – might be ready to clean up its act. One local paper mill says that after much expensive research they have been able to produce chlorine-free pulp. It doesn't look quite so pristine white but maybe the world is ready to accept that in exchange for a cleaner environment and the fresh water Vancouverites love.

THE SEX LIFE OF SALMON

The sex life of the salmon is one of sadness and inspiration. Born already orphaned it never meets its children, yet the last stages of its life are a struggle in which it sacrifices everything to ensure their future. When it leaves the ocean, fully mature and ready to spawn, it can travel close to 50 km (30 miles) a day, dodging sea-lions, bears and other predators and battling fiercely against adverse currents to return to the place of its own birth.

There, with exactly the right temperature and climatic conditions, it fulfils its date with destiny, females depositing several thousand eggs in deep gravel and males fertilising them before both drift away to die. The gravel beds, flushed by water that bears oxygen and removes wastes, protects the young until they can swim downstream and then in their turn grow to maturity in the ocean. The cycle is inexorable.

"Any real concern for self-preservation has largely left them," wrote conservationist Roderick Haig-Brown about the reckless drive of spawning salmon. "They are obsessed with sexual purpose and the imminence of death leaves no leeway for other concerns. Successful spawning is the preservation of the race."

Among the salmon's predators, of course, none is more deadly than man. From the earliest times native Americans knew well the salmon route. It was easy to catch them as they cautiously bypassed the currents and eddies, gathering for their magnificent waterfall leaps on the way upstream. Along both the Columbia and Snake rivers many villages held age-old rights to fish with – depending on the season – hook and line, seine (a net which is used to encircle a school of fish), spear or the bag-shaped dip net attached to a pole. Sometimes wickerwork baskets were used and here and there wooden "fish wheels" would block specific channels acting like miniature Ferris wheels to scoop them up. In Alaska salmon were hunted with bow and arrow aimed from birch bark canoes.

There was once a famous annual gathering of the tribes at the Celilo Falls on the Columbia River, near the present site of the community called Wishram, where the salmon fishing was accompanied by trading market in hides, blankets, food, baskets and other necessities.

The first salmon of the season to be caught was celebrated with singing, dancing and praying – ceremonies that have survived to this day. On the 9,000-hectare (22,000-acre) Tulalip reservation north of Everett in Washington state's Snohomish County, drummers and singers head for the water when Big Chief King Salmon is landed. If it is treated well – even if it is eaten – legend insists, many more salmon will follow and the fishing will be good.

"O Swimmer, I thank you that you are willing to come to us. Don't let your coming be bad, for you come to be food for us," was part of the address made by Kwakiutl Indians at their First Salmon Ceremony. Like most tribes they assigned the salmon as much importance as their counterparts on the plains did to the buffalo. In recent years some conservationists have speculated whether the salmon was not destined to suffer the same depleted fate. Officials from Canada's Department of Commerce, electric power authorities and conservationists have been at odds over whether the Snake River sockeye salmon are "endangered" or merely "threatened".

Millions of dollars are at stake because releasing more water over the dams to help the fish migrate has repercussions for electric power use, barge traffic, irrigation and fishing. Everybody agrees that the declining numbers have been caused by overfishing, poor water quality and obstacles created by the dams. What nobody can agree on is how to solve the problem.

When Simon Fraser in 1808 first descended the river which now bears his name, he subsisted on the same type of dried salmon that had been subsistence for the natives. Dehydrated in the sun or smokehouses, the pulped flesh was packed tightly into baskets of grass or cedar strips already waterproofed with a lining of stretched skins. The resulting packages were ideal in both size and shape for transportation by canoe. The Fraser River is even today still abundant with salmon with one of its tributaries, the Adams, being responsible for the largest production from a single river.

In the 1830s the Hudson's Bay Company began buying salmon from the Indians and shipping it to Asia, eviscerated, scrubbed, salted and packed into barrels. At that time virtually every coastal river and creek from California to Alaska teemed with the fish. Until the completion of the railroad in 1886, in fact, salmon was briefly British Columbia's major export.

Puget Sound's first salmon cannery, set up at Mukilteo in Snohomish County in 1887, was soon absorbed by the Alaska Packers Association, but by the end of the century there were dozens of companies, and destruction and devastation were under way. Extremely long traps wiped out entire runs as the fish-lazy "sportsmen" casually tossed dynamite into pools (most of the dead fish sank to the bottom); canneries dumped tons of fish to rot because it wasn't red-meat sockeye; the mining and lumber industries polluted some rivers beyond redemption.

With a wasteful policy of catching virtually everything that swam by, there was too much to handle even for the busy canneries whose primitive art had not progressed much beyond testing individual cans for leaks by holding them under water and then lacquering them to inhibit rust. When attention turned from sockeye (the word is

Artificial hatcheries to improve the fish supply were first introduced more than a century ago but today even some of these are being criticised for releasing their breed to mingle with fish born in the wild and thus diluting the natural strain. Attempts to transplant Pacific Northwest salmon to other parts of the world have been largely unsuccessful, except for flourishing schools off New Zealand's southern coast.

Recently the dispute has taken a different turn with the enormous growth of foreign salmon farms – Norway, Scotland, Canada and Chile are the major sources – shipping hundreds of millions of pounds of fish each year, lifting their market share in a decade to 30 percent eventually to rival that of Alaska. Ironically Alaska's thousands of

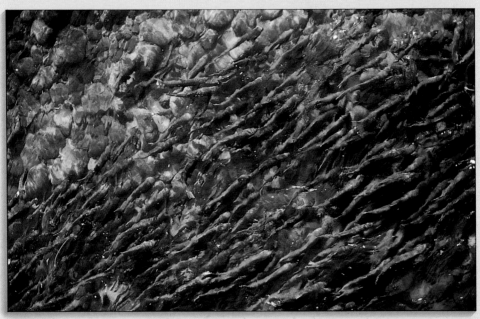

a corruption of the Salish *sukleigh*) to the pink-fleshed coho, a new marketing slogan was born: Warranted not to turn red in the can.

There are three principal salmon types: chinook (king), blue back with silvery sides; coho (silver) slightly larger with blueish green back later turning red; and sockeye (red), bright blue back (later red) with whitish belly. All of them head inland from May to October – the major flow being in August – bypassing the river obstructions and dams by means of specially constructed "fish ladders".

Above, sockeye salmon spawning in the Adams River, after which both male and female will die.

miles of undeveloped coastline would be ideal terrain for salmon farming, but in a misguided attempt to protect its fishermen the state discouraged it until recently. Most people in the industry see the future in terms of improving domestic consumption. "The room for growth is here with 250 million people who eat salmon only twice a year," says one packer.

Three new salmon farms about to open in the Pacific Northwest area had first to satisfy ecologists that waste droppings from thousands of fish would not unduly pollute the water and threaten other marine life. To the delight of local headline writers the operators agreed to study the feasibility of "fish diapers" to solve the problem. ∎

"Eco-terrorist" is the latest buzzword in the forests of British Columbia. It is a harsh term being used in a bitter campaign that is pitting father against daughter, husband against wife and an ever growing number of individuals against some of the largest corporations in Canada's most western province.

The headlines scream of people who hurl their bodies in front of logging trucks, chain themselves to tall and ancient trees and hammer dangerously long nails into the hearts of magnificent timber to stop the loggers from tearing down some of the oldest natural forests in North America.

It is a battle that has turned the names Carmanah Valley, Meares Island, Stein Valley, Clayoquot Sound, Moresby Island, Robson Bight, Walbran Valley and countless other forested regions into household names throughout British Columbia.

But this is not a simple story of long-haired hippies fighting it out against multi-national corporations. Like elsewhere around the world, the controversy over the old-growth forests in BC is attracting a new breed of environmentalist that includes high school honours students, doctors, lawyers, artists and housewives. It's hardly the picture of communist radicals once painted by the multibillion dollar lumber companies.

Virgin forests: At stake are the last virgin forests in Canada, places virtually untouched by human hands where the wildlife and plant life have prospered undisturbed since Christopher Columbus made his journey across the great waters.

The latest symbol in these battles has become the Carmanah Valley, 160 km (100 miles) north of the thriving capital city of Victoria, where the climatic conditions of over 600 cm (250 inches) of annual rainfall and thick, nutrient-rich soils help the Sitka spruce grow to enormous stature. This is the home to the Carmanah Giant, the tallest tree

in Canada, estimated at more than 500 years old and 95 metres (312 ft) tall.

This rare valley has several hundred Sitka spruce that measure almost that height, but despite assurances from the lumber companies that the oldest trees will not be touched, the protesters come to prevent logging on nearby hillsides that they say will do irreparable harm to the sensitive eco-system.

It is probably fitting the Carmanah is not far from Friendly Cove on Nootka Sound

where Captain James Cook, sailing with the *Resolution* and *Discovery*, landed in 1778 and became the first white man to chop down one of the giant trees for masts, spars and fuel for his wood-burning stoves. Cook discovered a 1,600-km (1,000-mile) coastline blanketed with untouched forest and he didn't need long to appreciate it.

Within 10 years of the region's initial exploration, the first real logging operation in British Columbia was undertaken by Captain John Meares, on orders from the Merchant Proprietors of London to load up as much raw lumber as he could possibly stow

Preceding pages: autumn leaves. **Left,** Cathedral Grove on Vancouver Island. **Right,** seedling for a replanted forest.

aboard and head to China for the first sale of British Columbia lumber. "Indeed, the woods of this part of America are capable of supplying with their valuable materials, all the navies of Europe," Meares wrote on that long but lucrative voyage.

The perception that the forests would last forever was the start of the whole problem. The practice of "cut and run" – chopping down massive areas of forest without replanting – was widespread and unchecked. Before the mid-1800s, British Columbia, like the Wild West of the US, was virtually without any government and raw resources were plain and simply there for the taking.

ered sawmills, chain saws, railways and eventually helicopter logging, was a natural occurrence in attempts to get at more logs faster and more efficiently. With a frontier mentality determination, the logger barons became very wealthy men.

Captain Stamp's bargain: By the year of Confederation, 1867, when Canada was declared a country, several million board feet of lumber were exported from the province of British Columbia. Captain Edward Stamp built the famous Hastings Mill plant in what is now the centre of downtown Vancouver. Under the Land Ordinance Act of 1865, the first piece of forestry legislation in the prov-

At first, BC logs were simply shipped overseas for processing, but on 24 November 1848, the enormous Hudson's Bay Company opened the first machine-operating, water-powered lumber mill near Victoria. Things were looking rosy when the mill shipped masses of finished lumber to San Francisco during the California Gold Rush.

But like any other resource-based industry, the logging companies that began proliferating around the coast were subject to a highly volatile boom-and-bust economic cycle. The drive to automation, starting with steam power and moving to electric-pow-

ince, Stamp was able to acquire the rights for virtually all the timberland in what is now metropolitan Vancouver, an area of almost 200,000 hectares (500,000 acres), for the princely sum of $1 per acre.

British Columbia came into the international limelight when Ross McLaren Sawmills spent $350,000 for construction of the Fraser Mills plant, the world's largest, about 30 km (20 miles) from Vancouver in January 1889. But Fraser Mills faced some tough times in its early days. With poor weather conditions, an illness that eventually killed company president Ross McLaren, a change to new equipment and the need for channel improvements on the Fraser River, the first exports did not leave until 1906.

As logging rose to the number one business in British Columbia, international pressures came to bear on the industry. An early indication of these outside influences arrived in 1907, when the first big financial bust hit the marketplace. A set of temporary American tariffs meant it was cheaper to import US lumber than it was to produce Canada's own. Wages dropped from $35 to $25 a month. But less than three years later, spurred by the impending opening of the Panama Canal, the boom times hit. A total of

"An epoch, sir, is drawing to a close – the epoch of reckless devastation of the natural resources which we, the people of this fair young province, have been endowed by Providence."

Although the warning bells were rung long ago, the tense and sometimes violent standoffs have only begun to be felt. Today, environmentalists are fighting to turn pristine valleys into dedicated parks, native bands want the return of their ancient land, conservationists argue against the destruction of habitat for rare and endangered species, and sometimes even the fishermen protest against logging that could damage some of the most

$65 million was invested in the BC lumber industry by US industrialists and speculators who acquired 90 percent of the growing provincial logging and lumbering industry.

Knock on wood: These developments virtually forced the provincial government to call the first British Columbia Royal Commission of Inquiry on Timber and Forests, and few people were surprised when W. R. Ross, Minister of Lands, delivered this stunning verdict on the state of the industry in 1909:

<u>Left</u>, Vancouver's first real estate office, 1880s.
<u>Above</u>, Stanley Park's hollow tree, 1890s.

important salmon-breeding streams and rivers in North America.

The complexity of the issue of land use disputes is comparable to the size and scope of the province and its forest industry. British Columbia has a landmass which is more than the US states of California, Oregon and Washington combined. Fully two-thirds of this is covered in trees. The provincial forest industry is estimated to be worth a total of $13 billion and provides 80,000 direct jobs. Even more important, the forests are indirectly responsible for half of the total 1½ million jobs in the province.

But if the employment statistics look rosy, don't be fooled. British Columbia forestry companies use the most technologically advanced equipment in the world and have managed to pare their work force to a mere 1.05 jobs for every 1,308 cubic yards of wood logged. That figure is the lowest in the world, comparing to 2.2 jobs created in the rest of Canada, 2.52 in Sweden, 3.55 in the United States and 5.0 jobs in New Zealand. Although the production of lumber has jumped 15 percent in the past decade, the number of jobs has dropped by an equally large percentage.

With a growing threat that more jobs will

be lost because of the environmentalists, the usually antagonistic union members have joined their employers in the campaign to discredit the so-called "tree huggers". The incidents of violence when loggers meet the protesters are becoming more common.

When the initial land protests began in the late 1960s and '70s, in remote places like the Queen Charlotte Islands, the forest industry was able to keep the conservationists at bay. But the environmentalists established a firm foothold in British Columbia that was not going to be so easily shaken.

The first eco-warriors from this part of the

world, Robert Hunter and Paul Watson, gained international attention when they formed Greenpeace, the ground-breaking environmental action group, in 1971. The loose-knit society had unprecedented success when it mustered more than 10,000 people to its first protests against nuclear weapons tests in Alaska. Soon, the organisation moved on to fight against the Arctic Ocean seal hunt, the slaughter of whales in the Pacific Ocean and the acid rain from steel and chemical mills on the east coast.

Save the trees: Within a decade, the large corporations and governments knew they weren't facing just another fad. This environment thing was catching on. The Green Party, a political group devoted to ecological issues, was beginning to see the first signs of electoral success in Europe. Big-name musicians were joining the rallying cry to save the Amazon rainforest. And in British Columbia it was no different.

The hippie radicals of the 1960s were becoming the yuppie business people of the 1980s and the face of the environmental movement was changed forever. These new protectors of ecology were doctors, lawyers, school teachers, students and even young children who feared for their own future in a world that might be smothered in pollution. With names like the Western Canada Wilderness Committee, the Friends of Clayoquot Sound, and even the Raging Grannies, people ventured out into the forests to sing the new folk songs and save the trees.

Thousands of people willing to join the front lines have created some interesting sidelines. In 1990, after Indian bands and ecological groups blockaded access to one proposed logging site in the interior of BC, the foresters responded by shutting down the road to the native lands. On the other hand, a small group of unionised loggers recently refused to chop down a 10-hectare (25-acre) patch of timber on Vancouver Island because the stand included a rare mix of old-growth Douglas fir, balsam, hemlock, spruce, red cedar and cottonwood. Recent opinion polls rank concerns with the forests as the number one environmental problem in BC.

Inflammatory words and phrases like "eco-terrorist", "tree-spiking" and "jobs versus the environment" have succeeded in confusing the average citizen. But while the sensational headlines go to the protesters chaining themselves to trees and throwing themselves in the paths of mammoth bulldozers, the more intelligent and organised of the environmentalists know the bravado and daring in the forests is just a sideshow to the real issue. With thousands of forestry jobs at stake, the small groups of the conservationists are looking for economic alternatives.

Getting the public to understand what is wrong with the management of the forests will take even harder work. One glance at such complex subjects as Tree Farm Li-

Further damaging the economy is the amount of raw lumber – with merely the branches pulled from the trunks – that is being shipped overseas to the primarily Asian marketplaces. Even labour unions, enemies of the environmentalists, agree the creation of new industries like furniture factories and other "value added" wood-processing plants would bring back thousands of jobs lost in the industry.

At times it seems the environmentalists are gaining ground against practices such as clear-cut logging – an unsightly act that literally wipes away every tree on a hillside – especially in areas like Robson Bight where thousands of tourists travel each year to

cences, Public Sustained Yield Units and Allowed Annual Cut ratios can deter anyone from delving any further into economics of lumber. But the environmentalists have found some convincing arguments that BC's forests are not being properly managed.

On the world market, softwood lumber from BC fetches rock-bottom prices – sometimes less than a quarter of what it would command if it came from New Zealand.

Left, environmentalists think the forests are being destroyed. **Above**, at a Walbran Valley protest, about 30 people were arrested.

watch the whales. But real changes are not going to be easily achieved. The timber companies have retaliated with a sophisticated PR campaign. They are defending the clearcut system as the most economical and efficient way to reach logs on mountainous terrain and are stressing the fact they are planting 50 million seedlings a year.

The BC situation is unique. On one side is a determined environmental lobby and on the other is a giant $13 billion forest sector indirectly responsible for employing 750,000 people. Jobs versus the environment. The controversy will likely continue for years.

Vancouver ranks enviably high on the Good Life Meter. You can see that in the faces of bikinied windsurfers at Jericho Beach. You can spot it in the lazy lope of visitors to Gastown and in the comfortable stride of weekend fitness nazis who hike the circumference of what someone once termed "the 1,000-acre therapeutic couch that is Stanley Park". You can identify it in the media back-patting that's followed Vancouver's improved reputation as a fine restaurant town.

The Good Life is equally obvious during a walk through the arts-and-crafts area of Granville Island or along the up-scale blocks of fashionable Robson Street. Most of the people you see *want* to be here; they don't just *have* to be here. This includes the Hong Kong entrepreneurs who, having been driven from their homeland by the 1997 deadline for the return of Hong Kong and Macao to mainland China, are resettling in Vancouver by the thousands each year – and bringing with them not only large families but, in some cases, millions of investible dollars. One such immigrant, Victor Li, son of the richest man in Hong Kong, owns the old Expo 86 site on the north shore of False Creek, which he's turning into a housing and business district that will expand the size of Vancouver's downtown area by one-sixth.

And this is a city that, agreeable as it is, people can't wait to get out of – not to escape Vancouver itself but to enjoy some of the awesome charms that surround it. They head north and east to the mountains for skiing, hiking, invigorating air or just the inspiring views; south to the lovely Gulf Islands, the US border or Victoria. Across the Georgia Strait Vancouver Island, at whose southern end Victoria sits on a busy harbour, stretches northwards for more than 400 km (250 miles) dotted with enough attractions to demand a week of anybody's time, from big-city museums to small-town fishing piers.

Thousands of people travel on boats every day around the waters of Vancouver. If places were judged by the quality of their water-front, this city would rate about as high as they come. Not only does it have hundreds of miles of waterfront, but its vast harbour is one of the world's most spectacular.

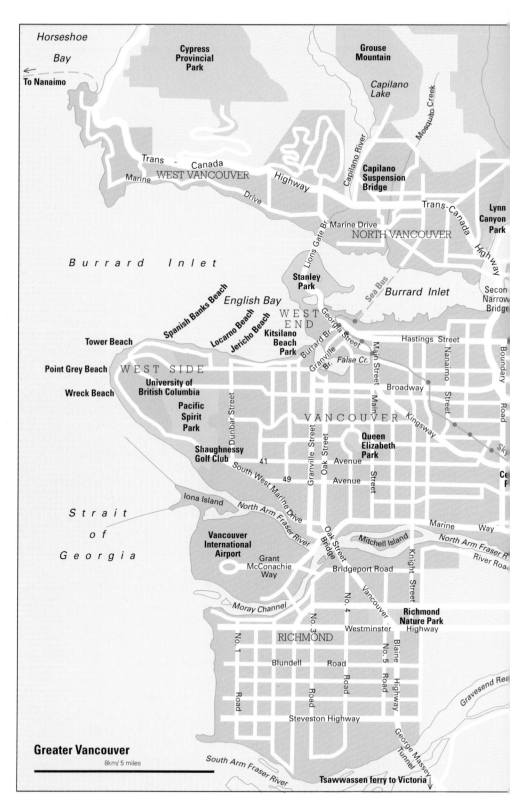

Greater Vancouver

8km/ 5 miles

120

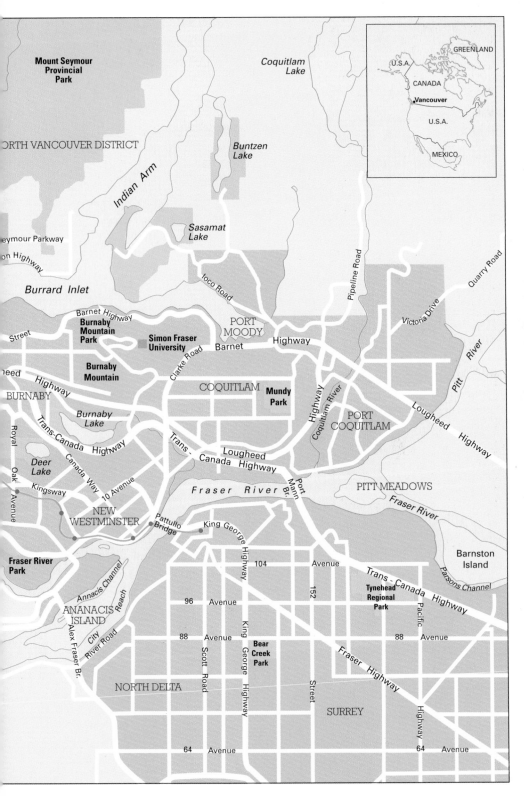

Mount Seymour Provincial Park

Coquitlam Lake

GREENLAND

U.S.A.

CANADA
Vancouver

U.S.A.

MEXICO

NORTH VANCOUVER DISTRICT

Buntzen Lake

Indian Arm

Seymour Parkway

on Highway

Sasamat Lake

Ioco Road

Pipeline Road

Quarry Road

Burrard Inlet

Barnet Highway

Burnaby Mountain Park

Simon Fraser University

PORT MOODY

Barnet   Highway

Victoria Drive

Pitt River

Street

Burnaby Mountain

Clarke Road

COQUITLAM

Mundy Park

Coquitlam River

PORT COQUITLAM

Lougheed Highway

Highway

BURNABY

Burnaby Lake

Trans-Canada Highway

Canada Way

Trans-Canada Highway

Lougheed Highway

Highway

PITT MEADOWS

Fraser River

Royal

Deer Lake

Oak

Avenue

Kingsway

10 Avenue

Fraser River

Port Mann Br.

Barnston Island

Parsons Channel

NEW WESTMINSTER

Pattullo Bridge

King George Highway

104   Avenue

Trans-Canada Highway

Pacific

Fraser River Park

Annacis Channel

Reach

96   Avenue

152

Tynehead Regional Park

ANANACIS ISLAND

City

River Road

Alex Fraser Br.

88   Avenue

Scott Road

King George Highway

Bear Creek Park

88   Avenue

NORTH DELTA

Fraser Highway

Street

SURREY

Highway

64   Avenue

64   Avenue

DOWNTOWN

Vancouver is a city whose geography one needs to understand as early as possible. For an overall impression, it would be hard to beat the view from Canada Place, or from the observation deck of the Harbour Centre across the street. From the exterior levels of **Canada Place**, the various landmarks are clearly and interestingly identified by means of carefully-positioned plaques at the edge of the various decks overlooking the water.

Looking to the west, **English Bay** laps at the shores of the peninsula which separates Vancouver harbour from the **Strait of Georgia**, the northern part of the peninsula looking much as it must have done when it was occupied by the Salish Indians whose only means of transport were canoes carved from red cedar trees. The first roads were built from the piles of shells salvaged from their refuse tips. In 1863, when Canada was still unsure of its mighty US neighbour, this land was set aside as a military reserve; eventually by a stroke of good fortune it was turned over to the city undeveloped and became Stanley Park. Indented under Stanley Park's south shore, Coal Harbour – a seam was worked here briefly a century ago – is host to shipyards, yacht clubs and a floating restaurant.

Almost immediately adjoining Canada Place itself, the old **Canadian Pacific Railway terminal**, which in 1914 replaced a magnificent chateau-type building on the site, is now a terminal for the **SkyTrain** (monorail) system and also the city's **SeaBus**. When CPR's first train, festooned with flowers, steamed into the station here on 23 May 1887, the whole town turned out to celebrate. An endless stream of grain, lumber, even immigrants, could now travel with relative ease from coast to

Left, downtown skyline.

coast and at last Canada had a deep-water port from which it could trade with the exotic Orient on a regular basis. The old CPR building is one of the city's most impressive, its attractive interior decorated with romantic pictures of the Rocky Mountains by the wife of a long-dead railway executive.

Wooden ships: CPR quickly developed the harbour with wharves and hotels; by the time of World War I, North Shore shipyards were turning out a non-stop stream of cargo and supply ships, tugs, icebreakers, fishing boats and barges, many built with wooden hulls because steel was scarce. Today, 60 million tons of materials and ships leave from the score of terminals here every year, bound for the ports of 80 different countries.

The first ferries chugged across the inlet in 1900; early forerunners of today's SeaBus which takes approximately eight minutes to cross to Lonsdale Quay, the North Shore's upmarket shopping centre. **BC Ferries**, with 39 vessels, serves more than 40 ports up and down the coast and on nearby islands.

A bridge crosses Burrard Inlet in the east, latest in a long succession of bridges which were damaged by ships and eventually demolished. Rare sightings of killer whales have been made in the harbour; they are lured here to feed on salmon which were once in plentiful supply but are now mostly to be found in the big, red **Canfisco building** where they have been processed and canned since 1918, the continuation of an industry then almost a century old.

On a clear day another view from Canada Place, which also contains the city's **Trade & Convention Centre**, is of 3,000-metre (10,000-ft) **Mount Baker**. It is named after Captain George Vancouver's third mate and is fully 80 km (50 miles) south of the Canada/US border. A possibly-extinct volcano (its last eruption was in 1843), it has been popular with mountain climbers since the first known ascent in 1868 and offers skiing on its rugged slopes.

There are two eating places which

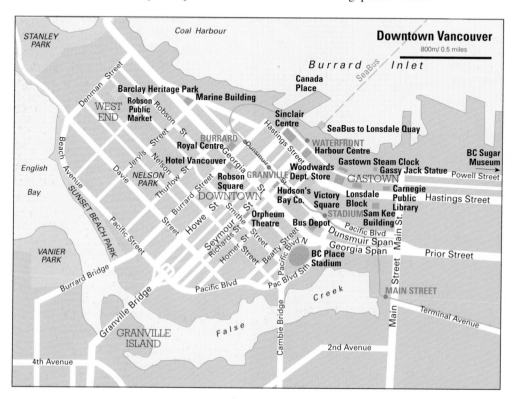

overlook the harbour at the end of Canada Place: an inexpensive cafeteria and the classy Prow Restaurant. Visitors can watch ships traverse the harbour, identifying their flags or silhouettes from explanatory charts beside one of the Canada Place stairways. A glass elevator connects the different decks and floors; down below are promenade shops, fast-food counters and an immense arrival hall to serve the arriving and departing cruise ships.

At one end is the stylish Japanese-owned **Pan Pacific Hotel**, which has thick carpets, soft sofas, waterfalls, a piano bar and big windows overlooking the harbour. Outside is a clock that lights up with times around the world, plus another waterfall. Across the street is the 23-storey **Waterfront Centre Hotel**, one of the CP chain.

Just east of Canada Place, towering above the corner of Hastings and Richards streets, is the 169-metre (553-ft) tall **Harbour Centre.** Both the revolving restaurant and the observation deck offer what is perhaps the best view in the city. Skip the 12-minute "multi-image extravaganza" which is one of the more banal examples of its kind, and concentrate on the view. During the summer months, there's a nightly salmon dinner "theme show" in the restaurant.

Gastown: Standing at the corner of Cambie and Water streets, Gastown begins with a unique sight: the world's first **steam-powered clock**. Every hour crowds of spectators assemble to watch synchronised jets of steam announce the time from noisy whistles far above their heads. Built by horologist Ray Saunders, who maintains a basement workshop nearby, the clock was not erected until 1977 but the original design for its mechanism dates back to a century earlier. It certainly looks it. An outer bronze case hides an elaborate system of steel weights on a chain, plus a music box which plays the Westminster chimes every 15 minutes, all powered by an underground steam source.

The sidewalk tables of the **Water

The city's charm lies in its natural setting.

Street Café, opposite the clock, are crowded on non-rainy days, which for most of the year are all too infrequent. "Rain dominates Vancouver," wrote Donald Stainsby 30 years ago. "To understand the city you must study rain and its variants, wet snow and fog. Rain affects the life of the whole city. Even the absence of rain is notable." Once rain starts, Stainsby said in his book *Vancouver Sights and Insights,* "you don't make a dash for the bus hoping it will clear up; you put on a raincoat and prepare to use it for several days."

The first commercial business in the new city after Hastings Mill was established in the 1860s, was a wholesale grocery firm built by Bavarian-born David Oppenheimer. His brick warehouse at Columbia and Jackson, now **Pier One Imports**, was followed by other neighbourhood businesses. Oppenheimer, along with his brothers Isaac and Charles, had built up a fortune by supplying wagon trains en route to the Cariboo goldfields. By the time he

arrived in Vancouver in 1885, Oppenheimer was rich enough to buy all the land between the present-day streets of Carrall and Gore. He fought constant battles with the Canadian Pacific Railway who were trying to expand the town further to the southwest.

When CPR built the **Hotel Vancouver** the following year, its location at Georgia and Granville was felt to be "way out in the woods". Oppenheimer, by then the city's mayor, gave a boost to his part of town in 1889 when he and brother Isaac established the Vancouver Street Railway company to run trams along Powell Street between Main and Campbell Avenue. "There is no doubt," remarked the *Vancouver Daily World* on 14 January 1890, "that the electric light wire is dangerous, that it has killed a great many people… (but) the situation is not dissimilar to half a century ago when railways began to supplant stage coaches. But notwithstanding frequent appalling accidents we now know that railway travelling is much less dangerous than travelling by coach. It will be so with electric lighting." The city finally abandoned its streetcars in favour of buses in the 1950s.

Gastown's main drag, **Water Street**, is composed mostly of souvenir shops and touristy restaurants but also includes a **wax museum**, a photography studio that will dress you in 1890s style and the **Inuit Gallery**, which sells exclusively native arts and crafts.

Woodwards department store, whose mail-order catalogues supplied isolated western communities for decades after it was founded in 1892, has a Water Street entrance, but its main building – the roof bearing an enormous revolving "W", a landmark seen for miles – has stood at the corner of Hastings and Abbott since 1902. This end of Hastings is now a seedy but interesting mélange of cheap hotels, cut-priced restaurants and low-budget shopping; be sure to note Sikori's Classical Records near Abbott. Also check out **Funky Winter Bean's Pub** with its brass rails, marble-

The view from the centre's observation deck is far-reaching.

topped bar, wooden balustrades and silent-movie nudes.

One block north, at 21 West Cordova (where sailors once caroused in the stand-up bar of the anything-goes Stanley Hotel), stands the **Pig & Whistle Pub.** The old Travelers Hotel (now a residence) in the white, four-storey **Fortin Building** (1893) and the **Lonsdale Block** (1889) across the street recall an earlier age.

The **Old Spaghetti Factory** restaurant, with its charming, antique-filled interior, occupies the ground floor of what was once the warehouse built by Staffordshire-born William Harold Malkin. Malkin left England as a teenager and arrived in Vancouver in 1895 to start a wholesale grocery business which provisioned prospectors heading for the Kootenay goldfields. In 1928 he became mayor of Vancouver, at least partly because of his campaign pledge to eliminate the CPR crossing at Carrall and Hastings where shunting trains held up traffic several times each day.

His successful firm was responsible for constructing three warehouses on Water Street – at Nos 139, 353 and 57. "Malkin's Best" proclaimed the huge sign on his rooftop, matched by the Nabob sign advertising the coffee of his rivals, Robert Kelly and Edward Douglas, down the block. The Kelly-Douglas firm – its warehouse is now **The Landing** – also served the mining booms. Douglas, in fact, was on his way back from a summer visit to the Klondike, his order book filled and $50,000 cash in hand, when his ship hit an iceberg and sank. Kelly, who got his training working for David Oppenheimer, continued to prosper: his Nabobettes singing group became an early hit on commercial radio and his 1940 lemon-scented ad in the Vancouver *Province* for a new soap was at the time a sensational new advertising gimmick.

The Landing is a delightfully user-friendly shopping mall, two levels filled with eating places and such stylish stores as Ralph Lauren, the Edinburgh Tartan

Curled up in the sun.

Shop and Snowflake. The boast of **Pastel's Café**, that it offers a "beautiful view of the North Shore", is correct.

Hotel Boom: Water Street's turn-of-the-century boom encouraged Angelo Colari in 1908 to replace his Hotel Europe with a reinforced concrete, flat iron-shaped version, the structure that today still dominates the eastern end of the street; it is now an apartment house. "Our autobus meets all trains and boats," boasted the hotel which was only a few blocks from the Union Steamship wharfs. Among a score of the city's oldest buildings dating back to this era, at least half a dozen were Gastown hotels: the 1900 Dominion (its brick arches added in the 1960s) at **92 Water Street**; the Carlton (1899) and Commercial (1896) hotels at **300** and **340 Cambie Street**; the Italianate Grand Hotel, built in 1890 at **26 Water Street**; the bay-windowed Terminus whose customers were mainly sailors, miners and loggers, two doors away; the Kings Hotel at **208 Carrall Street**; and the deluxe Alhambra with fireplaces in every room for which guests paid as much as $1 a night when it first opened in 1887. The **Edward Hotel** at 300 Water Street was built in 1906 on the site of the Regina Hotel which had been the only building in Gastown to survive the fire of 1886.

Twenty years earlier, a river boat pilot named Jack Deighton, a Briton who had been running a saloon in New Westminster, landed near here in a canoe with his Indian wife and a yellow dog, rolled a keg of whisky ashore and started a saloon in an old wooden shack. Soon he was advertising that his establishment was replete with all the comforts of home.

His prices, he said, would be found "to suit the times". A rival saloon keeper, Joseph Manion, later described him as "a man of broad, ready humour, spicy and crisp and everflowing of grotesque Falstaffian dimensions." Deighton died in 1875 but when the hotel burned down in the Great Fire (13 June 1886) its new owner needed less than 24 hours to be back in business dispensing "encouragement" from an open-air bar consisting of nothing more than a plank resting on two kegs.

Today, at the corner of Carrall and Water streets, a life-sized bronze **statue** of **Gassy Jack** atop a barrel stands at the site of where not only Gastown but the city itself began. In 1885 an old maple tree grew here and it was under the shade of its branches that the pioneers met to choose the name Vancouver. The tree was one of the town's better known landmarks, sloping at such a steep angle that one man had trained his dog to run up the trunk to retrieve things. It was on this tree that the notice of the first civic election was posted in 1886. (A local paper, the *Herald*, urged citizens to "vote early and vote often".)

The **Byrnes Block** building behind the statue went up that very year, one of the first to be constructed after the fire; behind it is another reminder of that era: **Gaoler's Mews**, now a brick-floored alleyway with ivy-covered walls, shady trees, lanterns and a **carousel clock** that musically greets the hour. The mews was the site of the log-cabin police station of Gastown's first police chief and postmaster, Jonathan Miller. Miller had his prisoners, lightly chained at the ankle, work on road-clearing projects. Behind the mews, **Blood Alley Square** still has a cobbled yard with iron stairways and a sleepy air.

Across Water Street beside the railroad tracks, **Le Railcar Restaurant** occupies a renovated and extended 1929 CPR carriage in which diners can enjoy French cuisine while watching the occasional train shuttle back and forth. Gastown ends here, just beside the building that once was Angelo Colari's Hotel Europe, the first fireproof hotel in the entire city.

Eastwards along **Alexander Street** from Gastown is an industrial area of warehouses and small businesses of little interest to visitors except possibly for the usually deserted BC Sugar Museum. An early sudsmaker, the Columbia brewery, stood on the north side of Powell Street between Wall and Victoria in what was then Cedar Cove at the edge of the forest.

In the years preceding World War I, Alexander Street was rife with brothels, their doors wide open to the street into which flowed the melodious tones of piano rags. At 623 Alexander, the "House of all Nations" offered (according to a 1912 edition of *The Truth*) "everything from a chocolate-coloured damsel to a Swedish girl." The following year saw a police crackdown that netted 133 "keepers of bawdy houses" and 204 "inmates". By 1914 the red-light district was no more.

The ageing warehouses of BC Sugar dominate the eastern end of Powell Street. The **BC Sugar Museum**, at the foot of Rogers Street, recounts the saga of 24-year-old Benjamin Tingley Rogers who founded the company in 1890 and agreed to employ only white labour in return for 10 years of free water and 15 years without taxes.

Mayor David Oppenheimer was an early investor in this firm, the city's first industry not based on fishing or forestry. Today the company's raw cane comes mostly from Australia and generations of Canadians are familiar with Rogers' Golden Syrup whose pails have served as lunch buckets. Thousands of empty sugar sacks were transformed into aprons and pillow-cases prior to 1948 when the company switched to paper bags. Although the museum is free and is open every weekday it gets very few visitors, possibly because of its location.

At the foot of Dunlevy, named for a Victorian rancher and hotel owner Peter Dunlevy, the 1906 office of the **Hastings Mill**, with its broad verandah and large windows, was built by the province-wide timber company that acquired both the Hastings and Moodyville mills. Nearby is a 1966 monument by sculptor Gerhard Glass on the site of the old Hastings Mill Store, which is now located in Pioneer Park (*see page 154*).

Gassy Jack marks the spot where the city began.

NEAR THE STADIUM

Apart from Chinatown, the triangular area between East Hastings Street and the end of False Creek is a bit of a neglected wasteland. All this will change, however, if developments planned for the old Expo 86 area are carried to fruition.

Hastings Street, dotted with cheap hotels, beer parlours and wandering sailors, has long been skid row but where it crosses Pender it becomes more ethnically mixed with the spillover from Chinatown. The old **Carnegie Public Library**, which opened with 800 books in 1903, was once a museum. It now serves a largely Asian clientele. Vancouver's Chinatown, the third largest (after San Francisco and New York) in North America, began with the influx of gold seekers in 1858, augmented by the need for labour to build the railroads.

Stroll along **Pender Street**, admiring some of the city's oldest buildings with their characteristic recessed iron-fronted balconies: the **Chinese Benevolent Association** (1909), the **Ming Wo Cookware** with its dramatic green banners; and especially the **Wing Sang Building** (1889), probably the oldest on the street, behind which lurks **Market Alley**. This once housed one of the area's many opium factories in the days when the manufacture of the drug, but not its consumption, was legal. The street is even livelier at night with its fanciful neon signs. Of particular note are those of the **Sun Ah Hotel** and the **Niagara Hotel** (four blocks west).

Everybody comes to stare at the world's thinnest building, no wider than the outstretched arms of Barbara Chow whose father Jack owns it and from which he operates his insurance business. Subject of countless magazine stories and featured in the *Guinness Book of Records*, the **Sam Kee Building** at the corner of Carrall and Pender streets is a mere 2 metres (6 ft) wide and 30 metres (100 ft) long, enlarged with bow windows on the upper floor and a basement under the sidewalk with a glass-panelled roof. When the city widened the street 75 years ago, "Sam Kee" (whose real name was Cheng Toy, a poor immigrant who became a successful import merchant) was left with a narrow space which appeared to be useless until an ingenious architect devised the solution. It is now highly publicised by Chow, who jokes: "We have no secrets; we can't hide anything in here." A local magazine described the building "as much showbiz as real estate".

In the 1930s, Chinatown was regarded with suspicion by the white establishment which prohibited white women from working in Chinese restaurants. "In view of the conditions under which the girls are expected to work," said police chief W.W. Foster as he closed down two cafés for infraction of this by-law, "it is almost impossible for them to be so employed without falling victim to some immoral life."

The **Chinese Cultural Centre** on Pender Street is the main focus for the community today, with changing exhibitions and activities of various kinds. There is always one permanent attraction: the small **Dr Sun-Yat-Sen Classical Garden**, modelled after the Ming Dynasty garden in Suzhou, Jiangsu province, by artisans from that Chinese city. Contained in the garden is a tranquil pool, a waterfall, rockeries and lots of lovely flowers and although tours are organised it's pleasant just to meander on one's own. No power tools, only traditional methods, were used on the wood and tile work.

At the *Chinese Times*, located in a 1902 building at the corner of Carrall and Pender streets, you can peer through a window to watch typesetters laboriously setting type one character at a time from the 5,000 at their disposal. For those in search of a little variety in their diet, the basement of the **Sun Wah Centre** on Keefer just east of Main Street houses a well-stocked Chinese supermarket.

First public square: Between Cambie and Hamilton on Hastings Street is one of downtown's few parks. **Victory Square** was once the site of the city's domed courthouse, the first major building outside Gastown. After the Great Fire it became a public square. The old courthouse was torn down before World War I and the vacant lot was at first used for military recruiting. The Southam family, then owners of the city newspaper the *Province*, donated money for the square's rehabilitation which included the erection of the **Cenotaph** in 1924. Today homeless people mingle with Chinese families in the square, and office workers bring brown-bag lunches on sunny days. "In Vancouver," wrote Eric Nicol in a biography of the city, "a heat wave is defined as a warm sunny morning followed by a warm sunny afternoon."

Almost immediately after the 1886 fire the city's senior alderman, Lauchlan Alexander Hamilton, who had arrived in the city six years before as a civil

Chinatown began in 1858.

engineer working for the railway, set up a tent from which city hall business was conducted. One of his first tasks was to decide on the names for the new city's streets. As the first stake was driven into the ground near what is now Victory Square he declared: "We will call this Hastings Street, and this shall be named Hamilton after myself, and these trails leading off into the bush we will name Cambie and Abbott streets." (Hastings was Admiral George Fowler Hastings, Commander in Chief of the Pacific Naval Station; Abbott was H. H. Abbott, general superintendent of the CPR in British Columbia; Henry John Cambie was CPR's consulting engineer who selected the route for the railway in British Columbia.)

The 14-storey **Dominion Trust Building** was the tallest building in the British Empire when it went up at Cambie and Hastings in 1910, but within two years its title was taken by the nearby 83-metre (272-ft) **Heritage Building** constructed in 1912 as the headquarters for *The World* newspaper. It is a stylish structure, with Charles Marega's naked nymphs supporting the cornices. One of the publishers, Louis D. Taylor, four times mayor of the city, nevertheless died destitute in 1946 in a seedy rooming-house.

The land on which the oddly-shaped, maroon and orange Dominion Trust Building was erected cost $100,000 – more than six times its price only five years earlier. *The World*, which had been founded in 1888 by Canada's first female editor-publisher, Mrs J. C. McLaglan, folded only three years after moving into its new headquarters, but 22 years later when a moving and storage company vacated the building, it was taken over by the *Vancouver Sun,* which announced its presence with a spectacular neon light until it moved to its current premises on Granville Street in 1965.

Its tenancy of the green-topped Heritage Building coincided almost exactly with a fallow period in Vancouver real

The Sam Kee Building is in the *Guinness Book of Records*.

estate when new building – initially halted by the Depression – was at a standstill and the city's skyline barely changed. The Heritage/World building, still beautifully preserved, is now occupied by lawyers and government offices but is not open to the public.

On the north side of Pender Street at Beatty, was once an old drill shed which sheltered the 298-member Yukon Field Force en route to the Klondike in 1898. It had opened a decade earlier as the Imperial Opera House but was never as popular with the loggers, miners and sailors as the Grand Theatre on nearby Cordova Street, where audiences paid 25¢ to sing along to crudely tinted lantern slides spelling out "On the Banks of the Wabash" before the silent movie programme began.

Today, only a block or two away is the busy and popular **Queen Elizabeth Theatre** which has concert and recital halls as well as a playhouse. Behind the theatre is the **bus depot** across the street from a SkyTrain station.

Old Expo site: The 60,000-seat **BC Place Stadium**, at the end of False Creek, claims that its 4-hectare (10-acre) roof is the largest air-supported domed stadium in the world. When it went up in 1982 for the Expo ceremonies it was the first covered stadium in Canada, a roof of Teflon-coated fibreglass that though stronger than steel lets in 20 percent of the daylight. According to a reassuring brochure, 16 revolving fans provide the air pressure and if they all failed and the roof deflated it would still clear the seating area by some distance. The stadium, home of the BC Lions football team and the scene of numerous horse shows, concerts and exhibitions, has hosted several Grey Cup championship games. There are also daily tours.

The former Expo site adjoining the stadium, once a wasteland of derelict railroad lines and abandoned warehouses, is scheduled for development with plans for apartments, museums, a theatre and parkland. Nearby, one of the **Sun-Yat-Sen Garden.**

136

city's best-known landmarks is the giant, silvery geodesic sphere containing **Science World** whose exhibits, simultaneously fascinating and educational, demonstrate the principles of sound and light as well as offering whole rooms full of ingenious games and puzzles, devices to create gigantic bubbles, music studios enabling anybody to compare melodies from simply-explained synthesisers and sudden flashes of light that imprint visitors' images on the wall. "Our world is immersed in light," says one placard. "We use it to tell us about galaxies beyond our own and worlds too small to visit. Its majesty is preserved by poetry; its mystery probed by science."

Advertising itself as "the most curious place on earth", this futuristic museum with its talking dinosaurs also features **Omnimax films**, a stupendous experience when plunging into the Grand Canyon or making a closeup inspection of the world's volcanoes. Each frame is 10 times the size of conventional 35mm movie film, complete with wraparound sound.

A SkyTrain station lies just across from the Science centre not far from the majestic, old CN station (now VIA) sitting since 1919 on land reclaimed from False Creek but now standing "in majestic isolation… a wonderful survivor of its era," according to architectural columnist Robin Wood. **False Creek**, still 3 km (2 miles) in length, once extended all the way east to Clark Drive but over the years has been filled in extensively to provide more industrial land. City officials never liked the name – given by the Royal Navy – and in 1891 unsuccessfully petitioned the Dominion Government to change it to the much more attractive appellation of Pleasant Inlet.

In Vancouver's early days, hunters and loggers wanting to cross False Creek would wave a stick with a rag on the end to summon an Indian from the nearby reserve. For a small sum he would take passengers across the creek by canoe.

Chinese takeaway; the Dominion Trust Building.

MIDTOWN AND
THE WEST END

One of Vancouver's oldest landmarks, a mere 15 years younger than the city itself, is the four-sided clock which has been at the corner of Georgia and Granville streets since 1913 when the century-old, Montreal-based jewellery store outside which it stood in 1902 moved from Hastings Street. From **Birk's clock** south on Granville, a local author wrote in 1962, lies "Vancouver's gaudiest avenue".

Tree-lined street: But that was three decades ago. An 1895 newspaper carried a picture of the aftermath of a wild westerly gale which had toppled one of the 30-metre (100-ft) trees on the crest of Granville Hill on to a nine-passenger coach, killing the driver. All such trees were harvested in the early days of the city but new, young replacements were planted along Georgia in 1962 and the area is more attractive now. The street's name comes from the Strait of Georgia which, in turn, was named after George III. Birk's store adjoins the massive **Vancouver block**, at the top of which is the biggest clock in the city.

Almost immediately after the 1886 fire, foundations for the wooden, four-storey **Hotel Vancouver** were laid at the corner of Georgia and Granville, moving the new city's centre further inland. Ten months later, one week before the CPR's first trans-continental train arrived on 23 May 1887, it was open for business. The building survived until 1916 when it was replaced by a larger hotel on the site of the present Eaton's department store which was replaced in its turn just before World War II.

The hotel in its various forms has played host to royalty, writers and business tycoons (Mark Twain, J. Pierpont Morgan, Rudyard Kipling, Winston Churchill, Clark Gable, Jane Fonda, Indira Gandhi and Romania's Queen Marie are among those who have signed the register), meeting in spacious suites that, reported *The Vancouver Sun*, "seem so strangely and commodiously out of place in this day of cubbyhole bedrooms and smart supper places."

The third (and present hotel) has 508 rooms, many elegantly furnished with antique mahogany and Chippendale, which are among the biggest in town. The five-bedroom Royal Suite was inaugurated within days of the May 1939 opening, when King George VI and Queen Elizabeth arrived on their first royal visit to Canada. A decade later a dishevelled and unshaven Bing Crosby, returning from a backwoods fishing trip, was at first refused admission to the hotel until the manager was summoned and recognised the famous singer in his unfamiliar, casual state.

The hotel's green chateau roof is reflected attractively in the golden glass windows, a full block away, of the **Transport Canada Building**. The TCB building lies across from the excellent public library, scheduled for relocation to a new site opposite the Georgia Street post office by mid-decade.

Across Burrard Street adjoining a mini-park with a waterfall is the century-old **Christ Cathedral**, its stained-glass window depicting Captain Cook and its beamed cedar roof soaring to the skies. The cathedral, which was nearly replaced with an office building in 1973, shows visitors around on Sundays.

The **Hudson's Bay Company store**, erected in 1913 at the corner of Georgia and Granville, has large Corinthian columns that became an architectural trademark. It was the firm's fifth outlet in Vancouver. **Market Square**, an enticing collection of mini-shops and eating areas in the store's basement, should not be overlooked either. More shops on the mezzanine floor segue into the corridors and atrium of the rest of **Pacific Centre** whose 200 stores, many of them under the street, stretch over three blocks and are set against cascading fountains and a three-storey waterfall. **The Bay**, as it is known, vies with **Eaton's**, at the centre's western edge (and on the site of the old Opera House) for being the classiest store in town.

Opulently elegant: Two blocks further west is the extravagantly opulent, 2,800-seat **Orpheum Theatre** with its domed ceiling and dazzling crystal chandelier. Opened in 1927 as a combination vaudeville hall and movie palace to replace an earlier theatre dating back to 1891, the Orpheum was put up for sale and almost certain demolition in 1973 by its movie chain owners. It was refurbished at a cost of $7 million by the city after thousands of voters petitioned the mayor to save it. Charlie Chaplin, Bob Hope and Margot Fonteyn have graced its stage, which was also the scene of the Canadian premiere of *Gone With the Wind*. The Vancouver Symphony Orchestra now performs here; the theatre's lower level men's room was once nominated "the most glorious" in town by a local magazine.

Galloways, just west of Burrard on Robson, seems strangely but wonderfully out of place among all the chic stores along this block and it's worth dropping in just for the exotic aroma of spices and curries as well as jams, chutneys, nuts, dates, pulses and a thousand and one imported foods.

With its designer boutiques, **Robson Street** thinks of itself as Vancouver's answer to LA's star-studded Rodeo Drive. It has a distinctly European flavour, reminiscent of when the street was called Robsonstrasse and predominantly populated with German restaurants, some of which remain. Heavy traffic along Robson on weekend nights has prompted police crackdowns with roadblocks to prevent "cruising", much to the distress of local merchants who also complain that escalating rents are threatening to drive them away. There is a group of moderately priced hotels on Robson between Jervis and Broughton.

Lonely lions: The south end of Robson Street is dominated by trendy **Robson Square** and the **Vancouver Art Gallery** with its collection dating back to

Robson Square has an ice-rink in winter.

the 16th century and numerous paintings by local artist Emily Carr (*see page 147*). Once the city's courthouse, the building was designed by Francis Mawson Rattenbury with an entrance flanked by lions overlooking Georgia Street. Much was lost when the entrance was changed from the front to the back, writes architectural critic Robin Wood, leaving "lonely lions to guard a purposeless portico".

Although his studio once stood on this very spot, Trieste-born Charles Marega, one of the city's most prolific sculptors, is unrecognised in the gallery. "(He) was not honoured when he was living and he is not honoured now that he is dead," wrote Peggy Imredy in Chuck Davis's *Vancouver Book*, "but no other sculptor has as much work on display in Vancouver as this 'unknown' artist." Among his creations were the bust of David Oppenheimer in Stanley Park, the Captain Vancouver statue at City Hall and the Edward VII statue at the courthouse. Marega died penniless

Shopping on Robson Street.

in 1939, six months after the completion of his last work, the twin 6½-ton lions at the south end of Lions Gate Bridge. Pop into the **Hong Kong Bank** across the street from the square to admire Alan Storey's enormous sculptural work *Pendulum*. The plaza of Robson Square is used for concerts in summer and an outdoor skating rink in winter.

Most of the architecture around this neighbourhood is worth a look, particularly Arthur Erickson's stylish **courthouse** with its sloping, glass roof between Hornby and Howe. The area is a delight for pedestrians with its profusion of little plazas, waterfalls, seats and flowers. A good example is the open space beside the **Royal Centre**, Burrard and Georgia, a gleaming hotel and shops complex that replaced the legendary Glencoe Lodge whose plush interiors were a favourite with diplomats, politicians and the actress Ellen Terry.

One block away down Burrard, the complex known as the **Bentall Centre** which houses a **tourist information**

office, stands on what was once the wooded hillside site of Spratts Oilery, a series of shacks where fish oil was made for use in lubricating the skids over which logs were dragged to the harbour. Joseph Spratt, who had begun his business on a barge in Coal Harbour, gained something of an unpopular reputation in his day, especially among the local Indians, because his main method of catching fish was by throwing dynamite into the water.

The **Sinclair Centre**, at Cordova and Granville, is a textbook example of how to renovate with taste and imagination. Based on the original 1910 post office together with its 1939 extension and two adjoining buildings, it is an artfully appealing blend of old and new designs, an attractively lit atrium surrounded by shops and offices connected with a staircase. The "Dickensian-looking" former **Customs and Excise Building** (1912) at the corner of Howe and Cordova streets and the **Winch Building** (1909), in wildly different styles, complete the quartet, each facade preserved to reflect the good architectural taste of its era.

Richard Winch, who also commissioned a mansion on Comox Street with solid oak billiard tables, mahogany staircases and a 270-kg (600-lb) marble bathtub, made a turn-of-the-century fortune from his sawmill and salmon canneries. He loved to drive between his home and Vancouver's first major office building in one of his matching Rolls-Royces (which cost $10,000 each at a time when the Model-T Ford could be bought for $400).

Still dominated by banks, this part of town was always a business centre. Across the street from the **Bank of Commerce** was the old (1889) Strand Hotel, where shipowners and brokers met for business lunches. Among the customers was Captain Alex Maclean, a belligerent fur trader, said to have been the model for one of Jack London's characters in his novel *The Sea Wolf*.

The corner of Granville and Hastings was the site of two "firsts" – the city's first modern skyscraper, the **Royal Bank Tower**, erected in 1929, and the first traffic light installation. It was known as McKinnon's Corner in the 1920s after Constable Duncan McKinnon, whose white gloves and white baton were a familiar sight to motorists. He was hired by the newly created Traffic Department in December 1921, two weeks before the rule of the road was changed to enforce driving on the right-hand side of the road. Vancouver motorists expected a disaster.

"It was prophesied that there would be a scene of wild confusion... that there would be innumerable accidents; that people would be killed every 10 minutes and the gods of old customs would rise up and demand a continuous stream of sacrifices," said a columnist in the *Province*. "But there were no sacrifices and no confusion."

There are some fine buildings further northwest on Hastings, among them the **Guinness Tower** with its sculptured mural, across from the Oceanic Plaza.

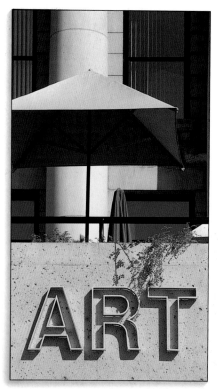

The Vancouver Art Gallery...

144

Where the tower now stands appeared, in 1862, the first cabin along this shore, built by a settler named John Morton who later settled at English Bay. He died in 1912 and a street was named after him: Morton Avenue, reaching from Denman Street to Beach Avenue, is the shortest street in Vancouver.

Past the opulent premises of the **Vancouver Club** (1913) are the gleaming, gold skyscraper of the **North Shore Credit Union** and the magnificent Art Deco **Marine Building** with its terracotta frieze of Neptune and sea creatures, decorative tiled entrance and elegant lobby complete with stained-glass window. "Its architectural conception," wrote its designers, McCarter and Nairne, "suggests some great marine rock rising from the sea clinging with sea flora and fauna, in sea green, flashed with gold."

This marine-type motif is echoed in one of Vancouver's largest murals, Robert Wyland's *Whaling Wall VIII* in the 1000 block of Dunsmuir. Another enormous mural nearby on Alberni Street depicting an 800-year-old forest has been sponsored by an ecology-minded group who financed it with contributions from people whose names were listed for a small fee.

The West End: Northwest along Robson Street at Bidwell is the delightful **Robson Public Market**, a glass-enclosed complex modelled after London's Crystal Palace and filled with spotlessly enticing stalls and snack bars. It is worth heading up here just to eat at the superlative Chopstix (1508 Robson) where prices are low and the food some of the best in town. This is Vancouver's **West End**, not to be confused with the West Side which is across the Burrard Street Bridge to the southwest.

Some of the city's oldest and most interesting wooden houses, whose attractive gingerbread-type facades include balconies and stairways, are in the area around Nelson Park, Comox and Bute, which the city would like to expand, demolishing "unworthy" struc-

...was once the city's courthouse.

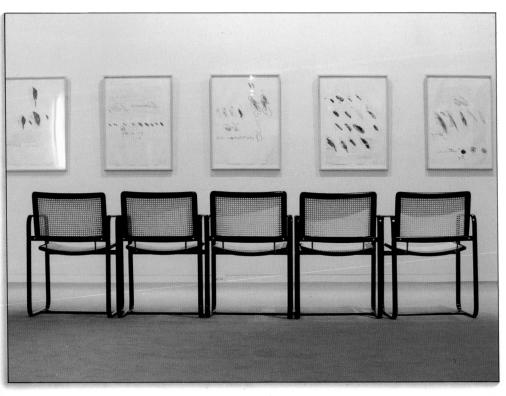

tures to clear the space. Some of these Edwardian and Queen Anne buildings played a significant part in the city's history; one was the home of a former mayor and another, at 1147, served as the French Consulate in 1898. Nine old homes have been transplanted to Nicola and Barclay where, renovated by the city as the **Barclay Square Heritage Park**, they are used as community activity centres.

One of them, **Barclay Manor** in the 1400 block, was built in 1904 for Frank Baynes, manager of Gastown's Dominion Hotel. At Lord Roberts School on Comox Street, elementary school children are introduced to the concept of urban gardening.

In the 1960s and '70s developers ran riot in the West End, replacing large, handsome, single-family homes and inexpensive rentals with ugly concrete blocks of flats and flashy condominiums. Through a series of angry public meetings, residents finally fought back and a stand-off ensued.

Denman Street and **Commercial Drive** are together the nearest thing that Vancouver has to a European ambience. Impassable by car on summer evenings they are chock-a-block with locals patronising the many small shops, restaurants and outdoor cafés. There's serious jazz and great food at Café Django and excellent fish and chips at Bud's between Nelson and Comox.

On the northeastern side the marina and moorings on **Coal Harbour**, together with controversial condo developments, created considerable dispute in the past decade but the developers appear to have won their battle. It is expected that this area will be the first beneficiary of Vancouver's new by-law which mandates a percentage of construction budgets being set aside for public art. On the southwestern side **Sunset Beach**, running all the way up to the south entrance of Stanley Park on English Bay, is a popular venue for political rallies and the annual Earth Day celebration in April.

Miles of aisles.

146

AN ARTIST'S LIFE

Emily Carr, one of Canada's most important artists and an award-winning writer, was considered an eccentric character in the Victorian times in which she lived. In her shapeless coat, sturdy laced shoes, her grey hair tucked into a hairnet with velvet band, and with only a dog or parrot for company, she often went sketching and camping in remote forests and Indian reservations. Her "modern" style earned her much derision, but British Columbians are now proud to claim this remarkable woman as one of their own.

Daughter of a successful Victorian merchant, she was 19 when, in 1890, she persuaded her family to send her to San Francisco's California School of Art. When she returned to her studio in Victoria, a reconditioned barn, she taught art so she could pay her way to a London art school. Later, in France, she became influenced by the painters of the Fauve school.

This "new art", which in the main is so much lighter and brighter colured than her "Canadian" paintings, was still unacceptable to Vancouver or Victoria society, so Carr gave up teaching in 1912 in favour of other means of earning a living. Constructing a home on her father's land, she bred sheepdogs and made pottery, digging her own clay and wheeling it home in an old pram which doubled as a shopping cart. Her simple pots bore authentic Indian designs.

Carr's eight trips to sketch and paint the culture of northern British Columbia and Alaska in villages of the Nootka, Salish, Haida, Kwakiutl and Gitksen peoples, as well as her powerful renditions of totem poles, gave her credence with her peers, the reigning Group of Seven artists in eastern Canada, and increasingly with anthropologists seeking records of such artefacts.

In the 1920s Carr switched her affections from sheepdogs to Belgian griffons and expanded her menagerie: she had a cat, parrots, a cockatoo, a white rat named Susie and a Capuchin monkey called Woo for which she made pinafores so they could take winter walks together in the park.

She painted on manila paper, using oils thinned with gasoline or even house paint. Adding boxes to an old caravan for her pets,

Emily Carr's Street Scene, 1911.

she created a mobile shelter in which she could work on her visits to Goldstream Park and the Metchosin region of Vancouver Island. By the 1930s, her work was internationally recognised, but it had brought her scant financial reward.

While recovering from the first of four heart attacks, Carr began to write about her experiences. She was 70 when her first book, a collection of stories about her travels among the Indians of the Northwest, was published. It won the Governor General's medal for general literature. This first book, *Klee Wyck* (meaning "laughing one", the nickname given to her by the Indians of Ucluelet) is still in print, as are *The House of All Sorts* (about her days as a landlady), the *Book of Small* (based on her childhood) and *Growing Pains,* her autobiography.

Carr died in 1945 and her birthplace, 207 Government Street in Victoria, has been restored for public viewing. A museum of Carr artefacts is housed in the nearby Wharf Street building which her father owned and in which he operated a grocery store. The Vancouver School of Art on Granville Island is called The Emily Carr. ■

WEST SIDE STORY

An unwary visitor can easily be confused by the profusion of "wests" in and around Vancouver. West Vancouver is a separate North Shore municipality to the left of the Lions Gate Bridge. The West End's residential apartments and beaches join downtown Vancouver to Stanley Park. The **West Side** of Vancouver, stretching from Cambie Street to the **University of British Columbia**, has been home to upper-income Vancouverites since the early 1900s. Their ability and willingness to vote tax dollars for improvements shows in the preponderance of parks and handsomely landscaped boulevards.

False Creek, the West Side's northeast boundary, was originally a 5-km (3-mile) inlet extending east from English Bay through marshlands and mud. Its south shore now harbours one of the most vibrant spots in the city. **Granville Island** isn't really an island, but a narrow-necked peninsula: 15 hectares (38 acres) of mud flats built up by dredging and dykes.

Shopping island: Seventy years ago when False Creek extended slightly further east, Granville Island was part of the industrial heart of Vancouver. Sawmills, processing plants, cooperages and foundries smoked and clanked under the **Granville Street Bridge** right up to the 1950s. As industry declined, the almost derelict area became a political embarrassment to the city and to the Canadian government, which still owns the site. After years of indecision, the Granville Island Trust was formed in 1973, with ambitious redevelopment plans. Today, the island represents everything Vancouverites like best about their city.

The heart of the island is the **Public Market**, housed in what were once industrial warehouses. It's a real farmers' market, offering fresh seafood and good local produce, as well as imported gourmet items. West-siders head here for Thai spices, fresh pasta and more than 150 different types of cheeses. Take-out stalls, bakeries, dairies and greengrocers provide the makings for spontaneous casual meals, eaten inside the market itself or outside on the pier among pigeons, masts, musicians and jugglers. A portion of the market is set aside for craftspeople, who display their ceramics, jewellery and art between kettles of fudge and mounds of strawberries.

Get a free map of the island at the **Granville Island Information Centre**, across Johnston Street from the market, and watch a short video on the island's history. Then head for **Granville Island Brewing Company** on Anderson Street. BC's peculiar and restrictive liquor laws didn't allow cottage breweries until 1984, when Granville Island Brewing opened its doors with the aim of making a good old-fashioned beer. It takes as its gospel the Bavarian Purity Law of 1516: unpasteurised beers and ales contain no chemicals or preservatives. There are free tours and tasting sessions daily. Granville Island's atmosphere is overwhelmingly marine-based. The **Maritime Market** deals in boat sales, charters, repairs and sea-going hardware. **Sea Village**, behind the **Emily Carr College of Art and Design**, is a permanent enclave of costly floating homes. Boaters get three hours of free "parking" when they tie up at the dock beside the Public Market.

Aside from the market, the most interesting eating places are Isadora's (run by a cooperative association), which specialises in delicious combinations of innovative foods and seasonings; Mulvaney's, the first restaurant to take a chance on the island's post-industrial future; and Bridges, convivial and trendy, with a great view of False Creek.

The island also features a **mainstream theatre**, a **revue stage** and one venue specialising in **experimental theatre**. Working studios display art, ceramics, weaving, dyeing, glass-blowing and paper-making studios, and visitors are welcome, or at least tolerated. Children have a two-storey department store all their own – the **Kids Only Market**, one of the more than 260 businesses and facilities now occupying the island. Just past the Information Centre, a solitary cement factory provides the only active reminder of Granville Island's colourful industrial past.

There are several ways to get to Granville Island. For sanity's sake, put the automobile at the bottom of your list. Although there are 1,100 free three-hour parking spaces and several pay lots inside renovated warehouses, you are more likely to circle endlessly around the cobbled one-way streets.

A more relaxed approach is via the mini-ferry boats which chug to the island from the Vancouver Aquatic Center off Beach Avenue (False Creek Ferries), or from the foot of Hornby Street on the north side of False Creek (Aquabus). Ferries operated by these two rival services depart every few minutes from early morning till 8pm. For the price of the bus fare, you'll get a seal's-eye view of water birds, expensive yachts and towering luxury condominiums. You can also get to Granville Island on foot, by bicycle or by BC Transit bus.

Sea, sand and sail: Most things of interest on the West Side lie along a roughly circular route from the beaches at the western end of the Art Deco-style **Burrard Street Bridge**, around Point Grey and back to the Granville Street Bridge. **Kitsilano Point** was once home to the Kitsilano Indians. In 1870 their village, called Snauq, became the centre of a government-decreed reservation with Indians forced off the land in 1901 and relocated on the North Shore. Provincial authorities tried to use the Point as an industrial site, but CPR influence helped turn it into a residential area.

Today, Kits Point is the location of three parks, a popular beach and some worthwhile scientific and cultural attractions. **Vanier Park** off Chestnut Street contains the **H. R. MacMillan**

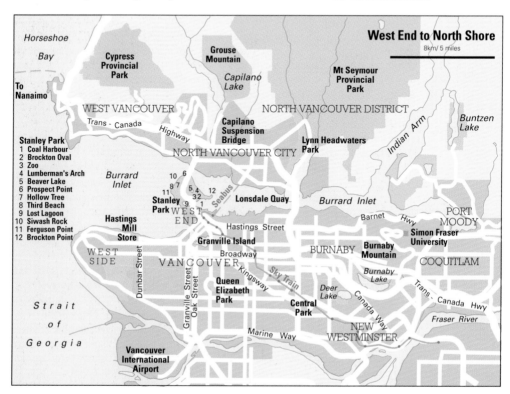

Planetarium, featuring laser light shows projected on to its domed interior; the **Vancouver Museum** (local cultures charted back to 6,000 BC); the **Gordon Southam Observatory** (free star-gazing on clear nights); and the **Vancouver Academy of Music**.

Where False Creek meets English Bay, the **Vancouver Maritime Museum's Heritage Harbour** accommodates restored old vessels. Visiting Tall Ships dock here, too. The harbour-side A-frame building which contains the museum's permanent gallery is also the *St Roch* **National Historic Site**. The *St Roch* is a Royal Canadian Mounted Police ship which gained international fame from her 1930s and '40s voyages through Canada's Arctic waters and was, in 1950, the first ship to circumnavigate the North American continent.

Kitsilano Beach occupies the west side of the Point. In the summer, the grassy areas close to its tennis court are packed with unbearably fit single people, waiting for their turn at the nets and "catching some rays". Kits Beach includes **Kitsilano Pool** – the largest saltwater pool in the British Empire when it was built in 1931.

West of the pool, Point Grey Road leads past assorted sailing clubs and expensive waterfront homes to **Pioneer Park**. This is the site of the **Hastings Mill Store**, the oldest building in Vancouver, built in 1865 (*see page 154*). After Vancouver's disastrous fire of 1866, which destroyed virtually the entire town, members of the stunned community gathered in the store to plan their future. As Vancouver was slowly rebuilt, the store was forgotten and in 1929 scheduled for demolition. The Native Daughters of British Columbia (white, not Indian) arranged for the building to be placed on a barge and transported from its downtown location to Pioneer Park, where it now serves as the city's most fascinating and probably least appreciated museum.

Open daily in summer (weekend afternoons only in winter), it is a wonder-

Granville Island.

HASTINGS MILL

Not many cities can point to a solitary log cabin as "the place where it all began", but no building in Vancouver could make a better claim than the Hastings Mill Store. As the hub of the tiny community on Burrard Inlet since its beginnings in 1865, the store was one of only a handful of buildings to survive the city's devastating Great Fire of 1886.

The Hastings Mill (which began as the headquarters of the British Columbia and Vancouver Island Spar, Lumber & Sawmill Co.) was the town's first employer and its store the first meeting house, the first post office and the first church. After clearing some adjacent land, the mill then built Vancouver's first school. All this took place at the foot of what is now Dunlevy Street, a site marked today by a cairn which commemorates the mill's first export of lumber back in July 1867. The cargo was destined for Australia, "thus beginning Vancouver's prime function, the supply of her great timbers to the world" as the

inscription on the granite monument puts it.

"Magnificent Douglas firs and Western red cedars... some of the finest timber the world has ever seen" was grist for the mill around which the settlement of Gastown quickly developed. Today the old mill store is located 8 km (5 miles) from its original site, preserved as a museum in Pioneer Park at the foot of Alma Street.

Captain Edward Stamp's mill was not the first on Burrard Inlet; that honour goes to one on the North Shore which, after various financial problems, was eventually acquired by Sewell Prescott Moody and which spawned the town of Moodyville. But Stamp's mill was better situated and the decision of the Canadian Pacific Railway to run right into Vancouver clinched its leading role.

The demand for wood in the 19th century was almost insatiable: masts and spars for sailing ships, sturdy timbers for European mansions and beams and immense planks for the palaces of Oriental emperors. Between 1867 and 1868, Vancouver's legendary timberman Jerry Rogers felled and shipped 2,000 spars, which even in those days fetched $200 apiece. Each massive, 800-year-old tree would take a day to bring down by axemen working from "springboards" notched into the tree several feet from the ground and 10-foot saws whirring away at the other side.

Captain Stamp's lease for the mill cost what was then the equivalent of about $250; until it was ready for operation he busied himself building the harbour's first tug. Within weeks of the mill starting production it was loading as many as four ships simultaneously. Soon Stamp converted to steam power and his mixed crew of Indians, penniless gold prospectors and deserters from sailing ships were working around the clock to ship the timber out, spending their free time in Gassy Jack's tavern. On 11 April 1869 the mill transmitted the first message (to Moodyville across the inlet) on a newly-installed telegraph line.

By the time of Vancouver's disastrous fire, Captain Stamp was long gone – he returned to his native England after heavy financial losses – but, almost alone among the town's buildings, the mill survived.

Catch a No. 4, 7 or 32 bus running along Fourth Street to Alma Street, then walk three blocks to the museum. **Hastings Mill: Vancouver's oldest ■ building.**

fully appropriate clutter of glass cases and rickety shelves piled with old dolls, sewing machines, Indian baskets, patchwork quilts, wooden kitchen chairs used in early trams, an oil lamp from the Brockton Point lighthouse, a piano brought from England in 1894 for a bridal gift and an embroidered portrait of Queen Victoria.

The end of Point Grey Road is one of several entrances to **Jericho Park**: 45 hectares (111 acres) of nature trails, picnic sites, 640 metres (2,100 ft) of beachfront and the **Vancouver Youth Hostel**. "Jericho" is a distortion of "Jerry's Cove", named after legendary 19th-century logger Jeremiah Rogers. A Federal Government military air base tied up the property for decades; it was finally turned over to the City in 1973. The **Vancouver International Folk Festival** is held here annually in July, attracting thousands of music fans from throughout the US and Canada.

Beautiful beaches: West of Jericho, **Locarno** and **Spanish Banks** offer almost a mile of continuous sand. **Locarno** is the board-sailing capital of BC's Lower Mainland; tides at **Spanish Banks**, where Captain George Vancouver exchanged civilities with two Spanish captains in 1792, retreat as much as half a mile off shore. On a good day (and if you're a good swimmer), it's possible to wade far out toward the shipping channels in English Bay.

These two beaches are the very best in the city for swimming, sunsets and ship-watching. Every day a cavalcade of fishing boats, oil tankers, container vessels and grain ships makes its way through English Bay to port facilities on Burrard Inlet.

Northwest Marine Drive leads from Spanish Banks into the campus of the **University of British Columbia**, the third largest university in Canada and the oldest in British Columbia. UBC was incorporated in the first decade of the 20th century, but World War I and financial crises stalled construction. Disgruntled students, fed up with tempo-

MacMillan
Planetarium
and much-
loved "crab".

rary quarters, made their Great Trek of 1922 to focus public attention on the delay. The buildings are a hodge-podge – seven decades-worth of architectural trends and fads – but glorious trees and gardens help unify the campus visually. The land belongs to the BC government, and owners of the luxurious older homes close to the northern entrances pay their property taxes to the provincial government rather than the city.

First peoples' culture: On the water-side of Marine Drive, between Gates 3 and 4, the **Museum of Anthropology** draws attention to the grandeur and intricacy of the local cultures that European immigrants and their descendants once tried so hard to exterminate. This outstanding building was designed by Vancouver's Arthur Erickson, an architect of international renown responsible for the impressive courthouse complex downtown.

Hugging the slope on a cliff overlooking the Strait of Georgia, the 1976 structure evokes the ghost of a traditional Northwest Coast Indian village and is a superlative setting for huge, turn-of-the-century totem poles as well as masterworks by contemporary Indian carvers and artists. A teaching museum, the MoA, uses an innovative sliding storage tray system that lets the public view thousands of smaller artiefacts from other indigenous cultures collected from around the world.

The **Nitobe Memorial Garden**, just beyond the museum, is a serene example of Japanese gardening art containing a carp-stocked lake, a tea garden, several very old lanterns and other traditional features. Admission is free.

From June to September, you might encounter a mini-traffic jam not far from the museum. The attraction is the city's only nudist beach, 237 steps below the cliffs. The steep descent doesn't deter either the 100,000 people who gather monthly on **Wreck Beach** to soak up Vancouver's sporadic sunshine, or the entrepreneurs who serve them. Beer, fast food, jewellery and novelties are for

Wedding in Queen Elizabeth Park.

sale here, as well as other more exotic substances. The very idea of Wreck Beach isn't overwhelmingly popular with more sedate local residents, but their fellow Vancouverites have been coming to this 6-km (4-mile) strip of foreshore since the late 1920s, and the beach's clothing-optional status is now unofficially official.

A small unmarked road to the right of Marine Drive leads to a close-up of one of BC's top three industries. Fir, cedar, alder, cypress and hemlock logs come by barge here from all over the BC coast and are stored until they can be sorted and "boomed" – assembled in loose "rafts" for towing up the lower Fraser River to waiting timber processors.

The entrance to the **UBC Botanical Garden** is just past the storage grounds turnoff. Begun in 1916, the garden now encompasses three major attractions and many pleasant surprises. **The Asian Garden** occupies a patch of virgin forest, a former Royal Navy Reserve that supplied timber for the masts of George

"Clothes-optional" Wreck Beach.

Vancouver's sailing ships. Some of the trees here are over 60 metres (200 ft) high, and their trunks are frequently a mass of climbing, flowering vines. This garden contains one of the largest collections of Asian plants in North America, including 300 different species of rhododendron.

Through a circular Chinese Moon Gate, and a tunnel under the highway, lie the **Alpine Garden**; the **BC Native Garden**, a series of aromatic trails through woodlands, meadows and a peat bog; and the **Physick Garden**, a typical 16th-century medicinal herb garden begun with plants from the famous Chelsea Physick Garden in London, England. Herbalist favourites such as datura, comfrey, valerian and witch hazel thrive here; the symptoms they treat are often described on accompanying signs.

Pacific Spirit: The woods to the right of 16th Avenue heading east back toward town belong to **Pacific Spirit Regional Park**: 763 hectares (1,885 acres) of

native flora criss-crossed by a 50-km (31-mile) network of riding and jogging trails. The use and jurisdiction of these former UBC Endowment Lands has been the subject of seemingly endless dispute over the past 50 years, until in 1988 the government dedicated the area as regional parkland. This decision handily ignored outstanding land claims by the Musqueam Indian band, who have never given up their aboriginal title to the area.

A right-hand detour off 16th Avenue to Wallace and 29th Avenue will bring you to the site of the former **Convent of the Sacred Heart**, a girls' Catholic boarding school from its construction in 1912 until the late 1970s. The building's granite facade, set in beautiful wooded grounds, is relieved by a Gothic port-cochère and countless parapets and bay windows. Now operated as a prestigious private boys' school, the building may not be long for this world, as the massive interior renovations needed to bring it up to present earthquake and

comfort standards may turn out to be prohibitively costly.

Several miles east of UBC, 16th Avenue enters the world of Vancouver's early aristocracy. The Canadian Pacific Railway was granted mammoth land holdings in Vancouver in return for constructing the railway that crossed the length of Canada. In 1901, it turned much of this land bank into an exclusive residential area called **Shaughnessy Heights**, named after its chairman, Sir Thomas Shaughnessy.

Within two decades, virtually every influential family in Vancouver had a Shaughnessy address. Their mansions reflected a wide variety of architectural styles, from imitation Georgian to American Gothic, with a predominance of half-timbered Tudor Revival.

In the 1920s, the area was the centre of a social scene which revolved around costume balls, croquet and Cadillacs. The streets lying between 16th Avenue and King Edward still curve along the contours of the land in a leisurely, heavily-landscaped fashion that reeks of planning and old money. It's easy to get lost along them.

A 1922 city by-law prohibiting any subdivision of the spacious grounds has only recently been relaxed, so many of the original homes can be seen in all their glory. Of the three best examples, only **Villa Russe**, at 3390 The Crescent, is still a home. Built by a Russian émigré in 1921, this building once hosted such international figures as composer/pianist Serge Rachmaninov and the Grand-Duke Alexander. Thirty-room **Hycroft House**, at 1498 McCrae Avenue, was constructed between 1909 and 1912 and is now the University Women's Club. The beautiful pillars and porte-cochère of this Italianate mansion are visible from the gates.

The gem of the collection is **Glen Brae**, at 1690 Matthews Avenue. Built in 1910, its twin domes were an area landmark; the floor of its third-floor ballroom, laid over a padding of seaweed to give it spring, quickly became **Net gain.**

the talk of the neighourhood. Glen Brae's neighbours had even more to talk about in 1925, when the Kanadian Knights of the Ku Klux Klan paraded up Granville Street to take possession of their newly purchased headquarters. Their proprietorship didn't last long. Today the building, with its memorable wrought-iron fencing and gates, is a private and restful hospital for the elderly (*see picture on page 81*).

Costly shopping: If you have to ask the price you probably shouldn't be shopping on South Granville between 10th and 16th avenues. Along this corridor, there's an array of stores which sell upscale fashions, oriental rugs, antiques, art and home-furnishings – products designed to match the incomes of nearby residents.

A little further east are two more major attractions for garden-lovers: **VanDusen Botanical Garden**, 37th Avenue at Oak Street, originally part of a massive land grant made to the ubiquitous CPR in the mid-1800s, offers thousands of ornamental plants including fuchsia and rhododendron, a hedge maze and intriguing sculptures on its grounds; and **Queen Elizabeth Park**, at 33rd Avenue and Cambie Street. Built on **Little Mountain**, the highest point in the city at 150 metres (500 ft) above sea level, Queen Elizabeth Park offers splendid panoramic views. This basalt hill was the source of much of the crushed stone used to cover Vancouver streets until 1908.

Today, the grassy slopes of the park are filled with picnicking families, and wedding parties line up to have their photos taken in the **arboretum** created from an abandoned basalt quarry. Colourful birds fly inside the triodetic glass dome of the **Bloedel Conservatory**, a home to 500 varieties of tropical plants and fragrant, blooming flowers.

The park also contains a **Henry Moore** bronze sculpture, *Knife-Edge (Two Pieces)*, as well as tennis courts and reflecting pools that are built over two city reservoirs.

Sunset, Kits Beach.

STANLEY PARK AND NORTH VANCOUVER

Both Stanley Park and North Vancouver lend a special "fresh-from-the-woods" quality to Vancouver which few other urban centres can claim. Stanley Park, a wilderness area set in the heart of a metropolis, is the reverse image of Vancouver itself – a city set in the heart of the wilderness. If visitors need a potent reminder of just how close to the wild Vancouver lies, North Vancouver, across Burrard Inlet, is a cogent example. City parks on the outskirts of North Vancouver, only minutes away from quiet middle-class neighbourhoods, sport signs at the entrance to hiking trails explaining exactly what to do if attacked by a bear. Bears admittedly are rare, but the untamed beauty of the city's wooded areas is one of Vancouver's greatest attractions.

Monumental park: In 1935, when the **Lions Gate Bridge** across First Narrows was constructed, mostly to enhance the value of the vast land holdings of the Irish Guinness family on the opposite shore, citizens decried the venture: "The road will destroy the serenity of our beloved Stanley Park!" Although the road certainly did alter the park, it is still a fine area of sylvan calm, with enough activities and sights to fill the longest day. **Stanley Park** is encircled by a promenade, confined by a low sea wall which begins beside Vancouver's first public monument: a bronze **statue of Queen Victoria** paid for with contributions by local schoolchildren on her death in 1901.

Near the park's main entrance (at the western end of Georgia Street) is the **monument to Lord Stanley**, a former Canadian Governor General, after whom the park was named. Its creation was due to the tireless energy of another city benefactor, J. S. Matthews, who raised the necessary funds when the city cried poverty. Welsh-born Major Matthews devoted four decades of his life to building up invaluable archives of the city's earliest days.

One-way traffic is mandatory on the 8-km (5-mile) road that loops anti-clockwise around the park. It travels first along the shore of **Coal Harbour** past the moored craft of the Vancouver Rowing Club and Royal Vancouver Yacht Club and the cannon fired nightly at 9pm (originally as a reminder that fishing is prohibited) out to **Brockton Point**. A causeway leads to **Deadman's Island**, a former Indian burial ground. Further east is **Hallelujah Point**, once a rallying ground for the Salvation Army's rousing picnics. Brockton Point itself takes its name from the chief engineer of *HMS Plumper*, the first ship to first survey this area, in 1859.

Most of the park's totem poles, representing various coastal Indian tribes, are clustered around the **Brockton Oval Sports Field** (on which you may see white-clad sportsmen playing cricket in summer), but one can be found beside the **Zoo** which cuts north across the park

Preceding pages: Stanley Park's marina. Left and right, North Vancouver's Capilano Suspension Bridge.

east of the **Malkin Bowl**. This area is the site of an **open-air night-time theatre**, the **children's zoo**, a **miniature railway** and the **aquarium**, where dolphins and whales can be viewed through underwater windows. There are numerous galleries exhibiting different types of fish, and impromptu shows by some lovable sea otters.

Among the monuments in this section of the park are a **statue** (sculpted by Charles Marega) **of Warren Harding**, commemorating the US president's 1923 visit to Vancouver, and the **Japanese War Memorial** in a lovely setting of spring-blooming cherry trees. The nearby **Rose Gardens** contain 5,000 bushes which bloom in early June.

Rejoining the circular road just beyond the *Empress of Japan* **figurehead** (a fibreglass replica from the CPR ship that serviced the Pacific route from 1891 to 1922) and the *Girl in Wetsuit* **sculpture**, the next landmark is the **Lumberman's Arch**, a 1952 replacement of one built to welcome the Duke of Connaught who visited the city in 1912 as Governor General. Before the white man arrived, this area of Vancouver was the Indian village Whoi-Whoi.

Just before the 2½-mile mark along the circular road, **Ravine Trail** heads inland to **Beaver Lake** whose bewhiskered inhabitants were removed elsewhere after their persistent attempts to flood the surrounding area by damming the lake's outflow. Waterfowl and herons frequent the lake today, in addition to colourful water lilies and wild flowers.

West of the road leading to the Lions Gate Bridge, the park's northernmost section, **Prospect Point**, was the site of an early semaphore station – which failed to prevent BC's first steamship, the *SS Beaver* from capsizing on the nearby rocks back in 1888. A cairn commemorates this event. The Prospect Point Restaurant is a pleasant spot from which to contemplate the traffic crossing the bridge high above the First Narrows, but in summer many prefer to head slightly further into the park to an organised picnic area. This is located atop a now filled-in reservoir which early in the century supplied the city with drinking water.

The Hollow Tree: One of the park's most famous landmarks, an immense **red cedar tree**, was already hollowed out when the first Europeans arrived more than a century ago. It now stands supported by iron bars as a symbol of the great forest that once covered the area. In attics and bottom drawers all over Canada are faded photographs of people in cars, carriages, horseback and alone or in groups, that were taken by a photographer who plied his trade beside the tree in the early years of this century.

Trails from the tree lead to the offshore **Siwash Rock**, which Indian legend holds was once a young man who was turned to stone as a "reward" for his unselfishness. At least one person has died while diving from Siwash Rock; consider this a dangerous spot to explore from close up.

Next comes **Third Beach** (further

Cricket players in Stanley Park.

164

down are Second Beach and the beach at English Bay) followed by **Ferguson Point**, named for an early member of the Parks Board, and the nearby teahouse which is all that remains of what was once a World War II defence station. The park's only marked grave is near here: that of a local poet, Pauline Johnson, who wrote lovingly about the city for most of her life and specifically requested burial in the park.

Below **Second Beach**, with its **swimming pool**, is a large recreational area which adjoins Lost Lagoon. There are **playgrounds**, a **miniature golf course**, **tennis facilities** and an **outdoor dance floor** on which various ethnic groups perform folk dancing open to all. The lagoon once flowed into Coal Harbour. Now that it is denuded of water at low tide, **Lost Lagoon** is a haven for a delightful variety of birds including heron, Canada geese and black swans.

Stanley Park ends where the sea wall terminates in front of the offices of the Parks Board on Beach Avenue. Opposite is a **statue** by Charles Marega of Vancouver's four-times mayor, **David Oppenheimer**, who died in 1891. There are bicycles for rent in the park (cycle paths adjoin the promenade) and it is also possible to make a tour of the park even on rainy days in a horse-drawn covered wagon.

North Vancouver: A trip across Burrard Inlet to the North Shore (the SeaBus runs from just beside Canada Place in downtown Vancouver) offers visitors a chance to see the city to its best advantage. A trio of Cypress Mountains peaks – Grouse, Seymour and Cypress – are all accessible and have skiing facilities, but only **Grouse Mountain** has the attraction of an enclosed gondola ride to the top. And you don't have to wait for the ski season to get a chance to see the breathtaking view because the mountain is open all year round.

Try the ascent on a crisp evening when you may be able to catch the lights of Victoria 80 km (50 miles) away; on cloudy days, you may only get the view

Girl in Wetsuit.

of the top of the cloud cover, a treat none the less as you break through the mist. The restaurant and bar at the top will give you the time to wait for the clouds to clear. Be sure to wear warm clothing – a jacket or a sweater – for this upward journey, as it can be chilly.

Many people consider North Vancouver simply to be a few exits on the main road that leads to the ferries. In fact, North Vancouver is a separate city established in 1907, a time when the municipality extended all the way from Horseshoe Bay eastwards to Deep Cove.

This side of the Burrard Inlet was the site of the earliest saw mill, Moodyville, and to this day logging trucks laden with the massive trunks of trees cut from stands of timber to the north and east rumble through the streets of this mostly dormitory suburb of Vancouver proper. Moodyville ceased to be a separate entity when it was swallowed up by North Vancouver in 1915.

The waterfront area of North Vancouver is still very much a working port with grain elevators and shipyards and, of course, sawmills. The **Lonsdale Quay Market**, the landing point of the SeaBus and the easiest way to reach North Vancouver (the bridges across the narrows are frustrating in the rush hour) is a collection of quaint shops oriented to the discerning tourist. The ferry-ride itself is as pleasurable as it is pragmatic, offering stunning views of Vancouver.

Capilano Suspension Bridge is the most recent version (built in 1956) of a cedar plank bridge that an early settler named George Grant Mackay built with the help of local Indians, August Jack and Willie Khahtsahlano, back in the 1880s. A second bridge replaced it in 1903 and a third, also of wire, in 1914. The Capilano has always been a tourist attraction, offering a minor thrill to adventurous visitors who delight in crossing the 107-metre (350-ft) wide canyon at a height of 70 metres (230 ft) above the river. It is not a trip for acrophobics, however: the bridge does sway, but the view down the gorge of clear river amidst

dense forest is certainly well worth it.

The first **totem poles** in the park adjoining the bridge were created by two Danish immigrants, Aage Madsen and Karl Hansen, in the 1930s, the others carved by local Indians, Mary Capilano and Chief Mathias Joe Capilano. More have been added since.

On the far side of the bridge are miles of well-marked nature trails, culminating at the end of Capilano Park Road in a **salmon hatchery** and **Capilano Lake**.

A mile or two to the east is the **Lynn Headwaters Park**, which has the dubious honour of being the city's most popular lover's leap. One couple found dead in the chasm in 1991 were still entwined in each other's arms. No one knows if they jumped, leaped or just got carried away in the throes of passion on the edge of the precipice.

The best trail for a short jaunt into the wilderness is the **Lynn Loop/Cedars Mill Trail**, a relatively easy hike of two hours that will lead you on a well-marked trek through the mountain wilderness.

Ravens and thunderbirds are often depicted on totem poles.

TOTEM POLES

Complicated and mysterious, bold and forceful, totem poles have become a powerful symbol for one of the world's great "primitive" arts. For centuries these massive columns, carved from western red cedar by skilled Pacific Northwest Coast Indian carvers, were raised in tribute in local coastal villages.

A totem pole tells a story of a family's history and lineage, or an historical event. The raven, the thunderbird, the bear, the whale and the frog are animals that are often depicted on the poles. This custom can be traced to a time when it was thought that humans could transform into animals and animals into humans. The right to use an animal's likeness in effigy was earned when the creature was overcome, killed or made human. The privilege was passed on to descendants, so a totem pole also maintained a link with ancestors.

Many totem poles have fallen down or rotted in abandoned native villages, and traditional skills and carving techniques were dying until their revival, largely due to the dedication of master carver, jeweller and artist Bill Reid.

"Bill found the dry bones of a great art and, shamanlike, shook off the layers of museum dust and brought it back to life," wrote art historian Bill Holm for a retrospective exhibit of Reid's work at the Vancouver Art Gallery in 1974.

Reid was born in Victoria in 1920, his mother a Haida from Skidegate in the Queen Charlotte Islands; his father a Scottish-German American. He began his career as a broadcaster, but while living in Toronto became inspired by a Haida pole at the Royal Ontario Museum. It originated in his grandmother's village of Tanu.

He enrolled in a jewellery-making course and began incorporating Haida designs into his argillite, silver and gold jewellery, copying from photographs and museum pieces. The break from broadcasting came when he accepted an invitation from the University of British Columbia to recreate a traditional Haida village for the Museum of Anthropology, a project that lasted from 1958 to 1962.

His experience of carving totem poles consisted of 10 days he spent working alongside a master Kwakiutl carver, Mungo Martin. (The pole on which they worked can be seen at the Peace Arch border crossing at Blaine, Washington.) Martin, who died in 1962, was the last of the master carvers; he had worked on an early Museum of Anthropology restoration programme and also Thunderbird Park at the Royal British Columbia Museum in Victoria.

Reid was able to "indulge in a lifelong dream" when a totem pole he carved and donated was raised in 1978 in Skidegate. It was the first pole to be raised in his mother's village in more than a century, and it was Reid's way of offering thanks to the great Haida artists of the past.

He told author Edith Iglauer: "I've never felt I was doing something for my people, except what I could to bring the accomplishments of the old ones to the attention of the world. I think the Northwest Coast style of art is an absolutely unique product, one of the crowning achievements of the whole human experience. I just don't want the whole thing swept under the carpet without someone paying attention." ∎

Carving out the past.

167

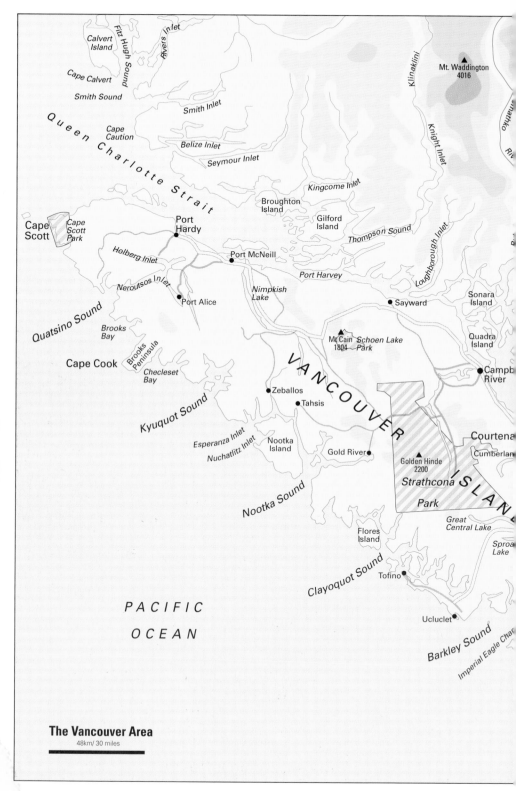

Rivers Inlet

Calvert Island

Fitz Hugh Sound

Cape Calvert

Smith Sound

Smith Inlet

Klinaklini

Mt. Waddington
4016

Cape Caution

Belize Inlet

Seymour Inlet

Kingcome Inlet

Knight Inlet

Broughton Island

Gilford Island

Thompson Sound

Loughborough Inlet

Cape Scott

Cape Scott Park

Port Hardy

Port McNeill

Port Harvey

Sonara Island

Holberg Inlet

Nimpkish Lake

Sayward

Quadra Island

Neroutsos Inlet

Port Alice

Quatsino Sound

Brooks Bay

Mt Cain 1804

Schoen Lake Park

Campb River

Brooks Peninsula

VANCOUVER

Cape Cook

Checleset Bay

Zeballos

Tahsis

Courtena

Kyuquot Sound

Esperanza Inlet

Nuchatlitz Inlet

Nootka Island

Gold River

Golden Hinde 2200

Cumberlan

Strathcona Park

ISLAN

Nootka Sound

Great Central Lake

Flores Island

Sproa Lake

Clayoquot Sound

Tofino

Ucluelet

Barkley Sound

Imperial Eagle Cha

PACIFIC

OCEAN

Queen Charlotte Strait

The Vancouver Area

48km/ 30 miles

172

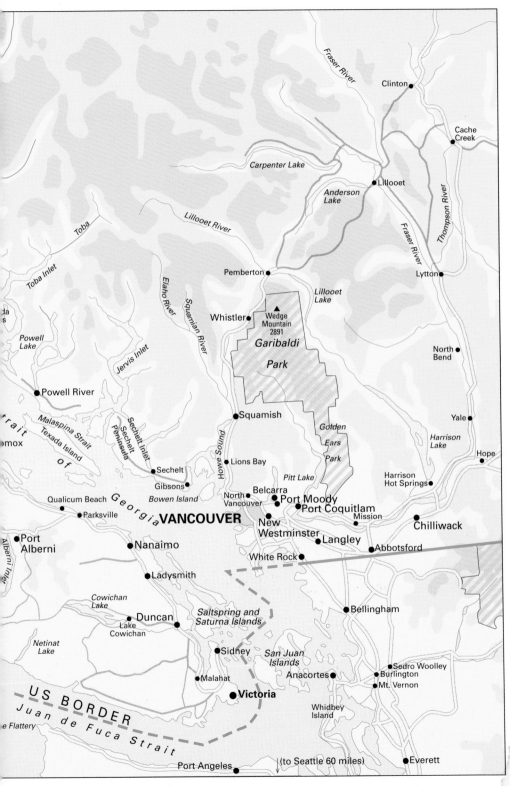

Clinton

Fraser River

Cache Creek

Carpenter Lake

Anderson Lake

Lillooet

Thompson River

Lillooet River

Fraser River

Lytton

Toba

Toba Inlet

Pemberton

Lillooet Lake

da s

Powell Lake

Elaho River

Squamian River

Whistler

Wedge Mountain 2891

North Bend

Jervis Inlet

Garibaldi Park

Powell River

Malaspina Strait

Texada Island

Sechelt Peninsula

Squamish

Golden

Yale

Harrison Lake

mox

of

Sechelt Inlet

Howe Sound

Ears

Hope

Sechelt

Lions Bay

Park

Harrison Hot Springs

Strait

Gibsons

Pitt Lake

Qualicum Beach

Georgia

Bowen Island

Belcarra

North Vancouver

Port Moody

Mission

Parksville

VANCOUVER

Port Coquitlam

Chilliwack

Port Alberni

Nanaimo

New Westminster

Langley

Abbotsford

White Rock

Ladysmith

Alberni Inlet

Cowichan Lake

Saltspring and Saturna Islands

Bellingham

Netinat Lake

Duncan

Lake Cowichan

Sidney

San Juan Islands

Sedro Woolley

Burlington

Malahat

Anacortes

Mt. Vernon

US BORDER

Victoria

Whidbey Island

Juan de Fuca Strait

e Flattery

Port Angeles

(to Seattle 60 miles)

Everett

VICTORIA

The largest island on the west coast of North America, Vancouver Island lies to the west of its namesake, with good ferry links between the two. The island's principal city is Victoria, located so far to the south as to be nudged into a geographical corner with the United States mainland surrounding it on two sides. In fact, Victoria is equidistant between Vancouver and the US city of Seattle; 183 km (114 miles) by ferry to either. Although this proximity to its southern neighbour should imply shared characteristics, Victoria is not only thoroughly Canadian, but more British than Vancouver. Some would go so far as to say this pretty, gentle town was more British than even Britain itself.

Visitors can take the ferry, fly or take the bus from Vancouver, because the return journey, plus sightseeing, can be accomplished in a long, action-packed day. More pleasant would be to emulate the leisurely pace of Vancouver Island and to spend several days touring around. Whatever the choice, Victoria is the logical place to begin.

Capital city: British Columbia's capital city, like many other towns in the province, began as a Hudson's Bay Company fort. The site was chosen by the HBC's James Douglas, who described the spot as "a perfect Eden". By the turn of this century it was clear to the city's boosters that although CPR was not about to make Victoria its western terminus by connecting it to the mainland with bridges, regular ferry services would be a major enticement to visitors. "Built on gently undulating ground – such as is characteristic of old England – the very location of Victoria differs from that of American cities on the Sound," wrote Henry T. Finck in 1907. "Nor are the streets laid out with the geometrical regularity so universal in the United States. The ladies on horseback, the numerous churches, the ani-mated streets on Saturday evening, the abundant beef markets, the pirated American novels in the bookstalls, the substantial appearance of the houses and many other things remind one of the fact that here we are in America indeed, but not in the United States."

Many of the earliest visitors had been prospectors from California who first touched down in Fort Victoria in 1858 on their way to search for gold in the Cariboo mountains, a trip that became easier with the establishment of Francis Barnard's BC Express Company. Three decades later, Barnard's lawyer son George teamed up with riverboat captain J. W. Troup to promote Victoria as a tourist destination. Barnard got himself elected to the city council, then as mayor, and with his partner persuaded CPR to build a fast ferry to operate to and from the Canadian mainland. They went into partnership with the city to construct a luxury hotel, hiring as their architect the talented Francis Mawson Rattenbury who had been responsible

Preceding pages: BC Ferry from Vancouver to Victoria; on the rails. **Left, Parliament Buildings. Right, a touch of Britain in British Columbia.**

for the city's **Parliament Buildings**.

Even after the plans were agreed in 1904, it took years of work dredging the harbour, filling in the mudflats, driving piles and using horse-drawn wagons to shift the debris, before the 116-room **Empress Hotel** – after costs of more than $1.3 million – was ready. "Beautiful in its magnificent stateliness," one observer described it on opening day, 20 January 1908. It has dominated the city's harbour ever since. Resting on what its official biographer, Godfrey Holloway, describes as "a massive yellow crumpet" of clay, planking timber and concrete, the hotel was "not so much a commercial enterprise as a civic development".

Today, with 480 rooms and with an international reputation for style and civility (*see page 181*), it is probably the best-known local landmark, although its importance to the city has not prevented the occasional dispute. In 1972, for example, after the then manager, Louis Finnamore, complained that the greed of tourist operators had led barkers "not unlike panhandlers" to besiege his guests with pamphlets, one of the city aldermen – who happened to be part-owner of one of the tours – retorted: "The Empress Hotel pretends not to be part of these happenings when in reality they are the biggest offender."

Tours to various parts of the city and the island leave from outside the Empress, but the city's compact size lends itself well to do-it-yourself sightseeing. Pick up a map or have questions answered at the helpful **tourist office** in the 1931 Art Deco building across the street from the hotel. The **Victoria Clipper Dock** sits on the harbour below the tourist office; fast catamarans operating daily make the trip from here to Seattle in about 2½ hours. Half a dozen of the city's principal tourist sites are located in or around the harbour area. Easy to reach and easy to recognise, they making strolling around town a pleasure.

Time will be needed to do proper justice to the imaginatively organised

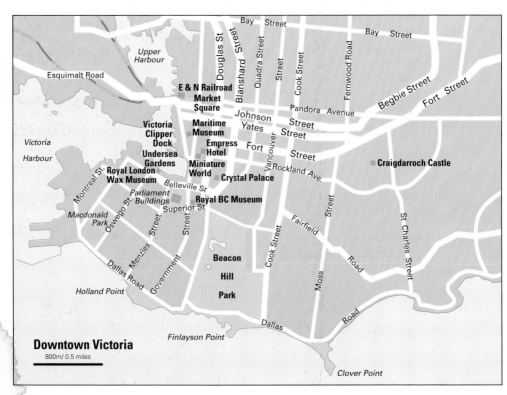

Downtown Victoria
800m/ 0.5 miles

Royal British Columbia Museum. There is always a queue for the **Open Ocean trip**: get a (free) ticket early, on the second floor, and join one of the small groups that walk through this intriguing adventure. Everywhere in the museum are floor-to-ceiling photographs, totem poles, artefacts and pictures of native peoples, layouts of tidelands with ducks and wild fowl, or stuffed seals basking on rocks. Climb into the reconstructed 18th-century charthouse of *HMS Discovery* to see how the captain lived; inspect a sawmill, its yard strewn with implements of frontier farming; reminisce over the old newspapers and magazines, a clunky 1950s TV set, bakelite cups and saucers, cloche hats, a steam iron.

There is an entire cobbled street lined with livery stable, drapery, a garage with a 1913 car, a railroad station waiting-room with sounds of passing trains and the Roxy moviehouse still showing Laurel and Hardy silent films. Outside, the museum's grounds include a totem pole park, native plant gardens and an ancient schoolhouse.

Long, slender dogfish shark and silvery salmon nudge the glass inches away from tourists in the harbourside **Underseas Gardens**, where big fish are seemingly as curious about you as you are about them. Window-lined corridors contain rocky pools with shells and starfish; in the theatre visitors fill rows of seats facing the glassy wall separating them from scores of different species, including an elusive octopus named Armstrong.

Occasionally, while walking around town, you may find yourself confronted by a London bobby wheeling Queen Victoria along the sidewalk; if you're like most tourists you'll have your camera ready. These recreated figures are a walking advertisement for the **Royal London Wax Museum**, located in a building designed by Francis Mawson Rattenbury.

The immobile characters inside include figures from literature; Britain's

Victoria was built on gently undulating ground.

royal family, past and present; sports legends (like Gordie Howe, whose 32-year hockey career included his role as the game's first playing grandfather); a group of inventors (including Canada's Sir Frederick Banting, the discoverer of insulin); plus the usual array of popular movie stars from Ottawa-born Lorne Greene to America's Elvis Presley and Marilyn Monroe.

The **Crystal Palace** is another structure designed by Rattenbury, a glass-roofed "tropical paradise", with an adjoining shopping mall. The building houses a collection of fantastic fish, brightly coloured birds, flamboyant flamingoes, timid turtles, miniature monkeys and other curious and amusing animals all set among plants and flowers, pools and a cascading waterfall. The popularity of afternoon tea at the Empress has been copied – albeit less regally – at many places around town, and this is one of them.

Opposite the Crystal Palace, the **Collectors' Car Museum** is laid out in a series of pseudo-workshops and old gas stations, used as settings for obsolete Packards (last one manufactured in 1950), model-T Fords, DeLoreans, wood-panelled station wagons and a curious (1964) Amphicar which used 5 gallons of petrol an hour when travelling across water but never became popular enough to be mass-produced.

At street level on the northern side of the Empress Hotel is **Miniature World**, a collection of tiny tableaux ranging from scenes from Charles Dickens's novels, an operational sawmill and a delightful three-ring circus with animated acts, to medieval England and the Old West. Thousands of hours of intricate construction went into these elaborate models, the highlight of which is probably the world's longest miniature railway, depicting the story of the Great Canadian Railway. Squeezing 8,000 km (5,000 miles) of trans-continental track into a model only 34 metres (110 ft) long, with wooden figures and 10,000 trees patiently assembled branch by

Reminders of a genteel age.

branch took 12,000 man hours and cost $100,000 to build.

For more than half a century, until 1948, Victoria had a sleepy streetcar line on which in earlier days cows (and even the occasional cougar) could be found asleep on the track. Now an efficient bus service operates locally, but most of the things visitors want to see are within walking distance. A stroll around the harbour's edge along Wharf Street to Fort Street leads to the **Emily Carr Gallery** with its permanent exhibit of the works of the Victoria-born artist who died in 1945 (*see page 147*). Emily's father ran a grocery store on Wharf Street, which in the 19th century was the commercial hub of the city.

The **Maritime Museum** is in Bastion Square, housed in a building that was once the Provincial Courthouse. Around **Bastion Square**, the actual site of Fort Victoria, is some of the city's oldest and most interesting architecture. In the square itself is the 1887 **Burnes House**, once a luxury hotel, and also the cha-teau-like 1896 bank built by Rattenbury at 1200 Government Street. Two other notable structures are in the same block: Samuel Maclure's **Temple Building**, now a bookstore; and the **Bank of British Columbia** building (now a year-around Christmas store), which was designed in 1883 by W. H. Williams who was also responsible for the amazing Craigdarroch Castle.

Craigdarroch Castle was built by Scots-born Robert Dunsmuir to fulfil a promise made to his wife when she expressed her dislike of the new country to which he had brought her. Dunsmuir, a classic robber baron who became rich from his Vancouver Coal Company, died in 1889 before the castle (on Joan Crescent) was completed. It is a lengthy walk from town, but buses run along Fort Street.

Situated at 1900 Store Street is the distinctive **Capital Iron Building**, which became a mill in the 1880s and later a scrap iron works responsible for dismantling 100 ships. On Johnson

Waterfront civility.

Street, between Store and Government, the old Milne Building (1891) and Strand Hotel (1892) form part of the busy **Market Square** complex with its 45 shops and restaurants.

One block further north, **Fan Tan Alley** anchors what was once the largest Chinatown in North America and which is still rich in architectural treasures. South of the harbour, the Queen Anne home of William Pendray at 309 Belleville Street, with its interesting garden, and the house of his architect Thomas Hooper (243 Kingston) are especially attractive.

Proof of Victoria's love of gardens is within easy walking distance of downtown. The 74-hectare (184-acre) **Beacon Hill Park** was set aside as a recreational reserve by James Douglas in 1852, a sprawling green with duck ponds, colourful gardens, stone bridges, elegant trees and benches overlooking the sea. An exceptionally tall and narrow Kwakiutl totem pole rises 39 metres (127 ft) above the grassy field, incorporating the 16 ancestral figures of the Gee-Eskem clan.

Near the park's southwest corner is **Mile Zero** of the Trans-Canada highway (at the corner of Douglas Street and Dallas Road), marking the beginning of the highway that crosses the country to St John's, Newfoundland, 7,820 km (4,860 miles) away.

One of Victoria's most famous attractions, the **Butchart Gardens**, 21 km (13 miles) north of the city, were transformed to their current splendour from an abandoned quarry. No sooner had Robert Pim Butchart established BC's first Portland Cement Co. plant in 1904, than his ambitious wife Jenny began creating gardens from the limestone ruins. Winding paths lead past clumps of colour, endless fragrant blossoms of honeysuckle and roses, green lawns, ponds and fountains. After sunset, carefully placed lights show off the plants and pathways.

West of town on Lampson Street (take bus 24) is **Anne Hathaway's Cottage**, an authentic reproduction of the original house in a suburb of Stratford-upon-Avon, and furnished with period antiques. It's part of a complex of Tudor-style buildings which includes an inn serving typically English fare.

Finest food: Gourmet diners with a car and a sense of adventure should not miss a chance to visit the **Sooke Harbour House**, one of the best restaurants in the Pacific Northwest. The restaurant chef uses innovation and fresh, local food to create exquisite tastes. Specialising in local seafood with exotic flair, try geoduck, scallops or periwinkles, or meat from the nearby farms. Fresh herbs, edible flowers and vegetables all come from the local gardens. There is an inn attached to the restaurant so if you are an incurable romantic, or just too stuffed to move, you may want to stay overnight. To get there, follow Highway 1 north of Victoria to the Highway 1A underpass, which becomes Highway 14 leading west of Victoria. It's then 45 km (28 miles) to Sooke.

Sooke Harbour House.

THE EMPRESS HOTEL

A misguided robber, it's said, once attempted to hold up the Empress Hotel only to be confronted by a defiant receptionist. "This sort of behavior is unacceptable here," spluttered the indignant employee. The baffled robber fled.

Apocryphal or not, the story would sound perfectly credible to anybody familiar with Victoria's best-known landmark which has been rated among the world's top hotels since it opened in 1908. With its elegant airs and strictly enforced dress codes ("no jeans, ever, ever, ever," the Bengal Room's hostess has told rejectees) the hotel can seem somewhat intimidating. Nevertheless, it is this formality that lies at the heart of the Empress's fame.

Named after Queen Victoria, Empress of India, the hotel was designed by English-born Francis Mawson Rattenbury. It was renovated in 1987 at a cost of $45 million.

Two decades earlier a similar overhaul had replaced heating and electrical systems, laid 6 km (4 miles) of new carpeting, booked special looms for the creation of hundreds of new bedspreads and checked for period authenticity the thousands of new (i.e. old) pieces of furniture for the additional rooms, which now total 480. The new pastry chef arrived with references from Buckingham Palace. The entire operation took place under the demure name of "Operation Teacup".

Antique oak furniture and teacups, of course, are major motifs of this harbourside hostelry, whose architectural style has been described as a cross between French chateau and Scottish baronial. Architect Rattenbury, already rich from successful gold prospecting in the north when he arrived in Victoria in 1892, promptly won a contest to design the city's Parliament Buildings, so his design for the Empress would not have come as a surprise.

Afternoon tea at the Empress has achieved "mythic proportions", according to one writer who reports that the hotel constantly receives enquiries from around the world about how to brew and serve tea correctly. Should the milk be poured into the cup before the tea, or only added afterwards? Guests reserve a table ahead in order to find out. Each person is served dainty, crustless sandwiches, honey-buttered crumpets, scones with clotted cream and jam, French pastries and, of course, tea – a blend of Darjeeling, China black and orange pekoe.

The visitors who come for tea, as well as the hotel's overnight guests, seem a conventionally decorous bunch these days, but in his official "biography" of the hotel Godfrey Holloway recalls wonderfully eccentric former guests, usually elderly ladies, who cooked aromatic liver and onions or made strawberry jam on hotplates in their rooms, wore threadbare tennis shoes with elegant gowns, and asked for pots of hot water in which to steep their own teabags, or came for a weekend and stayed 20 years.

In 1974 a dozen streakers tore through the elegant lobby past astonished tea-drinkers. "They went so fast and were shouting at the top of their lungs," gasped Dorothy Hart, operator of the lobby newsstand. "They must have had a car waiting; they made a quick getaway."

In deference to Empress traditions, the otherwise-naked streakers were reported to be wearing ties. ∎

Tea for two.

VANCOUVER ISLAND

Vancouver Island's climate is benign, the lifestyle slow-paced and the scenery varied: it ranges from rugged snow-capped mountains in the centre to gentle farming areas on its east side and craggy coastlines with deep fjords, ferocious storms and fishing villages in sheltered bays on the west coast. Stretching for 453 km (282 miles) in length and spanning from 48 to 80 km (30 to 50 miles) across, the island is best seen by train or car. The train takes in the most popular sites, while hiring a car in Victoria gives access to the isolated western and northern coasts.

North by train: The Esquimalt & Nanaimo Railroad, known locally as the E & N, came about mainly through the efforts of industrialist Robert Dunsmuir who needed an efficient transport system to move the coal from his mines. Canadian Pacific, which had terminated its trans-continental line on the mainland because it saw no profit in crossing the Georgia Strait, did in fact do so 20 years later when the E & N proved to be profitable. In 1905 CPR paid $2.3 million for the line, including 600,000 hectares (1.5 million acres) of land, extending the E & N as far north as Courtenay. The outbreak of World War I prevented further expansion.

The line today still ends at Courtenay, a 224-km (139-mile) single track from Victoria that sees a solitary train traverse its route every day of the year, although it has been many years since it carried coal or lumber.

Today the Malahat Dayliner Route still leaves Victoria at 8.15 each morning, making 20-minute stops at Nanaimo and Courtenay before arriving back in Victoria at 5.45pm. The printed schedule draws attention to a multitude of sights en route, from the spectacular bridge over **Niagara Canyon** to the former mining town of **Cassidy**. But, truth to tell, unless you have sharp eyes,

apart from a few glimpses of homes, lakes and mountains, you'll see very little of anything except trees.

Still, it's a pleasantly relaxing excursion offering the chance to catch up on your reading or study the product of BC's major industry in its natural, living state. Among other varieties you'll see arbutus trees, which shed their red bark every year, and dogwood, whose white flowers are BC's floral emblem. The train's whistle, at first evocatively sentimental, will eventually begin to get on your nerves.

Just north of Victoria is **Shawnigan**, gateway to Shawnigan Lake with its busy schedule of summer festivities, its lakeside resorts and nearby campgrounds. **Cowichan Bay**, further north, is not on the railroad line but with its marina, maritime museum and good seafood restaurants, offers a pleasant diversion if you are driving. **Malahat**, an Indian word meaning "plenty of bait" (a reference to the fish-filled waters of the Saanich Inlet) is at the highest point

of a 180-metre (600-ft) climb over the pass. Between here and Duncan, dairy farms line both sides of the track and glimpses can be caught of skittish deer among the trees. Just before Duncan, the Cowichan River was subject to flooding, necessitating on one memorable occasion the dramatic rescue of stranded passengers by local Indians in dugout canoes.

At **Duncan**, an ambitious totem pole project has provided work for many local craftsmen who have produced 40 majestic poles, half of which line the highway with the remainder placed beside City Hall and the railroad station. Seven days a week between mid-June and October visitors can pay a small fee to tour the riverside **Native Heritage Centre** to watch totems being carved. According to legend, a rock at Cowichan is where whales rub themselves to be transformed into wolves so they can hunt on land.

Just north of town on the Trans-Canada Highway is the 40-hectare (100-acre) site of the **British Columbia Forest Museum** with its turn-of-the-century farm, working sawmill, logging camp and blacksmith shop as well as displays, films and demonstrations of forestry work. Beside the main museum building are a dozen fir trees, seeded from a mother tree 1,000 years old, which were planted to celebrate Canada's centennial in 1967. About 10 minutes' drive south of Duncan is the whimsically named **Whippletree Junction**, composed of reconstructed buildings from other regions: Wagonwheel Antiques was once a fish cannery at Sooke; the **Boardwalk Museum** formerly a post office and bank in Cobble Hill.

Further north, the little town of **Chemainus** is striving to become Canada's mural capital with 30 enormous murals depicting local history already finished and others planned. The programme, begun in 1982 to revitalise a town whose sawmill had closed down, has brought attention to Chemainus from all over the world. Each year 300,000

visitors stroll through **Waterwheel Park** and the downtown area, patronising the galleries, restaurants and antique shops and admiring the walls painted with ships, steam engines and ethnic themes. One batch of murals can be spotted from the train as it stops briefly at Chemainus station, but for those seeking a closer look, a tourist trolley operates on a route which passes all of them. A special fund pays for the original artists to return whenever the murals need touching up. Early in the year, eagles are sometimes seen in trees by the Chemainus River.

Ladysmith, named by its founder James Dunsmuir after the South African community that survived a siege in the Boer War, was one of BC's earliest boom towns. Dunsmuir, son of tycoon Robert Dunsmuir (who had one other son and eight daughters), preferred to house his miners here at the port rather than at his rich coal seams a few miles to the north (and now a ghost town). He bought the houses in Wellington, chopped them in half and shipped them

Chemainus has more than 30 murals depicting local history.

186

here on railway wagons. Reassembled on a hillside west of the harbour, some of them still exist today.

The mines were closed down 60 years ago, the lumber business followed in the 1980s and the town's major industry today is tourism. It has refurbished and publicised its historic heritage. A jewellery store now occupies a pre-World War I building on Gatacre Street that still bears an early ad for a men's clothing store. On the same block the **Black Nugget Museum** houses a collection of antiques and memorabilia set around a splendidly restored bar dating from the time when the building was a two-storey hotel in the 19th century. Altogether, 17 of the town's buildings have been restored and another 27 upgraded, winning Ladysmith numerous awards and congratulations for its new-old look.

Historic structures: Most of the work has been done along First Avenue, beginning with the **Other Hall Building**. This, now occupied by a beauty parlour, once housed a brothel upstairs from Mrs Smith's Chicken Restaurant (three-course meal, 35¢). The **Travelers Hotel** was, in 1913, the most luxurious of 18 hotels in a town that still had mud streets and wooden sidewalks. Almost opposite, the **Nicholson Cottage**, built by a member of the first town council in 1904, is now inhabited by his great granddaughter. The red-brick structure across from Gatacre Street was the Miners Union Hall in 1912 when the bitter, two-year strike against Dunsmuir Colliery first began.

The **Wigwam Café** now established on the premises has been the most popular local meeting place for 40 years. Next door the **Island Hotel** dates back to 1913 when it was preceded by another hotel. Four doors away, Johnson's Shoes began as a butcher's shop in 1901, then became Miss Forrester's Hat and Dress Shop. At the foot of Gatacre Street, George's Restaurant shares the **Comox Building** – once the headquarters of a giant logging company – with the **Ladysmith Railway Historical Soci-**

Swy-a-lana lagoon harbour, Nanaimo.

ety's exhibit of old locomotives. Adjoining it is the **Arboretum**, a free park in which different varieties of trees from around the world can be admired. Nearby is a **seafaring museum** operated by the Tall Ships Society.

Just before Nanaimo, the train slows down as a safety precaution because of the network of abandoned mineshafts and tunnels beneath the tracks, but also to make room for an elaborately fitted engine truck that sprays high pressure steam into the foliage lining the tracks – the most efficient way, the company has discovered, to kill overgrown weeds without any polluting side-effects.

Nanaimo (from the Indian phrase, *Sne-Ny-Mo*, meaning "where the big tribe dwells") is the biggest community between Victoria and Courtenay. It was prosperous as far back as 1850 when some Indians digging for clams uncovered "a black rock that burned", the genesis of the coal-mining industry from which the Dunsmuir family made its fortune. "Nanaimo is experiencing very prosperous and thriving times," observed *The Coast* magazine in May 1907. "The business activities were never better or as numerous. No one should visit Vancouver Island without making a run up to Nanaimo. The customs, the life, the welcome of the residents is sweet, wholesome and strengthening."

Bathtub boats: It is a pleasantly unspoiled town today, apparently less dedicated than its neighbours to slicking itself up for tourists. The town makes headlines every July when it stages the Great Canadian Bathtub Race across the 58 km (36 miles) of Georgia Strait. Regular ferries ply between here and the BC mainland, both to Tsawwassen and to Horseshoe Bay. Once disembarked in Nanaimo, it's possible to walk the mile or so into town along the **Harbourside Walkway**, then the **Queen Elizabeth Promenade**, a trip that can also be made by taxi. Sometimes the smell of cabbage will accompany your walk. It's a sign of bad weather: a westerly wind is blowing,

bringing fumes from the pulp paper mill across the island.

The promenade winds around the edge of the **Maffed-Sutton Park** and lagoon, ending at the hill atop which is the curiously shaped **Bastion** which houses the **historical museum** and **tourist office**. Built from squared logs fastened with wooden pegs, the Bastion is octagonal in shape, was commissioned by the Hudson's Bay Company in 1852, and was later turned into a city jail.

Down in the harbour is the city's major attraction: 286-hectare (706-acre) **Newcastle Island**, created as a swanky resort by CPR early in the century but now a popular wilderness park with camp grounds, picnic sites, beaches, trails and bicycle paths. Wildlife abounds and there are several old quarries and an abandoned coal mine. There are audio-visual displays and a restaurant in the **Visitor Centre** from which nature walks are operated. On summer days, ferries run to the island every hour.

Adjoining the **Harbour Park Mall**,

Nanaimo's famous Great Canadian Bathtub Race.

the **Nanaimo Centennial Museum** features an interesting 1900s main street and mock-up of a coal mine. Guided, eight-block strolls of the downtown area start from beside the museum twice each day. There is a small fee. **Front Street** is probably the most interesting to explore, beginning at the **Globe Hotel** (1887) and the monumental **Provincial Courthouse** designed by Canada's ubiquitous Francis Mawson Rattenbury. Three blocks from downtown is **Bowen Park**, which has an attractive waterfall.

Some of the nicest places to eat are out of town: the lovely **Marble House Restaurant** on Cedar Road at Hemer was opened by the Marble family, next door to what is now the oldest road house bar in BC. Further out in this direction is the waterside **Inn of the Sea** on Yellow Point Road, standing in tree-sheltered solitude with its outdoor swimming pool and incongruous helicopter landing-pad. Not far away, in dense woods, is the equally attractive **Yellow Point Lodge**, an immense log cabin complete with an airy lounge, a dining-room in which everybody shares the long tables, and all the usual luxurious facilities.

English-style country pubs are scattered around the region, a particularly attractive one being the **Cow and Gate**, about 13 km (8 miles) southeast of town on Cedar Road off the Island Highway. All the familiar English pub grub – steak and kidney pudding, shepherd's pie, and so on – are served (at exorbitant prices) in a lovely bar or outdoor terrace in a village green sort of setting with swans and ducks on the pond.

Further North: As the train climbs between Nanaimo and Wellington, the view eastwards is of **Long Lake**, noted for trout fishing, geese and ducks. **Wellington**, once a busy terminal for shipments of coal from Robert Dunsmuir's mines, had a thriving vaudeville theatre and staged bicycle racing in its heyday. The rail track descends into **Pleasant Valley**, passing **Brannen Lake** and **Nanoose Bay** where clam diggers are often busy. **French Creek**, crossed by a

Dog paddling.

319-metre (1,045-ft) trestle, teems with fish; the resort of Qualicum Beach is named for the Indian word denoting where salmon can be found. Beside the Big Qualicum River, beyond Dunsmuir, is a provincial salmon hatchery.

Qualicum Beach, one of the most beautiful spots on the island, is a popular tourist resort with seaplane connections to downtown Vancouver. The beach itself is only a few minutes' walk from the station where flowers surround an apple tree dripping with fruit. Local attractions include hiking on **Mount Arrowsmith**, visiting lakes and caves, picnicking at **Little Qualicum Falls** and admiring the 800-year-old fir trees in **Cathedral Grove**. The town offers golf, swimming, curling, tennis, horse-riding, fishing and water-skiing.

After some splendid views of the Coast Mountains eastwards across **Comox Harbour** and the beautiful **Forbidden Plateau** to the west, the train arrives at its final stop, **Courtenay**, the biggest town in the area and a skiing centre in winter. The Old House Restaurant on Riverside Lane is a pleasant place to eat.

In summer, the Blue Chair ski-lift transports visitors to the summit of "mile-high" **Mount Washington** from which there are spectacular views across the Georgia Strait. The Comox Valley Chamber of Commerce operates a **tourist information centre** on the main highway just south of town. In town, **Lewis Park** with its totem poles and the **Courtenay and District Museum** on Cliffe Avenue, a few blocks from most of the motels, are the main attractions. The main ski area, Forbidden Plateau in **Strathcona Provincial Park**, is about a 30-minute drive from town.

There are numerous beaches and camping grounds between Courtenay and **Campbell River**, after which the traffic thins out all the way up to **Port McNeil** and **Port Hardy**. Ferries operate to islands in the strait and also across to Prince Rupert on the mainland.

<u>Right</u>, Vancouver Island's climate is benign.

EAST, SOUTH, WEST AND THE GULF ISLANDS

East, south and west of Vancouver, the variety of landscape is spectacular. The fertile Lower Fraser Valley broadens out from the Strait of Georgia and eventually gives way to grassland plateaux, basins and quite high alpine mountains. The level, valley area is well-suited to agriculture, and, although suburbia and development are continually encroaching in the district around the city, fields of corn, berries, other fruits and vegetables, plus dairy farms offer pastoral vistas all the way to the optimistically named town of Hope. Fort Langley and New Westminster offer history in an accessible, cosy setting.

Southwest of Vancouver, off the shore of Vancouver Island, the Gulf Islands shelter marine life and provide delightful places to explore or relax as well as a tranquil lifestyle for their residents.

East of Vancouver: Two main highways head eastwards to the Fraser Valley and beyond: Trans-Canada Highway 1 (The Freeway) and the Lougheed Highway 7. The latter is a prettier route, but we'll deal first with **Highway 1** that crosses the **Fraser River** on the **Port Mann Bridge** and bypasses Surrey, Cloverdale and Langley. A few attractions, however, are worth noting which are within the Greater Vancouver Regional District. These can be explored before heading out on a longer route.

Take the Kensington exit, turn east on Canada Way and follow the signs to the **Burnaby Village Museum**, a living museum with staff in period costume (1890 through 1925), and more than 30 buildings and exhibits depicting typical village life. A blacksmith pounds out shoes for horses or oxen, a Chinese herbalist explains the traditional use for dried Canton lizard, and butter is churned. All this in what was originally a retirement home. The guides are chatty and very well-informed. If it's near lunchtime, walk along Deer Lake Avenue to the Hart House Restaurant which serves country-style food emphasising fresh produce, herbs and local products. Past the Canada Geese on the lawn behind the restaurant is **Deer Lake Park**, a serene and peaceful spot with a beach at one end.

Overlooking the park is the **Burnaby Art Gallery**, housed in an elegant 1909 mansion complete with fireplaces and lounges. Exhibits, changed frequently, include video and multi-media presentations. Behind the gallery, the bright marigolds, rhododendrons and Japanese maples of **Century Gardens** overlook the park. To get there by bus from Vancouver, catch the 120 New Westminster Station bus on Hastings Street between Burrard and Main.

Car buffs won't want to miss the **BC Transportation Museum** in Cloverdale. John Lennon's flashy 1965 Rolls-Royce, a 1911 passenger stagecoach car and a 1900 portable gas pump are among the exhibits (including over 180 cars, trucks, motorbikes and planes) that the museum has on display. Take the 176th Street exit to Highway 10, and turn right at 177th Street. Allow 40 minutes' driving time from Vancouver.

The **Vancouver Game Farm** is further east, off Highway 1 on 264th Street in Aldergrove. Over 110 wildlife species (ever seen a nilgai or guanaco?) can be seen roaming in large paddocks on this 50-hectare (120-acre) farm. The flat land between the Vedder Canal and Abbotsford was reclaimed from marshland by drainage of Sumas Lake and an ingenious network of canals, dykes and dams. Completed in 1924, the project created an additional 13,000 hectares (29,000 acres) of fertile farmland.

In Abbotsford every August is the biggest air show in North America. It's often one of the hottest weekends of the year, but that doesn't stop hundreds of thousands of spectators from joining the highway crawl to the **Abbotsford International Airshow**. There are stunts, drills, aerobatics, antique and war planes. World-class demonstrations

Preceding pages: Canada's lower left-hand corner. **Left,** shades of autumn.

have included the Canadian Snowbirds, USAF Thunderbirds, US Angels and the Soviet MiG-29.

The Canadian Military Engineers Museum at the Canadian Forces Base on Vedder Road displays weapons, tanks and items related to Canadian military engineers' history, some of which date back to the 1600s.

Lougheed east: The scenery is more absorbing along the Lougheed Highway 7, and drivers seem to be less harried. If one starts from **Broadway** and follows the north bank of the Fraser River through Coquitlam and Port Coquitlam, the landscape begins to open up at **Pitt Meadows**. Blending in with commercial and residential development are Holstein cows grazing in lush fields, fruit and berry farms, sloughs and creeks, dykes and farms.

A rewarding place to learn about woodland and forestry practices is at the **University of British Columbia Research Forest**. Spread over a network of walking trails in varying stages of

growth are demonstrations of reforestation, tree-planting, and clearcut logging. An arboretum has 120 tree species from around the world. The forest (open daily) is between **Alouette Lake** and the **Pitt Lake** recreational areas, 8 km (5 miles) north of Highway 7 on 232nd Street.

In **Golden Ears Provincial Park**, wryly named after the twin peaks that glow at dusk, activities include hiking, climbing, horseback riding, swimming, fishing, waterskiing, windsurfing, canoeing, and nature study.

The **Alouette Lake** area on the park's east boundary was used by the Coast Salish and Interior Salish Indians for hunting and fishing, but in the 1920s the timber was cleared and traces of early railway logging still remain among the second-growth forest of Douglas fir, western hemlock, and western red cedar. A lucky hiker might catch glimpses of deer, beavers, mountain goats, or black bears in the park.

The **Albion Ferry** will carry you at no cost across the Fraser River from the south end of 240th Street to the historic town of **Fort Langley**, a Hudson's Bay Company supply post originally built in 1827 as a fur trading-post. It was here that British Columbia was declared as a British Crown colony and where in 1828 the company's chief trader, Archibald McDonald, first began processing salmon for export. Despite the discovery that the Fraser River wasn't a navigable route to the interior, agriculture and fish-processing kept the trading-post in operation until 1866. It was restored in 1955 as a **National Historic Park**.

The only original building is the storehouse but the others are authentic representations of the 1850s. Staff in period dress demonstrate such tasks as barrel-making and blacksmithing.

Fort Langley can also be easily reached via Highway 1 or you may view it from the deck of an 1800s paddle-wheeler boat. The **Fraser River Connection** leaves from Westminster Quay in New Westminster and arrives two hours later at Fort Langley. The entire

Burnaby miniature railway.

cruise will take about six hours, depending on the current.

Early capital: The easiest way to get to the Westminster waterfront is via Sky-Train. **New Westminster** was established in 1859 by Governor James Douglas as the capital of BC and was named The Royal City by Queen Victoria. Nine years later Victoria was chosen by the Legislative Council as the province's capital. More of the area's history can be seen at the **Irving House Historic Centre** in the 14-room home built in 1865 for the riverboat king, Captain William Irving. The parlour and master bedroom contain original furniture imported from England.

There are lovely picnic spots along the Fraser River at Fort Langley, near to which are the **British Columbia Farm Machinery and Agricultural Museum**, one of the largest of its kind, with cultivators, mowers, farm wagons and horse-drawn carriages; and the **Langley Centennial Museum and National Exhibition Centre**, which displays a variety of Coast Salish Indian artefacts.

Continuing east on Highway 7, the low flood plain area of **Hatzic Lake** is the tranquil home to Benedictine monks at **Westminster Abbey**, completed in 1982 after 28 years of construction. Its impressive bell tower rises 180 metres (600 ft) above the valley and 64 colourful stained-glass windows decorate the lower portion below the dome. Visitors are welcome most weekday afternoons; head north on Dewdney Trunk Road and you should see the abbey.

The **Kilby General Store Museum** near Harrison Mills still has the character and appearance of the two-storey general store and nine-bedroom hotel built by Thomas Kilby in 1904. Three bedrooms, the dining-room, sitting-room, pantry, and post office look pretty much as they did when prospectors, railwaymen and loggers passed through this small community at the junction of the Harrison and Fraser rivers. The store is fully stocked with goods for viewing from the 1920s and '30s – tins of coffee

Burnaby is a living museum.

and tea, candy sticks in jars, galvanised pails, hand tools, brooms, sock and glove stretchers for shrinkable woollens. On hot summer days, you might get a sample of homemade ice cream in the dairy.

Nearby **Kilby Provincial Park**, with its sandy beach, picnic and camping facilities, is a good place from which to spot trumpeter swans and bald eagles (in the winter months only, alas).

The Gold Route: At Agassiz, Highway 9 north leads to the town of **Harrison Hot Springs**, a year-round resort spot at the southern tip of **Harrison Lake**. During the gold rush in the 1850s, the lake was awash with wild-eyed optimists en route to the gold mines of the Cariboo. The landmark **Harrison Hotel** has been a resort since 1926. Supplied by two sulphur-potash springs, a large pool near the hotel is open to all.

There have been reported sightings of the legendary Bigfoot or Sasquatch, which is the Salish word for "hairy men" or "wild men". Visitors are unlikely to see this supposedly friendly creature in **Sasquatch Provincial Park**, but who knows? Keep your eye out for gigantic footprints and a loping ape-like creature about twice the size of a man.

Between Harrison and the Trans-Canada Highway, with Mount Cheam in the background, the award-winning **Minter Gardens** comprise several separate gardens interspersed with jade green lawns, babbling creeks and graceful trees. Roses, ferns and rhodo-dendron have their own special spots and to complete the plan are meadow, formal and fragrance themes. There are also three aviaries and the largest collection of Penjing Rock Bonsai outside China. These are yin/yang arrangements of coral and unusual rocks. The gardens are open April through October, 9am until dusk.

Branching out: Three major mountain highways branch out from the town of Hope, gateway to BC's interior, 154 km (96 miles) from Vancouver. The Trans-Canada Highway 1 cuts through the Fraser Canyon to **Cache Creek** and the Rockies.

The newer Coquihalla Highway 5 is the fastest, four-lane toll highway to **Kamloops**. The Hope-Princeton High-way 3 passes right through **Manning Park** and on to the **Okanagan**.

Set on the east bank of the Fraser River and ringed by mountains, **Hope** is a beautiful place with many accom-modation options. At the Rainbow Junction of Highway 1 and 3, stop for tea at the restored **Canadian National Railway Station**, built in 1916 by the Great Northern Railway. Moved from its original site at Hudson Bay Street and Fifth Avenue, it is now a tea house and arts centre. The **Hope Museum** next to the **Travel InfoCentre** has displays on the fur trade, mining, logging and native culture. **Christ Church**, built from locally milled and hand-planed lumber, at Park Street and Fraser Avenue, is one of the oldest churches in BC. It has been in use since 1861.

A walk through the **Othello Quintette Tunnels** is especially fascinating. The

The Abbotsford International Airshow features world-class demonstrations.

Kettle Valley Railway, a subsidiary of the Canadian Pacific Railway, blasted five tunnels through the solid granite walls of the **Coquihalla Canyon** linking the Kootenays with the coast. It was an extraordinary and costly effort – one particular mile cost $300,000 back in 1914. The line operated until 1959. To reach the tunnels, take the Kawkawa Lake Road off Highway 5 or off 6th Avenue in Hope to Othello Road.

The Coquihalla Highway makes a long, steady ascent to **Coquihalla Summit**, which slopes up to 1,247 metres (4,092 ft). The landscape is gentler, with a more subtle beauty than the awesome **Fraser Canyon**. Notice, however, the avalanche paths where rubble collects and trees remain bent and crippled. In winter, be prepared to get caught crawling along behind a snowplough in a blinding snowstorm; in summer it's usual to see cars stopped on the shoulder with overheated radiators. Stop at **Coldwater River Provincial Park** for a cooling stroll along the river. Trees

become sparser, mountains smooth out and around **Merritt** it's dry, hilly, ranching country. To return via the Fraser Canyon, Highway 8 through the Nicola Valley to Spences Bridge and Lytton leads to the junction. The circular tour, starting and returning at Hope, is 150 km (93 miles); 320 km (199 miles) from Vancouver.

River-rafting: There are two small provincial parks in the area, **Goldpan**, just south of Spences Bridge, and **Skihist**, just east of Lytton. Open May through October, both offer overnight camping. River-rafting is a favourite activity near **Lytton** where the Fraser and Thompson rivers meet. Lytton was once an interior Salish town called Camchin, meaning "great forks".

The **Stein River Valley**, between the Lillooet River Valley on the west and the Fraser River Valley on the east, can be reached from Lytton. The valley is sacred to the Lillooet people and the Nlaka'pamux people who have hunted, fished, gathered plants and held spiritual

Dreaming of
The Right
Stuff.

ceremonies here for centuries. From the headwaters at 2,900 metres (9,700 ft), to the valley at 130 metres (430 ft), the geography, climate and vegetation are more diverse than in any park in BC. It encompasses two climatic zones, three small glacier systems, and four major lakes. Within its confines are arid plains, cedar glades and pine forests, nearly motionless swamps and rushing rapids. Wildlife includes grizzly and black bears, mountain goats, wolves, cougar, deer and marmots.

Yale, 63 km (39 miles) north of Hope, began as a Hudson's Bay Company fur post in 1848 and boomed with the gold rush, becoming a terminus of one of the largest sternwheeler operations on the west coast. By 1868 the feverish days when a saloon might take in $10,000 in a day were over. The CPR construction activity that followed was short-lived; Yale (population 500) is now a small forestry and service town.

The **Historic Yale Museum** colourfully depicts the 1858 gold rush as well as the building of the CPR; other exhibits include Indian artefacts and baskets and a national monument which commemorates the work of the Chinese construction workers on the railway. Their daily pay of 50¢ was half that of a white worker, and poor living conditions caused the death of hundreds from illness or accidents.

The **Hell's Gate Airtram** that zips 153 metres (502 ft) across the river offers spectacular views of the rapids and narrow gorge below, as well as both the CN and CP railway tracks. The fishladders were built to help salmon over debris from a 1913 rock slide that obstructed the channel for subsequent years and which caused huge losses to the salmon trade. This local resource can be sampled at the Salmon House Restaurant, which serves a delicious, hearty salmon chowder.

East on Highway 3: Most of the mountain highway routes in BC are subject to landslides, avalanches and flooding and the Hope-Princeton Highway 3 is no **Mountain-climbing.**

exception. In 1965, a small tremor triggered the release of 46 million cubic metres (60 million cubic yds) of rock, snow and debris from Johnson's Peak. It swept three vehicles and four passengers off the highway, dumping 60 metres (200 ft) of fill in the Nicolum Creek valley. The **Hope Slide** viewpoint plaque just east of Hope gives all the details.

A sprawling and diverse region in the North Cascades, **Manning Park**, 225 km (140 miles) east of Vancouver, offers some of the most accessible alpine splendour to be found. **Rhododendron Flats** is best in June when this indigenous evergreen shrub is covered with deep pink flowers. It's possible to drive as high as the sub-alpine meadows along **Blackwall Road**; in July and August the area is profuse with towhead babies and flowers like lupins and yellow snow lilies. There is an extensive trail system and skiing in winter. Information, maps and brochures are available at the Park Headquarters and **Visitor Centre**, half

a mile east of the Manning Park Lodge. Trailhead to the 3,780-km (2,350-mile) **Pacific Crest Trail** is east of the park headquarters. Six months is recommended for this awesome trek though the wilderness, which leads right to the Mexican border.

The **Skagit Valley Provincial Recreation Area** can be reached from trails within Manning Park or by following the Silver Skagit Road, 32 km (20 miles) southeast of Hope. The area is noted for its wide range of mammals such as deer, black bear, cougar, bobcat, beaver, coyote, mink, squirrels, hares and chipmunks. Over 200 species of birds have been recorded and more than 50 species of waterfowl. The **Skagit River** is famous for fly fishing. As with any other area in BC, get a licence and check the local regulations – it's catch and release fishing here.

South of Vancouver: Between Vancouver and the United States border, there are a number of attractions off the main artery, Highway 99. After the George

Fraser Canyon.

Massey Tunnel, exit right (west) on to the Steveston Highway, turn left on No. 2 Road, then south to Moncton Street. First stop will be the historic fishing village of **Steveston**, a great place to browse through shops, sample the fish and chips, then wander down to the wharves where the day's catch of salmon, rock cod, snapper, prawns, crab, shrimp, sole, and herring is sold right off the boat.

Japanese fishermen were attracted to the area in the past by the huge catches of salmon. They were evacuated by the federal government during World War II, but eventually returned and their influence is evident today. One of the largest canneries on the lower Fraser, the Gulf of Georgia Cannery, was built here in 1894.

The **George C. Reifel Waterfowl Refuge** on **Westham Island** at the mouth of the Fraser River supports the largest wintering population of waterfowl in Canada. The 340-hectare (850-acre) habitat and estuarine marsh serves

as a a sanctuary to more than 240 species of birds. In November, vast flocks of migrating snow geese stop here on their flight from their breeding grounds in the Arctic to the Sacramento River Valley in California.

Pathways and covered shelters with peeking windows allow visitors to observe without disturbing the birds, which include barn swallows, song sparrows, mallard ducks, Canada geese and the more uncommon black-crowned night heron, spotted redshank and gyrfalcon. The refuge can be tricky to find: follow River Road for 3 km (2 miles) south of **Ladner**. Turn right on to Westham Island Road, then cross a one-lane bridge and continue, following the signs.

Another good place to go bird-watching is at **Boundary Bay**, where you'll find salt marshes, mud flats, dykes and dunes. Look for eagles, gulls, herons, terns and ducks along the sandy tidal beaches. Go south on Highway 17, left (east) at 56th Street and left (east) again at 12th Avenue to Boundary Bay Road.

On the eastern side of Boundary Bay are some of the lower mainland's best beaches. Follow Highway 99 south to Canada's southernmost mainland community, **White Rock**, on Semiahmoo Bay. On the way, the **Canadian Museum of Flight and Transportation** displays Canada's third largest collection of vintage aircraft, jets and biplanes. Sharing popularity with pre-war planes in this large park are vehicles from Highway 86, a big favourite with kids at Expo 86 before they were brought here.

Crescent Beach and **Blackie's Spit** are the most popular beaches in the area, where strong-armed bathers can fantasise about swimming to another country. **White Rock** is an artistic seaside community where the work of local artists can be seen at the Station Art Centre in a restored Great Northern Railway Station, built in 1913. **White Rock Pier** extends 469 metres (1,538 ft) out into Semiahmoo Bay.

The Gulf Islands: Southwest of Vancouver and sheltered from Pacific Ocean

The Strait of Georgia contains 200 islands.

storms by Vancouver Island, are about **200 enticing islands** and islets in the Strait of Georgia. Most have dry woodlands, abundant marine life, sandy beaches and rocky outcrops. The beautiful scenery is complemented by the drier, mild climate. Residents on the few inhabited islands lead a simpler, more natural life (even the ones who commute to work in Vancouver) and, except for the developers, most wish the gates could be closed after they arrive.

A visit to any one of the islands is a refreshing respite from the Lower Mainland's gnarly traffic and relentless city strain. For those who can spare more than a day, the islands not only have a multitude of cosy bed and breakfast places, but most also offer camping facilities. Many of the larger islands can be reached easily by ferry from both Tsawwassen ferry terminal, 30 km (20 miles) south of Vancouver, and Swartz Bay, 32 km north of Victoria on Vancouver Island.

Saltspring Island is the most populated and developed, as well as the largest, of the five major Gulf Islands. The first permanent settlers were black immigrants, arriving from the US almost half a century ago. They began one of the earliest agricultural communities in the region and the island is still known for its sheep, fruit and dairy products.

The modern seaside town of **Ganges** is the largest community in the Gulf Islands and here you'll find all the usual shops and services. There's a pricey hotel, Hastings House, whose meals, theme rooms (the sealoft overlooks the ocean) and perfect setting once earned it the title of Canadian country house of the year by a widely-circulated travel newsletter.

At the other end of the accommodation scale, there is camping at **Ruckle Provincial Park**, where rocky headlands and coves along the shore can be explored. Also part of the local landscape is the sheep farm, and its original buildings, that has been run by the Ruckle family since 1872. The best view of

Retreat Cove, Galiano Island.

Fulford Harbour, Vancouver Island and the other Gulf Islands is from Baynes Peak on Mount Maxwell.

Galiano Island, long and narrow, was named for Dionisio Galiano, a Spanish navy commander who explored the area in 1792, although it was undoubtedly inhabited by the Salish Indians for thousands of years before he arrived. Archaeological surveys have found ancient Coast Salish sites and huge *midden* deposits in the area.

It is the driest island of the group, receiving only 46 cm (18 inches) of annual rainfall. BC's oldest marine park is on this island; **Montague Harbour Provincial Marine Park** offers well-protected anchorage for boaters, sandy beaches and the opportunity to do some clam digging or fishing. A tidal lagoon is the most likely place to see great blue herons. Birders can also watch for oystercatchers, pelagic cormorants and bald eagles. There are 40 campsites in this very popular park and some excellent restaurants on the island itself including

a local favourite, the Pink Geranium, plus another called La Berengerie; and one pub, the Hummingbird Inn.

Miner's Bay on **Mayne Island** became a major stopping point between Vancouver Island and the mainland during the gold rush which began in 1858. Its central location and development of hotels and lodges have made it a favourite retreat since the turn of the century. Mayne is much quieter and more peaceful than it was when the jailhouse, built in 1896, was needed. This jailhouse now serves as the **Mayne Island Museum**. The island itself is tiny and can easily be seen in a day.

North and **South Pender Islands**, best known for their many small coves and numerous beaches, are joined by a one-lane bridge between Bedwell and Browning Harbours. **Bedwell Harbour Resort** on South Pender is a Canadian port of entry from the United States. There is a waterfront pub here, the Whale Pod, and another at Port Browning Marina on North Pender, the Sh-qu-ala or "watering hole".

Saturna Island is the most remote southern Gulf Island and is less visited than the others since it requires a ferry transfer. It's a good day trip, or a longer destination for those who like to travel off the beaten track. Note, however, that **Saturna Beach** is the scene of the Gulf Island's biggest annual event – a lamb bake for Canada Day, which is held on the first day of July.

The **East Point Lighthouse**, built in 1888, is a must for lovers of scenic locations; the same visitors will also appreciate the sculptural sandstone formations, kelp beds and a shell and gravel beach at the end of a short, steep lane. Killer whales are often spotted from here in summer, but more common are seals, sea-lions, and sea birds such as cormorants, sandpipers and herons. **Winter Cove Provincial Marine Park** has mud and sand beaches and can be reached by land or water. Accommodation on Saturna is limited, and there is no camping.

Left, tide pools. **Right**, sculptural sandstone formations are common on the islands.

NORTH FROM VANCOUVER

"When people say they love Vancouver I suspect it's not so much the city they love but the setting," architect Arthur Erickson once said of his home city. And it's true – the setting *is* the best thing about Vancouver. The ocean, rugged mountains, lush vegetation, clear water lakes, rivers and abundant wildlife, all within minutes of downtown, make it a paradise for those who appreciate the outdoors.

Beyond the beaches scattered along an otherwise rugged shoreline, the **Coast Mountains** extend from the lowlands of the Fraser River north to the **Yukon** territory in an unbroken chain of glaciated peaks, deep valleys, fjords and coastal rainforest. If you decide to venture into the wilderness, make sure you are properly equipped and go with proper respect. Many hikers have lost their way barely beyond Vancouver's back yard.

And don't expect to see everything in one visit. Some local explorers lose themselves in remote mountain regions for weeks on end, claiming to find something new at every turn.

Of course, there are options other than adventurous outdoor activity. Relaxation is a natural complement to adventure and there are some excellent historic and cultural sites to see as well.

Heading north: Highway 99 to **Horseshoe Bay** and beyond is the only road leading directly north of Vancouver. From Horseshoe Bay, ferries run across to Nanaimo on Vancouver Island, a trip that takes over 90 minutes, and incurable island enthusiasts can also make the 20-minute crossing to Snug Cove on tiny **Bowen Island** in Howe Sound or to the Sunshine Coast, a peninsula isolated from Vancouver by both Howe Sound and the Coast Mountains.

The **Sunshine Coast** has a kind of *laissez-faire* island feeling that comes from its isolation and a 45-minute ferry ride. The most casual reader of the local newspapers will be able to pick out some bit of controversy that makes the undercurrent of this seemingly laid-back coastline all the more interesting. Typical residents include artists, writers, loggers, fishers and reclusive types, all of whom appreciate the 2,400 hours of annual sunshine and low level of precipitation.

The only land link is Highway 101 that extends for about 150 km (93 miles) up the coast to its northern terminus at the small fishing village of **Lund**. Scuba diving, fishing, cycling, hiking, kayaking, skiing, beachcombing, sunning and gazing at the scenery are among the favourite activities.

Follow lower Marine Drive to Molly's Reach Café in the fishing village of **Gibsons**, setting for CBC-TV's popular television series, *The Beachcombers*. Excellent fish and chips are served at the Gibsons Fish Market near the grocery market. The **Elphinstone Pioneer Museum** has a tremendous shell collection, as well as pioneer and Coast

Preceding pages: snow lies on BC's mountains all year round. **Left**, Horseshoe Bay. **Right**, ice maiden.

Salish displays. The first of several provincial parks is at **Roberts Creek**, 14 km (9 miles) northwest of Gibsons. Picnic or camp in the second-growth fir and cedar forest or walk down to the pebble beach. Low-tide marine life includes starfish, mussels, and oysters. There is saltwater fishing here, but the rugged coastline requires good navigation skills. There's a better beach for swimming at **Wilson Creek/Davis Bay** further up on Highway 101.

As one enters the town of **Sechelt**, the impressive Sechelt Indian band's **House of Hewhiwus** or House of Chiefs is hard to miss. The band's office is here, as well as a museum, native arts and crafts, a theatre and gift store. Sechelt itself is a busy service centre with access to scuba diving, fishing and boating, but it has very little character. **Porpoise Bay Provincial Park** is a good spot for cyclists to camp and for canoers and kayakers to "put in" and paddle in and around the **Sechelt Inlets Marine Recreation Area**.

Unless they have a particular destination in mind, most day-trippers don't venture beyond Sechelt. But one natural spectacle further up the Sechelt Peninsula is a must-see: the west coast's largest saltwater rapids at **Skookumchuck Narrows Provincial Park**. It's a beautiful drive past the peaceful **Pender Harbour** area, encompassing the communities of Madeira Park, Irvine's Landing, and Garden Bay. The park is on the northeast east tip of the **Sechelt Peninsula**, east of Egmont.

Watery spectacle: Skookumchuck, or "strong waters", refers to the rapids created as ebbing and flowing water is constricted in the narrow channel. The churning action of billions of gallons of water forced through Skookumchuck Narrows is awesome to watch. Check the tide tables (usually posted at the trailhead or in the local papers), and try to allow enough time to watch the transition from calm to seething water.

The greatest action off **North Point** occurs on the outgoing tide and on the incoming tide off **Roland Point**. At low tide extraordinary specimens of giant barnacles, sea urchins, sea anemones, and molluscs can be observed, attracting scuba divers from all over the world. The narrows are also known for the plentiful catches of salmon and cod, but extreme caution is advised for boaters or paddlers. It's a one-hour hike to Roland Point from the parking lot.

The highway continues to **Earls Cover** ferry terminal, 16 km (10 miles) beyond Madeira Park, where a BC Ferry crosses Jervis Inlet in 50 minutes. **Powell River** (pop. 13,423) is a popular summer resort location which claims to be the scuba-diving capital of Canada and several sunken ships attract octopi, wolf eels and lingcod. One of the world's largest pulp and paper plants is the mainstay of the economy. Another ferry trip links Powell River to Comox on Vancouver Island.

Sea-to-sky highway: Twisting and winding along steep cliffs and mountains above Howe Sound, Highway 99 is the

Eat and sleep like a king.

most scenic drive immediately out of the city. It's moody and dramatic when great grey banks of clouds hover low on the slopes, and arbutus and fir trees drip with captured rain. Change to sunshine and it all becomes a sparkling vista.

If you'd rather not drive, you can see the Sound by bus, boat or train. One trouble-free way to do this is to take a leisurely three-hour ride aboard the **Royal Hudson Steam Train** to Squamish and then back again on board the cruise ship *Britannia* (*see Travel Tips section*). The day trip from Vancouver allows for about an hour there – just time to take the bus trip to see Shannon Falls (*see page 212*) or a spectacular (but expensive) flight up to the mountain glaciers.

At the residential community of **Lions Bay**, 11 km (7 miles) north of Horseshoe Bay, beautifully designed homes perch precariously on the steep slopes below the western cirque of **The Lions**, the two prominent rock summits that highlight Vancouver's skyline. The

steep, switchbacking hike to the main ridge south of the West Lion is one of the most popular in the Lower Mainland. It begins at Lions Bay and takes about six hours for the round trip. The **West Lion** at 1,646 metres (5,401 ft) is the higher, but don't attempt to climb it unless you have climbing experience; there have been fatalities. The **East Lion** is in the watershed and it is illegal to approach or climb.

For a spectacular free show at sunset take the second turn-off at Lions Bay, drive a short distance up the hill and park beside the map adjoining the cascading river. The steps back downhill lead to a little park with seats beside what looks like a house but is actually a camouflaged water tank.

Across Howe Sound the clouds are settling into the crevices of the hills like heavy cream puffballs, and what appear to be giant-sized tubes of crumpled tissue paper edge southwards. In time these clouds thicken and form a belt that obscures part of the mountains, another

Sechelt, on the Sunshine Coast.

sea above the sea. As the sun sets, dull orange rays are reflected in nearby windows. In the mottled grey sky a luminescent patch of light remains. It may be the entrance to heaven.

Porteau Cove offers easy access for scuba divers, kayakers, windsurfers and fishers. The provincial park, only 39 km (24 miles) north of Vancouver, has camping right by the ocean, boat launching facilities and picnic areas. The highway continues up and along another rise, then winds down into **Britannia Beach**, a former mining town. The mine was the largest processor of copper in the British Empire, processing 7,000 tons of ore daily at its operating peak in the late 1920s and early 1930s. Underground tours are available at the **BC Mining Museum**, now a National Historic Site. The museum is filled with artefacts and working displays of slushers, muckers, drills and one of the world's last remaining gravity-fed concentrators. Building on a 45-degree slope conserved vital power and reduced maintenance costs in the processing operation.

Murrin Provincial Park is popular with fishers, picnickers, hikers and rock climbers. Its tiny roadside **Browning Lake** is regularly stocked with rainbow trout, and you can swim but the bottom is yucky. Further along, **Shannon Falls**, thundering 340 metres (1,110 ft) down a granite bluff, is a more spectacular sight. A short, easy walk through the forest gives you a close-up view of BC's third highest waterfall. The Klahanie Restaurant across the highway serves delicious butter tarts for those who have forgotten to bring a picnic lunch, or if – as too often happens – it's raining.

The **Stawamus Chief**, a 650-metre (2,140-ft) granite monolith, towers over the town of Squamish, 61 km (38 miles) north of Vancouver, and attracts climbers from around the world. Most days when it's not raining, colourful ropes can be seen trailing down route lines and tiny dots move with deliberation up the rock face. Ambitious non-climbers can hike up the back trail to any of the

Chateau Whistler, BC's premier ski resort.

Chief's three summits. The view from the top is blemished only by the distinct smell of pulp and smoke steaming out of the woodfibre plant across Howe Sound.

Squamish (pop. 12,000), a small logging town, has shops and pleasant restaurants (good espresso at Quinn's) as well as places to stay. Shortly after Europeans settled the valley around 1873, logging the giant cedar and fir trees became the leading industry. Recreational tourism is growing rapidly with the area's reputation as a premier rock-climbing and windsurfing destination. Still, the town is proud of its logging heritage and in August holds a loggers' sports show with such competitive events as springboard chop, power-saw bucking and a chokerman's race.

Squamish means "mother of the wind" or "strong wind" in Coast Salish and some of the best windsurfing in Canada can be enjoyed where the river flows into **Howe Sound**. A good place to view bald eagles, especially from November to February, is at the viewpoint further north along Highway 99 near **Bracken-dale**. They nest here and feast on salmon in the Squamish River.

The largest and most visited provincial park in the Lower Mainland, **Garibaldi Park** covers 197,187 hectares (487,260 acres) on the east side of Highway 99, beginning just north of Squamish and extending past Whistler. It offers incredible alpine beauty in numerous day-hiking options throughout the park. The glacier-fed, clear blue **Garibaldi Lake** with the granitic **Panorama Ridge** beyond is a breathtaking sight. A very popular hike is to the top of the stark black volcanic plug, Black Tusk, which ends in a scramble up a 99-metre (325 ft) chimney.

For those not sure-footed, the surrounding meadows, especially when covered in alpine flowers in late summer, are more than satisfying. Allow six hours for a return hike to the Garibaldi Lake or Black Tusk area from the trailhead. The park has 196 wilderness walk-in campsites at five locations, four

Whistler was chosen for Olympic ski development.

overnight alpine shelters and six day-use shelters.

Before 1960, when **Whistler Mountain** was chosen for Olympic ski development, the **Alta Lake Valley** was a remote summer destination and home to only a few hundred hard-core outdoor recreationists and loggers. Since then, the carefully designed development, with cobbled streets, quality shops and galleries, restaurants, a golf course created by Arnold Palmer, plus the geographical splendour that includes five lakes and virtually every type of recreational possibility, have made the resort village of **Whistler** one of the finest in the world.

It all becomes a bit pretentious when full of beautiful people comparing fashion, but go there anyway for recreation, relaxation, culture and beauty; there's much more to do than skiing. In summer, ride the lifts with a mountain bike in tow, hike the meadows (listen for marmots whistling) or check for the dates of musical concerts. The Van-

couver Symphony Orchestra has performed annually on top of Whistler Mountain since 1988.

There's windsurfing, horseback riding, hiking, fishing (a licence is required to fish in BC), paragliding, kayaking, swimming, canoeing, or whitewater rafting. Play tennis, go for a nature tour, charter a helicopter, or hire an adventure guide to see some back-country. **Blackcomb** and Whistler mountains, rising directly above the village, offer more skiable terrain than any other ski area in North America.

Impressive falls: North of Whistler 32 km (20 miles), a pleasant half-hour walk along the Green River leads to **Nairn Falls**. Although not particularly high, its powerful tumble is loud and very impressive.

Highway 99 traffic thins out towards the farming and logging town of **Pemberton**. East 64 km (40 miles) is the **Meager Creek Hot Springs**, a popular spot for weary skiers and hikers. Access is via the **Lillooet Forest Road** northwest of the town, then left up a logging road marked M24. The springs are the largest in BC, but it is an undeveloped site with no tourist facilities except for tenting spots and trailer or camper parking.

As you approach Lillooet, the vegetation changes from coastal fir, hemlock and cedar to dry sagebrush, cactus and Ponderosa pines. It's well worth a visit to the **Village Museum**, open mid-May until mid-October, to get an idea of what the town was like when it was overrun with thousands of hard-living pioneers lusting for gold.

There are other museums here, one of them devoted to Jack Lynn – the man who discovered gold here in 1859 – and also the intriguingly named Bridge of 23 Camels. June is the best time to be in **Lillooet**, when the historic town celebrates its colourful past with staged "train robberies" and other dramas with everybody costumed in gold-rush style. It is possible to link up with Hope and Yale on the so-called Nugget Route.

Left and **right**, the old man and the tree.

TRAVEL TIPS

GETTING THERE

Unless otherwise stated, all telephone numbers are preceded by the area code (604). Numbers beginning with 1-800 are toll-free if dialled in North America. All prices quoted are in Canadian dollars.

BY AIR

Vancouver International Airport is the second largest airport in Canada and the Canadian gateway to the Pacific Rim countries. Nearly 10 million passengers a year use the terminal, flying in or out of Vancouver by the many airlines the airport accommodates. The main terminal services both international and domestic flights. The international carriers include Air New Zealand, British Airways, Air China, Cathay Pacific, Japan Airlines, Korean Airlines, KLM Royal Dutch Airlines, Lufthansa, Qantas, and Singapore airlines. Carriers from the US include American Airlines, Continental, Delta Airlines, Horizon Airlines and United Airlines. In all there are over 325,000 take-offs and landings a year.

The airport is situated on an island at the mouth of the Fraser River 13km (8 miles) from downtown Vancouver. In addition to the main airport terminal, a smaller south terminal services regional airlines and smaller planes. If you need transportation between the two terminals, call the connecting airline and they will arrange transportation, or you can take a taxi.

The airport concierge service is open from 6.30am–midnight on level three and information booths can be found on levels one and two. The Vancouver International Airport has a "Green Coat" service to assist travellers. These friendly volunteers can be distinguished by their green cardigans and blue ties or scarves. They will assist with directions and information about the airport. Tel: 276-6101 from any public phone if you need additional help.

There are many other services in the airport including duty-free shops, gift shops, a coffee shop and restaurant/bar, post office, bookstore, bank machines, barber shops, newsstand, flower shop, credit card fax machines, video games room and an interfaith chapel. The money exchange bureaux are on each level. On levels one and two you will find hotel courtesy phones. You can make hotel reservations from the airport and also rent cars. (*See the Getting Around section for more information.*)

BY SEA

Vancouver is Canada's busiest port. In addition to serving as the main centre of distribution of goods shipped between Canada and Asia, the port is also visited by some of the world's top cruise lines. Each year from May until October hundreds of passengers arrive in Vancouver on these luxurious ships. Some of these cruise lines are: Costa Cruise Lines, Crystal Cruises, Cunard Line, Holland America Line, Princess Cruises, Regency Cruises, Royal Caribbean Cruises, Royal Cruise Line, Royal Viking Line, Salen Lindblad Cruising, Seven Seas Cruise Line, World Explorer Cruises.

If you arrive in Vancouver by cruise ship your vessel will be berthed at either the Canada Place Cruise Ship Terminal or Ballantyne Terminal. The Canada Place Terminal is located on the waterfront in downtown Vancouver. The berth is next to the Vancouver Trade and Convention Centre and the Pan Pacific Hotel, close to city buses, the SkyTrain and the SeaBus. Shops and theatres are within walking distance as are several sightseeing attractions including Gastown and Stanley Park.

The Ballantyne Terminal is located a short distance east of Canada Place about a 10-minute taxi ride from the downtown area.

The cruise ship terminals are a 25-minute taxi ride from the Vancouver International Airport. A complimentary shuttle runs to and from the terminals at Ballantyne or Canada Place. There is car storage at the Canada Place Parking, tel: 681-7311.

For more information about cruising:
Vancouver Port Corporation, 1900 Granville Square, 200 Granville Street, Vancouver, BC, V6C 2P9. Tel: 666-4452 (9am–5pm). Fax: 666-3916.

BY BUS

The Greyhound Bus is the only bus service connecting Vancouver with the rest of Canada and the United States. Foreign visitors who wish to enjoy the scenic beauties of Canada are reminded that North America is a vast country and distances are much greater than in other parts of the world. For instance, the distance from Montreal to Vancouver is 4,800 km (2,980 miles) and from Toronto it is 4,490km (2,790 miles).

Long-haul buses are made for comfort with lounge seats and toilet facilities. Some even have videos to watch during night travel. They make frequent stops and provide good service and a smoke-free journey. If you have time, there's no better way to see the country. The express bus from Eastern Canada takes three days and three nights. The Greyhound bus trip from the US is much faster. From Seattle, Washington the trip is approximately four hours. If you enter Canada by bus from the US there is a Canada Customs and Immigration office at the Douglas crossing, Blaine, Washington. American passengers will require adequate identification.

Foreign visitors need valid passports and/or visas.

The Vancouver bus depot is located on Dunsmuir Street near the heart of downtown Vancouver. Like most bus depots it is unattractive and not very comfortable. There is a coffee shop, magazine and gift shops and a left luggage depot or lockers. You can get a taxi right outside the front door or the SkyTrain rapid transit is across the street at the Stadium Station.

(For more about inter-provincial bus travel, see the Getting Around and Things to Do sections.)

TRAVEL ESSENTIALS

BY TRAIN

Transcontinental rail service in Canada was cut several years ago with the two major railways amalgamating their services into VIA Rail Canada Inc. Arrivals and departures are three times a week from the Canadian National Railway station at Main and Station streets in Vancouver. For information about the trains, tel: 1-800 561-8630 (toll-free in Canada). For arrivals and departures, tel: 669-3050.

For information on connection with AMTRAK for rail travel in US, tel: 669-0110. There is a SkyTrain station on Main Street across from the railway station for rapid transit to downtown Vancouver. Taxis are available right outside the door.

(For more information on inter-provincial rail travel see the Getting Around and Things to Do sections.)

BY CAR

Trans-Canada Highway One is the major land route into Vancouver from the east. This highway connects with the Vancouver freeway system, passing through east Vancouver, across the Second Narrows Bridge to the North Shore, and ending at Horseshoe Bay. To get into downtown Vancouver watch for the freeway exit signs and proceed west.

Highway 99 is the main route from the United States border, crossing the south arm of the Fraser River via the George Massey Tunnel. The US border is about an hour's drive from downtown Vancouver. Watch for the signs indicating traffic into the city centre. Just past the George Massey Tunnel the highway branches off into Highway 17 to the Tsawwassen ferry terminal and ferries sailing for Victoria, Nanaimo and the Gulf Islands. Highway 99 then runs north to the ferry terminal at Horseshoe Bay, then on to Squamish and points north. This is the highway you take to get to Whistler ski resort.

Highway 91 is another route from the US border into the eastern municipalities of Greater Vancouver.

There are no toll charges on the highways or bridges entering Vancouver. The highways are well maintained and policed so be aware of the speed limits and traffic indicators posted on the right-hand side of the road.

(For more automobile information see the Getting Around and Things to Do sections.)

VISAS & PASSPORTS

All foreign travellers entering Canada are required to show a valid passport or an alternative legal travel document. Some people may require visas to enter Canada. Before leaving your home country, inquire at the Canadian Embassy. Foreign visitors coming into Canada via the US should check with the US Immigration and Naturalisation Service to make sure they have all the necessary papers to get back into that country.

Citizens or permanent residents of the US do not require passports or visas; however they should carry proof of citizenship such as a birth certificate or driver's licence. Naturalised US citizens need a naturalisation certificate or proof of citizenship. Residents of the US who are not citizens are advised to carry their Alien Registration Receipt Card.

CUSTOMS

Visitors 19 years old and over will be allowed to bring in, duty-free, either 1.1 litres (40 oz) of liquor or wine; or 355 ml (12 oz) cans or bottles of beer, ale or equivalent. Any additional quantities of alcoholic beverages up to a maximum of 9 litres (2 gallons) may be imported on payment of duty and taxes plus provincial fees at the port of entry. If you are over 16 years of age you can bring in 50 cigars, 200 cigarettes and 1 kg (2.2 lbs) of tobacco duty-free. Any additional quantities will be charged duty and tax.

Note: Customs officers are authorised to conduct thorough searches of persons they suspect of carrying contraband materials. Certain food may be brought into Canada for personal use but bulbs, cuttings of plant, seeds, fresh fruit and vegetables are prohibited to prevent plant pests from entering and causing damage to crops and forests. All plant material will be inspected by an Agriculture Canada inspector when you enter the country. Canada has strict gun laws and there are regulations prohibiting the entry of firearms into the country.

For further information on customs procedures, contact the **Canada Customs Office** at 1101 W. Pender Street. Tel: 666-0545.

When you are leaving Canada, keep a list of all purchases you have made, keep sales receipts and invoices and pack your purchases separately for the convenience of customs inspection. If you are re-entering the US you will require proof of the right to re-enter. US residents returning from Canada after more than 48 hours are allowed to take back, duty-free, $400 worth of articles for personal use. Families travelling together may combine their personal exemptions. Included in the duty-free exemption are cigars (up to 100 non-Cuban); one litre of alcoholic beverage and 200 cigarettes (one carton) per person. Gifts may be sent to friends and relatives in the US duty and tax-free if the retail value doesn't exceed $50.

ANIMAL QUARANTINE

If you want to bring your pet into Canada, all dogs and cats must be accompanied by a certificate issued by a licensed veterinarian which clearly identifies the animal and certifies that it has been vaccinated against rabies during the preceding 36-month period. If you are planning to camp in BC notice the regulations regarding animals in campgrounds. Some parks do not permit dogs.

Animals are not permitted on public transport or in most taxis; however, in Vancouver, there is a special service for pet-owners. **BC Pet Taxi**, tel: 732-1013, will carry you and your pet to your destination. Other services for pets including boarding kennels and veterinarians can be found in the *Yellow Pages* telephone directory.

MONEY MATTERS

The Canadian money system is based on dollars and cents. American money is accepted in Canada at the current exchange rate. Currency should be exchanged for Canadian dollars at any bank or exchange booth at the airport or border crossing points. It's a good idea to have some Canadian funds with you before you arrive, in case the exchange booths or banks are closed. Traveller's cheques are the safest way to carry money and are universally accepted by banks and major commercial establishments but proof of identification may be required. Most major credit cards and bank cards are honoured in Vancouver. Banking hours vary but are usually between 9am and 5pm Monday to Friday. Some banks have extended hours Friday night and many are open for limited times on Saturday. There are several currency exchanges in Vancouver. **American Express**, 1040 W. Georgia Street. Tel: 669-2813. Open: Monday–Friday 8.30am–5.30pm, Saturday 10am–4pm. There is also an American Express office on the 4th floor of The Bay department store at Granville and Georgia streets. Hours of operation vary slightly. **Thomas Cook Foreign Exchange**, 617 Granville Street. Tel: 687-6111. Monday–Saturday 9am–5pm. **International Securities Exchange**, 1169 Robson Street. Tel: 683-9666; and 1036 Robson Street. Tel:

683-4686. Summer hours: daily 9am–9pm. Winter hours: Monday–Wednesday and Sunday 9am–6pm, Thursday–Saturday 9am–9pm. **Bank of America**, Vancouver International Airport. Tel: 273-8808. Open: daily 6.15am–8pm.

Most main downtown branches of banks have foreign exchange departments. There are 25 foreign banks in Vancouver. Check the *Yellow Pages* telephone directory.

GOODS & SALES TAX

In most provinces of Canada, a provincial sales tax is added to purchases of retail goods with the exception of groceries, books and magazines. In British Columbia the sales tax is 6 percent. In addition, the Canadian government has added a Goods and Services Tax (GST). This 7 percent tax is applied to almost everything you purchase except groceries. It's an unpopular and confusing tax but if you're a visitor to Canada it is possible to apply for a rebate on the items you have been charged for as long as they are for use outside Canada and are removed from Canada within 60 days of purchase. To claim a rebate you must obtain a form (Tourism Vancouver will have one), fill it out and mail it to Revenue Canada, Customs and Excise, including your receipts. You can also take these completed forms to some Canadian Duty Free shops for a cash rebate. If you have goods shipped out of Canada by the seller, you won't have to pay the GST and won't be eligible for a rebate.

GETTING ACQUAINTED

GEOGRAPHY & POPULATION

Vancouver is located in southwest British Columbia, Canada, 40 km (25 miles) north of the Canadian/United States border. It is only a 2-hour drive from the city of Seattle, in the US state of Washington. Seattle is 20 minutes away from Vancouver by airplane.

The population of metropolitan Vancouver is 1,477,760, making it the largest city in British Columbia and the third largest in Canada. The people who live in the Greater Vancouver area make up about half the entire population of British Columbia.

The city of Vancouver itself is a sparkling core of high-rises and residential areas built over slopes covering 116 sq. km (45 sq. miles) with a population of 455,908. The city is encompassed on three sides by water and cradled by the surrounding mountains. It is a city of parks and gardens where the grass is always green and flowers bloom all year round.

GOVERNMENT

Like most Canadian towns and cities, Vancouver is self-governing. The City Council consists of a mayor and 10 aldermen who are elected by the citizens for terms of two years. The mayor is chairman of the City Council and acts as the city's chief law enforcement officer. The mayor also brings matters of interest and importance concerning the community before the City Council. The City Council is responsible for governing the city and operates under a council-committee system with a series of boards and commissions.

The Greater Vancouver Regional District Board consists of 24 members appointed by the municipalities. The district consists of the City of Vancouver and outlying communities. Most of the city government's revenue comes from property taxes, but the city also depends on funds from the federal and provincial governments.

Vancouver City Hall is located at 453 W. 12th Avenue. It was built in 1936 in a geometric Art-Deco style and is one of the city's landmarks. It is possible to attend some City Council meetings, and there is public access to the building. There are photo displays and other exhibits of interest regarding the city's history. For information, tel: 873-7415.

CLIMATE

There are lots of jokes about the weather. British Columbia has been dubbed "The Wet Coast" and the people who live here have adopted an "I don't believe this weather" attitude. Even if it has been drizzling steadily for several days it doesn't stop Vancouverites from going swimming, hiking, jogging, camping, fishing or picnicking. "You don't tan in Vancouver," they say. "You rust."

The climate is generally moderate. The average temperature in January is a mild 2 C (36 F) and in July an equally mild 17 C (63 F), although by the beaches temperatures can be higher. The wettest season is during the winter, with an average precipitation of 117 cm (47 inches). During the winter there is only a moderate amount of snow. At the first hint of a sunny day Vancouverites head for Stanley Park for a brisk walk around the sea wall. In this climate, a variety of sports can be enjoyed from January to December.

Summer temperatures are pleasant, sometimes even hot enough to risk a sunburn, but always cool and comfortable in the evenings. The mild climate makes Vancouver a popular vacation and retirement centre, attracting people from other parts of Canada. There are some advantages to the rain. It washes away the pollution and keeps the air clear and fresh. The average daily highs in Vancouver are:

Month	°C	°F
January	5	41
February	7	44
March	10	50
April	14	58
May	18	64
June	21	69
July	23	74
August	23	73
September	18	65
October	14	57
November	9	48
December	6	43

WHAT TO WEAR

Come prepared for the rain when you visit Vancouver but don't expect a monsoon. It's more of a Scottish mist. Vancouverites are used to getting around in it, even without an umbrella, but if you come it's advisable to bring an umbrella, as well as a light raincoat or waterproof jacket that you can tuck into your bag when the sun shines.

Vancouver is a cosmopolitan city and any fashion is acceptable. Sports clothing and casual dress are worn most of the time. However, during the evening people dress up and some establishments do have a dress code.

Comfortable walking shoes are a must if you plan to enjoy the many scenic walks around the city. For mountain hiking, proper footwear is advised.

Vancouver is a city of beaches and there are many lakes in the nearby recreational areas, so bring your bathing suit. You'll need a sweater or jacket for the cool evenings from May to September, medium- to heavy-weight apparel for the autumn months.

Although Vancouver doesn't get much snow, during the winter you'll need a warm coat and waterproof boots. If you plan to visit the ski slopes, bring the appropriate clothing. Shops at the ski resorts are usually pricey. If you are unable to bring your own skis and boots, rentals are available. It is also possible to rent hiking equipment.

TIME ZONES

Vancouver is on Pacific Standard Time until the first Sunday in April when clocks are advanced by one hour and Daylight Saving Time comes into effect. Clocks revert back one hour the last Sunday in October. Using Pacific Standard Time, when it is noon in British Columbia, it is: 10am in California; 4pm in New York; 8pm in Britain; 4am the next day in Taiwan, Singapore and Hong Kong; 5am the next day in Japan; 6am the next day in Australia.

WEIGHTS, MEASURES & ELECTRICITY

Canada uses the International System of weights and measures. If you are unfamiliar with this system there are metric conversion charts at the back of the *Yellow Pages* telephone directory. Usually weather reports are given in degrees Celsius, gasoline is sold by the litre, milk and wine by the millilitres and litres. Grocery items are in grams and kilograms, clothing sizes in centimetres or Small, Medium, Large; fabric lengths are sold in metres and road speeds are posted in kilometres per hour.

An example of the metric conversion table is:

Speed:

30 mph	=	50 kph
60 mph	=	100 kph

Length:

1 inch	=	2.54 centimetres (cm)
1 yard (3 ft)	=	0.9 metres or 90 cm
1 mile (1,760 yd)	=	1.6 kilometres (km) or 1,600 metres

Mass:

1 ounce (oz)	=	28 grams (g)
1 pound (16 oz)	=	0.45 kilograms (kg) or 450 grams

Volume:

1 fluid ounce	=	28 millilitres (ml) 3.78 litres (l) or
1 US gallon	=	3780 millilitres

Temperature:

Fahrenheit to Celsius = $5/9 \times {}^{\circ}F$ minus 32
Celsius to Fahrenheit = $9/5 \times {}^{\circ}C$ plus 32

In Canada, standard 120 Voltage **electricity** is used.

CULTURE & CUSTOMS

Canadians are similar to the British in many of their customs of etiquette. It is usual to queue for service in stores, banks and while waiting for public transportation, such as buses and ferries. It is courteous to express your thanks when someone has given you help. To show your gratitude for service at hotels and restaurants it is usual to give a tip. Tips or service charges are not always added to your bills in Canada. In general, a tip of 15 percent of the total amount is given for service in restaurants. This also applies to barbers, hairdressers and taxi drivers. Bellhops, doormen, and porters at hotels, airports and railway stations are usually paid $1 per item of luggage. You do not need to tip in cafeterias or fast-food outlets.

BUSINESS HOURS

Most **offices** in Vancouver conduct business during the hours of 9am–5pm and are usually open Monday–Friday. Government offices, including post offices, usually close by 4.30pm.

Retail stores have an option of staying open seven days a week. There are varying hours on certain days. Some stores open in the evening Thursday to Saturday and close by 6 pm on Sunday. Retail stores in major shopping centres are usually open on holidays but smaller businesses may close.

Post office hours are 8.30am–4.30pm Monday–Friday, closed on weekends but you can buy stamps and mail letters or packages at small outlets in drug stores (pharmacies) on Saturday.

Grocery stores are open daily until midnight. Safeway supermarkets are open 8am–midnight. There are also all-night convenience stores such as 7-11 and Mac's.

Pharmacies (drug stores) usually close by 9pm; however, there are some that offer late-night service. (*See listings under Emergencies and Restaurants for more late-night services*).

PUBLIC HOLIDAYS

Government agencies, banks and businesses close for statutory holidays and schools are dismissed. These are the statutory holidays in British Columbia:

New Year's Day – 1 January
Good Friday and Easter Monday – date varies according to first full moon after Spring equinox. Not all businesses close Easter Monday.
Victoria Day – third Monday in May
Canada Day – 1 July
BC Day – first Monday in August
Labour Day – first Monday in September
Thanksgiving – second Monday in October
Remembrance Day – 11 November
Christmas - 25 December
Boxing Day - 26 December

FESTIVALS & EVENTS

All events in the metropolitan Vancouver area are listed in the newspapers. Phone ahead to confirm dates and locations of listings. Tel: 439-3311 "In Touch" system for updated information daily. See the *Yellow Pages* directory for listings.

VANCOUVER/COUNTRYSIDE

JANUARY

New Year's Day, the annual Polar Bear swim, English Bay.
Robbie Burns Scottish Weekend, Harrison.

FEBRUARY

Mardi Gras, Harrison.
Chinese New Year, celebrated with parades, fireworks, bazaars. Dates are flexible according to the Chinese calendar.

MARCH

Ching Ming Festival, celebrated at a special Chinese shrine in the Fraserview cemetery at 33rd Avenue and Fraser Street.
Carnevale, at the Italian Community Centre.

APRIL

Abbotsford-Matsqui International Band Festival Music Festival, Chilliwack.
Baisahki, a parade focusing on the beautiful draped holy book of the Sikh religion. Colourful processional to the Sikh temple.

MAY

Hyack Festival, New Westminster. May-pole dancing and fireworks.
Lillooet Lake Rodeo, Pemberton.
Annual Seabird Island Indian Festival, Agassiz.
La Fête Colombienne des Enfants, Fort Langley.
Delta Pioneer Days, Ladner.
Dixieland Jazz Festival, Chilliwack.
Chautauqua Arts Festival, Chilliwack.
Power Boat Races, Harrison.
Children's Festival, Vanier Park, Vancouver. International entertainers.

JUNE

Kite Festival, Harrison.
Squaredance Jamboree and **Children's Festival**, Chilliwack.
Children's Art Festival, Whistler.
DuMaurier International Jazz Festival, (June/July).
Golden Spike Days, Port Moody.
Canada Week Festivals, Pemberton and North Vancouver.
Festa de la Repubblica, Italian Cultural Centre.
Veille de Saint-Jean, French Canadian celebration.
Highland Games, Deas Island Regional Park.

JULY

1 July, Canada Day celebrations throughout the province.
Sea Festival
Harrison Festival, local arts festival.
Vancouver Chamber Music Festival, (July/August)
Vancouver Folk Festival, (June/July)
Italian Days, Vancouver Italian Community Centre.
Annual International Pow-wow, Mission.
Country and Blues Festival, Whistler.
Illuminaries, a spectacular lantern festival, Trout Lake.
Dragon Boat Festival, races held from Plaza of Nations, False Creek.
Obon Festival, Japanese. A day for welcoming the spirits of the ancestors.

AUGUST

Powell Street Festival, Oppenheimer Park, Powell Street. A Japanese celebration.
Mid-Autumn Festival, traditional Chinese festival with lion dances, Pender Street.
Vancouver Wooden Boat Festival, Granville Island.
Pacific National Exhibition, the second largest exhibition and fair in Canada.
Molson Indy Vancouver, world-class Indy racing at Pacific Place (August/September).
Hiroshima Day Lantern Ceremony, tel: 430-2330 for information.
Annual Festival of the Written Arts, Sechelt.
Squamish Open Annual Regatta
Classical Music Festival, Whistler.
Chilliwack Fall Fair, Rodeo Days.
Abbotsford International Air Show
Chilliwack Country Music Festival
Tsawwassen Sun Festival
Vancouver International Comedy Festival, Granville Island.
Symphony of Fire, Vancouver. International pyrotechnicians compete in this blazing festival of fireworks. Can be viewed anywhere around English Bay area.
BC Day Celebrations, Burnaby Village Museum (first Monday in August).
Whistler Summer Theatre Festival, Whistler.
International Triathalon, Vancouver.

SEPTEMBER

Bluegrass Music Festival, Chilliwack.
Sand Sculpture Exhibition, Harrison.
Jazz Festival, Whistler.
International Street Performers Festival, Whistler.
Coho Festival, West Van's annual Salmon Barbecue, Ambleside Park.

OCTOBER

Oktoberfest, Chilliwack and Whistler.
Vancouver International Writers Festival, Granville Island and other venues.
Davali, a major fall festival celebrated by Indo-Canadians (October/November).

NOVEMBER

Haney-Harrison Road Relay, Harrison.
Christmas Craft Fairs, throughout the Lower Mainland (November/December).

DECEMBER

Winterfest, a family holiday affair. BC Place Stadium.
Christmas Lights Festival, Harrison.
Carol Ships, in English Bay and Burrard Inlet. (For dates tel: 682-2007.)

Sinter Klaas, arrives by steamboat in New Westminster (tel: 522-6894).

Children's Winterfest, BC Place Stadium.

First Night, outdoors family celebration 31 December, Robson Square.

VICTORIA/VANCOUVER ISLAND

APRIL

TerrifVic, Dixieland Jazz Party.

Antiques and Collectibles, Vancouver Island.

MAY

Swiftsure Yacht Race

Victoria Day Parade

Heritage on the Hoof, various locations throughout Victoria.

Island Tough Guy Contest, Memorial Arena.

Horse Logging Demonstrations, Chemainus.

National Forestry Week, Duncan.

Flatwater Racing Regatta, Long Lake, Nanaimo.

Victoria Music Festival

Tea Cup Races, Inner Harbour.

Queen's Birthday Celebrations, various locations, Sidney.

Decorated Boat Parade, Inner Harbour, Victoria.

Victoria Exhibition, Memorial Arena.

Artists in Action Festival

Annual Gorge Regatta, Gorge Waterway, Inner Harbour.

JUNE

Oak Bay Tea Party

Jazz Fest

International Folkfest

Annual Cowichan Bay Boat Festival

Victoria International Boat Race

Bay Day Children's Festival, Union Bay Hall, South Island Highway.

Sidney Days

JULY

Victoria International Festival, (July/August).

Canada Day Celebrations

Saanich Strawberry Festival

Old Time Fiddle Contest and Jamboree, Coombs Rodeo Grounds.

Pacific Rim Summer Festival, Tofino and Ucluelet.

Sooke Festival, part of History Week.

Annual Moss Street, Paint-In, Victoria, established and emerging artists.

Nanaimo Bathtub Race, Nanaimo to Vancouver.

AUGUST

Annual Symphony Splash, Victoria Inner Harbour, Victoria Symphony.

First People's Festival, Royal BC Museum. Native activities.

International Air Show, Victoria International Airport.

International Festival of Dance

SunFest, a weekend of music and dancing.

Eagle's Annual Fishing Derby, Campbell River.

Classic Boat Festival, Inner Harbour, Victoria. Internationally acclaimed wooden boats, power and sail vessels, schooner race, Sail Past.

SEPTEMBER

Fringe Festival

DECEMBER

First Night, downtown Victoria New Year's Eve festival.

RELIGIOUS SERVICES

There are hundreds of churches of every religious belief and faith in Vancouver. You can find listings in the *Yellow Pages* directory. Some of Vancouver's churches are historic buildings and others are worth going to see for their cultural uniqueness.

St James Anglican, Cordova and Gore streets. This church was built in 1935, inspired by the Gothic Revival. The interior is Byzantine in style.

Vancouver Buddhist Church, 220 Jackson Avenue. Built in 1906 with traditional gable and corner tower.

St Francis Xavier Chinese Catholic, 579 E. Pender Street. This imposing brick-faced church was built in 1910. It was the first Swedish Evangelical Lutheran Church, then St Stephen's Greek Catholic, then St Mary's Ukrainian Greek Catholic; now it has a congregation of Chinese Canadians.

Our Lady of the Holy Rosary Cathedral, Dunsmuir and Richards streets. This impressive, Gothic-styled church was built in 1899–1900 and has served as a cathedral since 1916.

Christ Church Cathedral, Georgia and Burrard streets. This Anglican church, built in 1889–95, is the oldest surviving church in Vancouver and was recently restored. It is located in the heart of downtown Vancouver. Next to the church is a beautiful little park in Cathedral Square.

St Andrew's-Wesley United Church, 1012 Nelson Street. The rich stained-glass window in this church was made by Gabriele Loire of Chartres, France in 1969. The church itself was built 1931–33.

Sikh Temple, 8000 Ross Street, South Vancouver. This is the main temple of Vancouver's large Sikh population, designed in the geometric form of India with religious symbols and designs.

St George's Greek Orthodox Church, Arbutus Street and Valley Drive. The original St George's church is now the Kitsilano Neighbourhood House hall at 7th Avenue and Vine Street. The present church serves most of Vancouver's large community of Greeks who reside in this area.

St Paul's Indian Church, Esplanade, North Vancouver (walking distance from Lonsdale Quay). This is the oldest surviving mission church in the Vancouver area, built in 1884 on the Mission Reserve. Chief Snat, a renowned Squamish leader assisted by the Oblate missionaries, built the first church on this site in 1868. It is a designated historic site of Canada. Extensive restoration was done in 1979–83. Nearby is a monument honouring all native Indian servicemen who fought in World War I, World War II, Cyprus and Vietnam which reads *Kwetsi – Wit Na Nam Xevx* "Those who went to war."

COMMUNICATIONS

TELEGRAMS, TELEX & FAX

To send a **telegram**, go to the CNCP office at 175 W. Cordova, tel: 681-4231. CNCP offers a Telex and Fax service as well. This office is at 200 Granville Square. Tel: 662-1262, Fax: 662-1002, Telex: 04-508834. There is a **fax machine** in the Sinclair Centre lower mall which will fax anywhere and takes credit cards.

TELEPHONES

You can make a phone call within the area of metropolitan Vancouver from any pay phone. To call outside the Greater Vancouver area dial 1 + number. To call outside BC dial 1 + area code + number. If you wish to make a collect call dial "0" for operator assistance. The telephone directory white pages list all charges for long-distance calls but if you're in doubt you can request time and charges from the operator. You can make long distance calls from any public telephone and from hotels.

The *Yellow Pages* directory lists all businesses and public services. Community services are listed in a special section in the front. There you will find city transit maps, a map of Stanley Park; bus, ferry and airport information; a map of the University of BC; weather information and news.

POSTAL SERVICES

The address of the main post office in Vancouver is: Main Post Office, 349 W. Georgia Street, V6B 1Z1. Tel: 662-5725. There are sub-stations throughout the city, and the times they are open may vary. Most post offices are closed weekends unless they are located in drug stores or shopping malls. The main post office is open Monday–Friday from 8am–5.30pm. The Bay and Eaton's downtown stores have postal services. Postage stamps may also be purchased from newsstands and automatic vending machines located in most hotel lobbies, railway stations, airports and bus terminals.

In addition to regular mail, Canada Post offers special services such as Special Letter, Registered Mail, Security Mail and Priority Courier. Visitors may have mail sent to them c/o "General Deliver" which is the same as the international *Poste Restante*. Use the name of the main post office in the location where you will be staying. Mail must be picked up by the addressee in person within 15 days and you must show adequate identification.

RADIO

Vancouver has at least 20 AM and FM radio stations broadcasting in English, French and multilingual. These are usually listed once a week in the newspaper. The **Canadian Broadcasting Corporation** is the national network. The CBC Regional Broadcasting Centre is located at Georgia and Hamilton streets. If you want to tour the building and studios, tel: 665-6665.

Some of the local networks, with cable stations shown in brackets, are:

AM Radio Stations

690 CBU-CBC:	news, talk, classical music, no commercials (93.1)
730 CXLG:	top 40 (94.7)
980 CKNW:	news, talk, MOR music, sports (95.5)
1130 CKWX:	country (97.1)
1410 CFUN:	soft rock (100.1)
1470 CJVB:	multilingual news, talk (103.3)

FM Radio Stations

93.7 CJJR:	country (91.7)
97.7 CBUF-CBC:	French (102.3)
99.3 CFOX:	adult rock (99.7)
103.5 CHQM:	easy listening (106.1)
105.7 CBU-CBC:	classical music, talk, no commercials (107.1)

TELEVISION

There are numerous television channels to choose from in the Greater Vancouver area. These include local, national and US networks in addition to Pay TV. Consult the daily newspaper or television guide for your choice of channels.

In addition to weather and road reports, certain channels broadcast airline departures and arrival information and ferry schedules. Some TV channels on the North Shore are slightly different from those listed for Vancouver.

Over the page is a list of TV channels showing where they appear on the cable dial.

2 **KING**: Seattle NBC (also cable 16)
3 **CBUT**: Vancouver CBC
4 **Community TV**: Vancouver
5 **Knowledge Network**: Vancouver
6 **CHEK**: Victoria CTV
7 **CBUFT**: Vancouver CBC, French network
8 **KIRO**: Seattle CBS (also Cable 15)
9 **KCTS**: Seattle PBS
10 **KOMO**: Seattle ABC
11 **BCTV**: Vancouver CTV
12 **KVOS**: Bellingham
13 **CKVU**: Vancouver
14 **Home Shopping**
17 **KCPQ**: Tacoma FOX
21 **Rogers**: TV Listings Guide
24 **The Sports Network**
25 **YTV**: youth network
26 **CBC**: Newsworld
27 **House of Commons and Broadcast News**
29 **MuchMusic**: rock
30 **WeatherNow**
31 **Transportation/Weather**: including airline departure and arrival information

These are the Pay TV channels:
33 **Superchannel**
34 **Family Programs**
35 **Cathay TV**: Asian languages station
36 **Chinavision**: Chinese programmes
37 **Cable News Network**
38 **Cable News Network Headline News**
39 **Arts and Entertainment**
40 **The Nashville Network**
43 **Financial News**

NEWSPAPERS

Vancouver has two major daily newspapers, *The Vancouver Sun* and *The Province*. *The Sun* publishes every afternoon except Sunday. The Thursday edition contains complete entertainment listings and the Friday edition has the weekly *TV Times*. *The Province* is a tabloid-style newspaper and is published every morning except Saturday. The entertainment and TV listings are published on Friday. Canada's national newspaper *The Globe and Mail*, published in Toronto Ontario, is also available daily from coin boxes and news vendors. The best selection of out-of-town and international newspapers can be found at Mayfair News in the Royal Centre mall at Burrard and Georgia streets. In addition to the daily and weekly papers there are a number of popular publications available free from newsstands.

The Georgia Straight is an entertainment weekly published on Thursday. *Business in Vancouver* is a weekly tabloid published on Friday. *BC Bookworld*, is a literary newspaper which is available at most book stores.

Vancouver also has a number of ethnic newspapers. *The Chinese Times* is the oldest Chinese daily newspaper in North America. There is also a Native Indian publication called *Kahtou*. A list of all the local newspapers, including those published in other languages, is available in the *Yellow Pages*.

EMERGENCIES

HEALTH & MEDICAL SERVICES

British Columbia has one of the world's finest health care systems but you must be a resident of the province to qualify for it. Although medical costs are not as extreme here as in the United States, it can be expensive if you require hospital care. Therefore it is advisable for visitors to Canada to have travel insurance to cover medical expenses and emergency care. Visitors who require prescription medicines should bring a copy of the prescription in case it needs to be renewed by a doctor here.

Most hospitals have staff doctors on duty 24 hours a day. If you need an ambulance phone **Emergency: 911**. All the hospitals are listed in the *Yellow Pages*. The central hospitals that offer 24-hour emergency services are:

Lions Gate Hospital, 231 E. 15th Street, N. Vancouver. Tel: 988-3131.

Royal Columbian Hospital, 330 E. Columbia Street, New Westminster. Tel: 520-4253; Emergency tel: 520-4283.

St Paul's Hospital, 1081 Burrard Street. Tel: 682-2344.

St Vincent's Hospital, 749 W. 33rd Avenue. Tel: 876-7171.

University Hospital, UBC Site: 2211 Westbrook Mall. Tel: 228-7121; Shaughnessy Site: 4500 Oak Street. Tel: 875-2222.

Vancouver General Hospital and BC Health Science Centre, 855 W. 12th Avenue. Admissions: tel: 875-4300; Emergency: tel: 875-4995.

MEDICAL/DENTAL CLINICS

Medicentre, tel: 683-8138.
Dentacentre, tel: 669-6700.
Both are located on the lower level of the Bentall Centre, Dunsmuir and Burrard streets.
Dental: Dentist Referral, College of Dental Surgeons, tel: 736-3621.
Academy of Dentistry Denture Clinic, 750 W. Broadway. Tel: 876-7311.
REACH **Community Health Centre**, 1145 Commercial Drive. Tel: 254-1354; Dental Clinic: tel: 254-1331

Granville Mall Optical, 807 Granville Street. Tel: 683-4716.

Contact Lens Centre, 815 W. Hastings Street. Tel: 681-9488.

DRUGSTORES/PHARMACIES

At some of the large drug stores in Vancouver you can buy everything from prescription drugs to computer software. Non-prescription drugs can be purchased off the shelves but certain drugs can be obtained only with a valid prescription issued by a doctor. These drugs may be obtained from the pharmacy department of drug stores. You can find a complete list of drug stores and pharmacies in the *Yellow Pages* directory, but these are some located near the downtown area:

London Drugs, 1187 Robson Street. General Inquiries: tel: 872-0396; Pharmacy: tel: 669-7474.

People's Drug Mart, 1295 Davie Street. Tel: 684-4322.

Pharmasave, 1625 Robson Street. Tel: 682-1018.

Shoppers Drug Mart, Pacific Centre, 43D-700 W. Georgia Street. Tel: 683-0358. Pharmacy: tel: 683-0359.

Most large supermarket chains have pharmacies. The Canada Safeway Stores in the following locations have pharmacies open 8am–midnight every day. Canada Safeway, 2733 W. Broadway; 4440 E. Hastings; 1780 E. Broadway. Shopper's Drug Mart at Davie and Thurlow is open Monday–Saturday 9am–midnight and Sunday 9am–9pm.

CRISIS INTERVENTION & OTHER EMERGENCY SERVICES

Police, Highway Patrol, Fire, Ambulance: tel: **911**

Alcohol and Drug Services: tel: TRYLINE (toll-free) 1-800 663-1441.

Vancouver Crisis Centre Distress Lines: tel: (24 hours) 733-4111.

Aids Information Line: tel: (24 hours, taped) 660-3550.

Ambulance (non-emergency): tel: 872-5151.

RCMP **Freeway Patrol Emergencies**: tel: 911.

Sexual Assault Centre: for victims of sexual assault: tel: 872-8212.

Sexual Assault Crisis Line: (24 hours) Rape Crisis Centre, tel: 875-6011.

University Hospital: (Shaughnessy Site), tel: 875-2247.

Injury – Criminal: tel: 276-3129.

Victim Assistance: tel: (toll-free) 1-800 842-8467.

VD Clinic: (STD Control, 828 W. 10th Avenue), tel: 660-6161-VD. Information: (taped message) 872-1238.

SECURITY & CRIME

Although Vancouver ranks as one of the safest travel destinations in the world, like all big cities there are problems. Purse snatching, muggings and car break-ins are a common occurrence. Never leave your belongings unattended. It is advisable to carry with you only the cash you need. Traveller's cheques are preferable and use credit cards whenever possible. If you lose your traveller's cheques or credit cards, report the loss immediately to a bank and to the police. At hotels you can usually leave your valuables with hotel security.

It is not wise to walk alone in darkened areas of the city at night. Keep to the well-lit streets where there are other pedestrians. When walking in the parks, women should not venture off the main trails unescorted. Under no circumstances should children be left alone in park or playground areas.

Hitchhiking is illegal on the freeways, and picking up hitchhikers is also illegal. Note to women: hookers in the Greater Vancouver area use hitchhiking as a means of soliciting business. So if you want to avoid the hassles involved in this practice, don't do it.

There are a few other laws which savvy travellers should know about. The wearing of **seat-belts** in cars is compulsory throughout British Columbia. **Jaywalking** (crossing mid-street or not observing pedestrian "stop" signs) is an offence and if caught you can be fined. It is illegal to dispose of trash on the roadsides and streets, and, under the **Litter Act**, offenders will be penalised; in some cases the fines for littering can start at $500. You are not allowed to **drink alcohol** in public places such as beaches and parks.

Lost and Found: If you lose something on the BC Transit, go to the Lost Property Office located at the Stadium SkyTrain station. Open: Monday–Friday 9.30am–5pm. Tel: 682-7887. If you lose something of value, contact the city police Lost Property Room, tel: 665-2232.

Lawyer Referral (Canadian Bar Association): tel: 687-3221.

Legal Aid: Vancouver, tel: 687-1831; Burnaby/New West, tel: 437-4432; Surrey, tel: 584-8535.

GETTING AROUND

Here's a quick guide to geographical Vancouver, written in the local lingo. Vancouver is also known as Van (as in North Van and South Van).

The North Shore: Meaning the north shore of Burrard Inlet, location of the municipalities of North Vancouver and West Vancouver.

Upper levels: Highway One on the north shore between Second Narrows and Horseshoe Bay.

Marine Drive: This is the Lower Level, the road that runs along the shoreline of West Van from the Lions Gate Bridge to Horseshoe Bay. Don't confuse it with South West and North West Marine Drive in the Point Grey university area of Vancouver.

The Bridge: This can refer to any of the ten bridges in metropolitan Vancouver, but it usually means the Lions Gate Bridge.

The Lions: The twin mountain peaks visible beyond North Van were once known as the Two Sisters. They were renamed because of their resemblance to a pair of lions. The Bridge was named after them, as was Vancouver's football team, The BC Lions, usually just referred to as The Lions.

The Ferry: "Taking the ferry" means you're going on one of the BC Ferries from either Horseshoe Bay or Tsawwassen.

The Island: There are hundreds of islands off the coast of BC, the largest being Vancouver Island. Usually if you're heading for Victoria or Nanaimo, you are going to The Island.

The Sunshine Coast: The Sechelt Peninsula, a few kilometres northwest of Vancouver, has more sunshine than the mainland. Hence its name.

The Lower Mainland: The southern and eastern suburbs of metropolitan Vancouver.

Whistler: The world-class ski resort north of Vancouver.

The Valley: The rural areas of the Lower Mainland along the Fraser River.

New West: New Westminster is a city east of Vancouver on the shore of the Fraser River, part of the Greater Vancouver area.

RECOMMENDED MAPS

To help you find your way around the Greater Vancouver area, there are a number of good maps available from the **Vancouver Travel InfoCentre** at 1055 Dunsmuir Street. Shops with an excellent selection of both city and countryside maps are:

World Wide Books and Maps, 736A Granville Street (across from Eaton's), downstairs. Tel: 687-3320; Fax: 687-5925.

Also try the **BCAA**, 999 W. Broadway. Tel: 732-3911; Travel Agency, tel: 732-3977. Maps and books here are priced slightly higher if you are not a member of an Automobile Association.

FROM THE AIRPORT

The taxi ride to Vancouver will cost about $20. It's cheaper to take the **Airport Express bus** (tel: 273-9023). It leaves downtown every 30 minutes from major hotels and from the airport at the second level for trips into town. Public transit buses run from the airport, but if you have large pieces of luggage this may not be a convenient means of travel. Vancouver's taxi fares are among the highest in Canada, so be warned.

If you take the bus from Vancouver to the airport, take the #20 Granville south to 70th Avenue and transfer to the #100 Airport bus. Going from the airport, take the #100 Port Coquitlam/New Westminster Station and transfer at 70th Avenue to the #20 Victoria.

Air Limo has a 24-hour service between the airport and downtown locations. Tel: 273-1331 for bookings. You can rent cars at the airport from concessions on level two. There is a large parking area in front of the airport terminal and a free yellow shuttle bus that transports you from pickup spots in the lot. Valet parking is available on levels two and three. Drop-off rented cars in the main lot are at the end closest to the terminal.

The **Quick Shuttle** (tel: [604] 526-2836) operates between downtown Vancouver (Sandman Inn, 180 W. Georgia) and downtown Seattle in the United States (8th and Blanchard) and Seattle's SeaTac airport every two hours between 6.45am and 8.30pm, a trip taking 3½ hours and costing about $25 each way. Toll-free number is 1-800 665-2122.

CAR RENTALS

Hertz: 1128 Seymour Street. Tel: 688-2411; Airport: tel: 278-4001.

Avis: 757 Hornby Street. Tel: 682-1621; Airport: tel: 273-4577.

Budget: 450 W. Georgia. Tel: 685-0536; Airport: tel: 278-3994.

Dominion U-Drive: 990 Seymour. Tel: 689-0550; Airport: tel: 278-7196.

Thrifty Car Rental: 1400 Robson Street. Tel: 688-2207; Airport: tel: 276-0800.

Tilden: 1140 Alberni Street. Tel: 685-6111; Airport: tel: 273-3121.

BY PUBLIC TRANSIT

The Vancouver Regional Transit System operates a very efficient bus service throughout the Greater Vancouver district. Transit requires that exact coin fares, tickets or passes be used. The fares are the same on bus, SkyTrain or SeaBus; you can transfer to and from all three without extra charge. However, the Vancouver transit system is divided into three zones and during weekday rush hours your fare depends on the number of zones you cross. These extra zone fares are in effect during rush hours Monday–Friday before 9.30am and from 3pm–6.30pm. On weekends and off-peak hours you can travel across any zone boundary without paying extra.

Tickets and passes are sold by retail outlets which display a blue and red "Faredealer" sign. They can also be purchased from vending machines at the SkyTrain or SeaBus depots. A Daypass for a single zone is available; remember, if you are crossing a zone line during rush hour you will have to pay more. Transit operators do not sell tickets so when you board a bus you must have either the correct change or a ticket, pass or valid transfer. Transfers between journeys are good for 90 minutes and can be used in any direction. Your validated ticket can also be used as a transfer.

The **BC Transit system** is very efficient, and service on most downtown routes run frequently until 1am, then a scant service is offered until 3am. During the months of April and through the summer until October there is a special bus service around Stanley Park. Many of the Vancouver bus routes such as this one are scenic and provide a cheap and interesting way to see the city and the outlying areas.

The **SkyTrain** is Vancouver's sleek rapid transit system. It runs every three to five minutes for a distance of 25km (16 miles) from Surrey to Canada Place Pier downtown, at a speed of 80 kph (50 mph). The entire single line trip takes 35 minutes. The trains are run by computers but security and information officers patrol the trains and stations. You can be fined if you are caught riding without a valid ticket or transfer, so make sure you have purchased your fare before boarding. Because most of the SkyTrain route is on an elevated track it is one of the best ways to see the city.

SkyTrain connects with the **SeaBus** at the Waterfront Station. The SeaBus crosses Burrard Inlet every 15 minutes during the day, connecting Vancouver with North Vancouver and thus reducing traffic on the bridges. The 13-minute trip is a great way to see Vancouver's impressive harbour.

Detailed transit schedules and information are available at all public libraries, municipal halls, information and community centres, SeaBus and SkyTrain terminals and ticket outlets. There are also free transit guides called *Discover Vancouver*, describing all transit routes to points of interest around the metropolitan Vancouver area. BC Transit operators are very friendly and helpful, so you shouldn't have any trouble finding your way around the city.

BC Transit Information: tel: 261-5100.
West Vancouver Transit: tel: 985-7777.
HandyDart Custom Transit Service for Disabled Persons: tel: 264-5005.

BY TAXI

You can hail a taxi in downtown Vancouver or you can go to any large hotel to call one. Taxi fares are regulated, with the meter price starting at around $2. The GST tax is now added as well, making taxis a rather expensive means of transportation in a city where the public transport is quite efficient. But if you need to call one, here are some of the companies.
Black Top: tel: 731-1111. If you want to go in style, request a Checker car.
MacLures: tel: 731-9211.
Vancouver Taxi: tel: 255-5111. This cab has space for wheelchairs and oversize items.
Yellow Cab: tel: 681-3311.

Taxis do not carry animals and many of them are non-smoking cars. Ask before you light up.

BY CAR

If you have a valid driver's licence from Canada, the US or an International Driver's Licence you may drive in British Columbia. The speed limit on the highways is 100 or 110 kph (65 and 70 mph). Limits on rural two-lane highways are 80 or 90 kph (50 and 55 mph). On most urban streets the limit is 50 kph (30 mph). All speed limits are posted in kilometres on signs at the right-hand side of the road.

If you are travelling from the US on highway 99, the distance from Seattle to Vancouver is 225 km (140 miles). The distance from the US border to Vancouver is 50 km (30 miles). To drive from Vancouver to Victoria it is 69 km (43 miles), not including the ferry trip from Tsawwassen terminal. If you are in Victoria and wish to drive up the east coast of Vancouver Island to Campbell River, it is approximately 225 km (140 miles).

The major routes into Vancouver are Highway 99, the Trans-Canada Highway 1, and the Lougheed Highway (Highway 7).

One way the city has of combating traffic congestion and pollution from exhaust fumes has been to establish a "Park and Ride" system. These large lots, owned by BC Transit, are located at various areas throughout metropolitan Vancouver near BC Transit bus or SkyTrain stations.

If you belong to an automobile club affiliated with the British Columbia Automobile Association you can get 24-hour emergency road service by calling 293-2222. The BCAA will also help you with any questions and provide road maps. Their office is at 999 W. Broadway. Tel: 732-3911.

Fuels in BC are sold in the litres: 4.5 litres = 1 Canadian gallon; 3.78 litres = 1 American gallon.

WHERE TO STAY

Hotels in the Greater Vancouver and Victoria areas are noted as some of the best in Canada. Throughout BC a blue "Approved Accommodation" sign is awarded to accommodations that have met the Ministry of Tourism's standards. Should you have any complaints about these facilities, first discuss them with the manager of the establishment, then direct your comments and concerns to the Manager of Accommodations Program, Ministry of Tourism, 1117 Wharf Street, Victoria V8W 2Z2.

Most hotels offer Corporate, Family Plan and off-season rates. Reservations are usually made in advance with a deposit of the daily room rate to hold the accommodation. When making a reservation you should ask for the cancellation of deposit and refund policy applicable to the establishment. Most hotels accept all major credit cards and will cash traveller's cheques. The more luxury accommodations have valet service, swimming-pools, fitness rooms and other amenities. Others are simple accommodations, plain clean rooms with basic facilities. **Expensive** hotels range from $130 up for a double room. Hotels that are listed here as **moderate** charge $100 and up for a double. **Reasonably priced** hotels usually start at $50 for double accommodation. An 8 percent provincial hotel and motel room tax and the 7 percent Goods and Services Tax is also added to the price of rooms. In some cases an additional 2 percent tax is levied by local municipal government.

If you want to stay in Vancouver for more than one or two months there are several agencies you can contact who will locate furnished suites, townhouses or family homes. Minimum stay is usually one week. For a long-term stay this may be more economical than paying hotel rates. Book through:

Executive Accommodations, tel: 522-6669.
Room Finders Inc., tel: 736-1733.
WestWay Accommodation Registry, tel: 273-8293.

VANCOUVER

HOTELS

NEAR INTERNATIONAL AIRPORT

Skyline Airport Hotel, No.3 Road at Skyline Airport Hotel Causeway, Richmond V6X 2B6. Tel: 278-5161 (toll-free) 1-800 663-1106. Easy to reach by commercial airline, private plane, car or bus. Five minutes from the airport. Courtesy shuttle service. Fifteen minutes to town. Full service, wheelchair access, pets. Reasonable.

Delta Pacific Resort and Conference Centre, 10251 St Edward Drive, Richmond V6X 2M9. Tel: 278-9611; Fax: 270-2317. Close to the airport and Tsawwassen ferry terminal. Fifteen minutes from town. Specials for children. Air tours, bike rentals, horseback riding, golf. Full service, family plan, wheelchair access, pets. Moderate.

Delta River Inn, 3500 Cessna Drive, Richmond V7B 1C7. Tel: 278-1241 or (toll-free) 1-800 268-1133; Fax: 278-0969. Airport limo service, hotel marina, swimming-pool, family plan, wheelchair access, full service. Moderate.

DOWNTOWN AREA

Le Meridien Vancouver, 845 Burrard Street, Vancouver V6Z 2K6. Tel: 682-5511 or (toll-free) 1-800 223-7385; Fax: 682-5513. Luxury service, fitness centre, limo service, valet parking in an elegant traditionally European style. Rooms for handicapped, wheelchair access. Expensive.

Wedgewood Hotel, 845 Hornby Street, Vancouver V6Z 1V1. Tel: 689-7777 or (toll-free) 1-800 663-0666; Fax: 688-3074. An intimate, small, elegant hotel with an excellent dining-room and popular bar. Located across from Robson Square. Full service, wheelchair access, pets. Expensive.

Barclay Hotel, 1348 Robson Street, Vancouver V6E 1C5. Tel: 688-8850; Fax: 688-2534. A small heritage hotel in the heart of downtown near Stanley Park and English Bay. Parking facilities, restaurant, lounge. European style. Reasonable.

Best Western O'Doul's Hotel, 1300 Robson Street, Vancouver V6E 1C5. Tel: 684-8461 or (toll-free) 1-800 663-5491; Fax: 684-8326. Close to Stanley Park and the downtown shopping area. Small, quiet atmosphere. Indoor pool and exercise room. One of Vancouver's best restaurants. Family plan, full service. Wheelchair access. Expensive.

Hotel Georgia, 801 W. Georgia Street, Vancouver V6C 1P7. Tel: 682-5566 or (toll-free) 1-800 663-1111; Fax: 682-8192. This is one of Vancouver's most charming old hotels built in 1927 and recently renovated. Close to the Vancouver Art Gallery, BC Place Stadium and all the downtown shopping. Excellent restaurant and pub. Covered parking. Full service. No charge for children under 16. Expensive.

Pacific Palisades Hotel, 1277 Robson Street, Vancouver V6E 1C4. Tel: 688-0461 or (toll-free) 1-800 663-1815; Fax: 688-4374. One of the Shangri-La International hotels. Luxury accommodation, indoor pool, exercise room, restaurant and bar. Near Stanley Park and downtown shopping. Full service, kitchens available; wheelchair access. Expensive.

The Westin Bayshore, 1601 West Georgia Street, Vancouver V6G 2V4. Tel: 682-3377 or (toll-free) 1-800 228-3000; Fax: 687-3102. This resort hotel is right in the heart of town and has moorage for private yachts and landing facilities for seaplanes. Indoor and outdoor pools, games area, masseur and bar. Minutes away from Stanley Park and courtesy bus service to shopping uptown. Luxury accommodation with views of the mountains and inner harbour. Full service, wheelchair access. Children under 18 free when occupying same room as parents or guardians. Expensive.

The Holiday Inn, 1110 Howe Street, Vancouver V6Z 1R2. Tel: 684-2151 or (toll-free) 1-800 465-4329; Fax: 684-4736. Comfortable guest rooms and suites for business and vacation travellers. Wheelchair access. Handicapped rooms available. Indoor pool. Pets. Moderate.

Chateau Granville, 1100 Granville Street, Vancouver V6Z ZB6. Tel: 669-7070 or (toll-free) 1-800 663-0575; Fax: 669-4928. A Best Western hotel located in the heart of downtown on the main shopping mall. 20 minutes from airport, five minutes from cruise ship terminal and convenient to public transport. Comfortable rooms with a city view, underground parking. Wheelchair access, pets. Moderate.

Sheraton Inn Plaza 500, 500 West 12th Avenue, Vancouver V5Z 1M2. Tel: 873-1811 or (toll-free) 1-800 325-3535; Fax: 873-5103. Guest rooms with a city view; shops; parking. Near the City Hall. Seven minutes from airport; five minutes from downtown. Wheelchair access, family plan, pets. Moderate.

Ramada Vancouver Centre, 898 W. Broadway, Vancouver V5Z 1J8. Tel: 872-8661; Fax: 872-2270. Situated near Granville Island, BC Place Stadium and five minutes from downtown. Comfortable rooms, guest parking, family-style restaurant. Wheelchair access. Moderate.

Hotel Vancouver, 900 W. Georgia Street, Vancouver V6C 2W6. Tel: 684-3131 or (toll-free) 1-800 268-9411; Fax: 662-1937. Vancouver's grand old Canadian Pacific hotel in the heart of Vancouver. Executive class facilities and meeting rooms. Indoor pool and health club. Full service, family plan, wheelchair access, pets. Expensive.

Hyatt Regency, 655 Burrard Street, Vancouver V6C 2R7. Tel: 687-6543 or (toll-free) 1-800 233-1234; Fax: 689-3707. Comfortable rooms, restaurant facilities, indoor pool, full service, family plan, wheelchair access. Close to shopping areas and English Bay beach. Twenty minutes from airport. Expensive.

The Pan Pacific Hotel, 300-999 Canada Place, Vancouver V6C 3B5. Tel: 662-8111 or (toll-free) 1-800 937-1515; Fax: 685-8690. One of the most beautiful hotels in Vancouver located by the spectacular Canada Place Convention Centre and cruise ship docks. The Five Sails Restaurant is an award-winning seafood restaurant, racquet courts, health club and spa, indoor running track. Outstanding views of the harbour and mountains. Expensive.

The Dominion Hotel, 210 Abbott Street, (Gastown), Vancouver V6B 2K8. Tel: 681-6666. One of Vancouver's oldest historic buildings in the heart of

Gastown. The Lamplighter Pub downstairs was the first establishment in Vancouver to acquire a beer licence in 1925 and the first bar to serve ladies in Vancouver. Comfortable rooms, casual atmosphere, good dining, dancing and entertainment. Ski packages available. Reasonable.

Shato Inn Hotel, at Stanley Park, 1825 Comox Street, Vancouver V6G 1P9. Tel: 681-8920. Sleeping and housekeeping units, free indoor parking, two blocks to beach and Stanley Park. Off-season rates. No pets. Reasonable.

Sylvia Hotel, 1154 Gilford Street, Vancouver V6G 2P6. Tel: 681-9321. A gracious old hotel on English Bay, covered parking, restaurant, lounge, family plan, pets. Kitchens available. Reasonable.

The Buchan Hotel, 1906 Haro Street, Vancouver V6G 1H7. Tel: 685-5354. One of Vancouver's lovely old apartment-hotels located close to Stanley Park in a residential setting. Quiet, comfortable rooms. Reasonable.

Kingston Hotel, 757 Richards Street, Vancouver V6B 3A6. Tel: 684-9024. European-style hotel. Seniors discounts. Close to BC Place Stadium, theatres, restaurants and bus depot. Reasonable.

MOTELS & MOTOR INNS

Most motels and motor inns charge moderate or very reasonable rates and are conveniently located on or near major motorways entering the city or in the suburbs. In Vancouver you will find many motels along Kingsway.

NEAR INTERNATIONAL AIRPORT

The Blue Boy Motor Hotel, 725 Southeast Marine Drive, Vancouver V5X 2T9. Tel: 321-6611. Free shuttle service to airport. Free parking for extended periods. Comfortable air-conditioned rooms. Restaurant, lounge. Full service, family plan, wheelchair access. Reasonable.

Granada Inn, 9020 Bridgeport Road, Richmond V6X 1S1. Tel: 270-6030. Located between Highway 99, Oak Street Bridge and the airport entrance. Thirty minutes from US border; 10 minutes from downtown Vancouver; six minutes from airport. Tasteful rooms, kitchens, restaurant and lounge. Sauna and outdoor jacuzzi. Free airport transportation. Reasonable.

The Abercorn Inn, 9260 Bridgeport Road, Richmond V6X 1S1. Tel: 270-7576 or (toll-free) 1-800 528-1234; Fax: 270-0001. Seven minutes from airport; courtesy shuttle service. Twenty minutes from downtown Vancouver. Just off highway 99 linking to US Interstate 5. Twenty minutes from Victoria ferry. European-style country inn. Spacious rooms with jacuzzis. Dining room and lounge. Wheelchair access. Moderate.

DOWNTOWN AREA

Tropicana Motor Inn, 1361 Robson Street, Vancouver V6E 1C6. Tel: 687-6631; Fax: 687-5724. Situated in downtown Vancouver with easy access to shopping and sightseeing. Suites with kitchenettes, free parking. Indoor pool and sauna. Moderate.

Sandman Inn, 180 W. Georgia Street, Vancouver V6B 4P4. Tel: 736-7254 or (toll-free) 1-800 663-6900; Fax: 681-8009. Located in downtown Vancouver across from the bus depot. Near shopping and easy access to public transit for sightseeing. Buses to connect with Amtrak and Greyhounds from US stop here. Comfortable rooms, swimming-pool, restaurants. Discounts for seniors over 55 years. Moderate.

The Coast Atrium Inn, 2889 E. Hastings Street, Vancouver V5K 2A1. Tel: 254-1000 or (toll-free) 1-800 663-1144; Fax: 253-1234. A pleasant modern hotel with a unique indoor garden. Located near PNE, race track, Pacific Coliseum, shops and public transit. Moderate.

BED & BREAKFAST

Many bed and breakfast inns are located in heritage houses. Most accept children, some are wheelchair accessible and allow pets. Some meals in addition to breakfast may be available. Most take major credit cards and discounts are available for long stays. There are some agencies representing these homes:
Canada West Accommodations, PO Box 86607, North Vancouver BC, V7L 4L2. Tel: 929-1424.
Town & Country Bed and Breakfast, Hotel Accommodation Guide, PO Box 46544 Station G, Vancouver V6R 4G8. Tel: 731-5942.
A Home Away From Home, tel: 873-4888.
Best Canadian Bed and Breakfast, tel: 738-7207.
Old English, tel: 986-5069.
West Way, tel: 273-8293.

West End Guest House, 1362 Haro Street. Tel: 681-2889. Restored Victorian house with period furniture. Small guest rooms. No smoking.
Kenya Court Guest House, 2230 Cornwall Street. Tel: 738-7085. Small apartment building across from Kitsilano Beach. Immaculate 1920s guest house. Complimentary breakfast. No smoking. Multilingual hosts. No credit cards.
Catherine's Bed and Breakfast, in Queen Elizabeth Park, Cambie and 29th Avenue. Tel: 875-0738. Cosy atmosphere, convenient to airport, parks and downtown. Visa accepted. Reasonable rates.
Kitsilano Heritage House, 2455 W. 6th Avenue. Tel: 732-9004. Heritage house close to beaches and shopping areas. Ten minutes from downtown and UBC. Accessible to public transit. Kitchenettes. Family rates or single. No smoking.
Laburnum Cottage, 1388 Terrace Avenue, North Vancouver. Tel: 988-4877. Luxurious rooms and cottages in lovely garden setting. Close to Capilano Suspension Bridge.

Mountain View Guest House, 706 W. 23rd Avenue, Vancouver V5Z 2A8. Tel: 874-6087. A historic stone house with view of city. Quiet neighbourhood. Close to public transit. Families welcome.

The Dogwood House, 1222 W. King Edward Avenue, Vancouver V6H 1Z7. Tel: 733-7098. Immaculate character house in beautiful Shaughnessey area of Vancouver. Quiet luxurious neighbourhood. Swimming-pool. No smoking. Moderate rates.

BUDGET ACCOMMODATION

BC's hostels are members of the International Youth Hostel Federation. Annual membership cards are available from the Canadian Hostelling Association. The cards can be used at any hostel in Canada. Purchase an International Youth Hostel card before you leave home.

The Vancouver Hostel, 1515 Discovery Street (near 4th Avenue). Tel: 224-3208; Fax: 224 4852. This hostel is located right on the beach in Jericho Park, 20 minutes from downtown. There are facilities for individuals, families or groups but no facilities available for children under five or pets. Wheelchair access. Wholesome, cheap food is served or you can cook your own meals. Bring sleeping bags or rent linen. Coin-op laundry and storage facilities. Mountain bike rentals. Reservations and one night's deposit are required from June–September. Mastercard, Visa.

YWCA Hotel Residence, 580 Burrard Street, Vancouver BC, V6C 2K9. Tel: 662-8188 or (toll-free) 1-800 663-1424; Fax: 684-9171. Daily and monthly accommodation for women, couples, families and groups. Located in downtown area near public transit and sightseeing. Pool, fitness area, licensed childcare centre.

Simon Fraser University, Room 212 McTaggart-Cowan Hall, SFU, Burnaby BC, V5A 1S6. Tel: 291-4503. Residences available from May–August. No catering service but meals available from cafeteria on campus. Kitchen facilities, laundry rooms, TV lounge and parking. Wheelchair access. Twenty kilometres (12 miles) east of downtown. Near public transit.

University of BC, Walter Gage Residence, 5961 Student Union Boulevard, Vancouver V6T 2C9. Tel: 228-2963. Located 16km (10 miles) west of downtown on the UBC campus. Free visitor parking, meals available at SUB across the street. Limited rooms in fall and winter for which reservations are necessary.

CAMPING & TRAILER COURTS

About 85 percent of BC is forested with much of the recreation management handled by the Forest Service. There are six national parks and four national historic park sites in BC in addition to more than 300 provincial parks and 16 parks operated by the Greater Vancouver Regional District. There are camp sites in most national and provincial parks, maintained by the forestry or parks services. There is a small fee for staying and in some parks your stay may be limited. There is only one campsite in the GVRD parks and that is at Derby Reach Regional Park in Langley, a 35-minute drive from Vancouver. For information about BC Parks, ask at any TravelInfo Centre or write to: BC Parks, Parliament Buildings, Victoria BC, V8V 1X5.

GREATER VANCOUVER AREA

Capilano RV Park, 295 Tomahawk Avenue, North Vancouver BC, V7P 1C5. Tel: 987-4722. Located under the north end of Lions Gate Bridge close to centre of downtown Vancouver. Fully serviced, swimming-pool, supervised children's play area. Access to Park Royal Shopping Centre and close to parks. Ten minutes to BC ferries at Horseshoe Bay. Pets allowed.

Burnaby Cariboo RV Park, 8765 Cariboo Place, Burnaby BC, V3N 4T2. Tel: 420-1722. Beautiful surroundings near Burnaby Lake Regional Park. Easy freeway access. Close to shopping, public transit and sightseeing. Shuttle bus available. Open: all year round. New, modern, clean. Wheelchair access. Pets allowed.

Richmond Park RV Campground, PO Box 94073, Richmond BC, V6Y 2A2. Tel: 270-7878. Open: 15 April–15 October yearly. Close to ferry, 30 minutes from all sightseeing. Twelve kilometres (8 miles) from downtown Vancouver. Pets welcome. Wheelchair access.

VICTORIA

HOTELS

Dashwood Manor, 1 Cook Street, Victoria V8V 3W6. Tel: 385-5517.
Heritage tudor mansion overlooking harbour and Beacon Hill Park. Suites, fully equipped kitchens, laundry. Moderate.

Queen Victoria Inn, 655 Douglas Street, Victoria V8V 2P9. Tel: 386-1312. Downtown hotel with family suites, kitchens, penthouses with jacuzzis and fireplaces. Full service; free parking. Near Royal BC Museum and Thunderbird Park. Wheelchair access. Pets. Moderate.

James Bay Inn, 270 Government Street, Victoria V8V 2L2. Tel: 384-7151. Historic hotel in oldest residential area of Victoria. European-style guest house. Some shared baths; pub-style lounge; near downtown and Beacon Hill Park. Off-season rates. Reasonable.

Holland House Inn, 595 Michigan Street, Victoria V8V 1S7. Tel: 384-6644. Elegant, individually designed adult-oriented establishment. Full gourmet breakfast. Non-smoking. Near inner harbour, Parliament Buildings, ferries. Moderate.

Captain's Palace, 309 Belleville Street, Victoria V8V 1X2. Tel: 388-9191; Fax: 388-7606. Near US ferries, by Inner Harbour. Unique accommodation in three mansions; Full breakfast and coffee served by pinafored maids. Small pets. Reasonable.

The Empress, 721 Government Street, Victoria V8W 1W5. Tel: 384-8111; Fax: 381-4334. Victoria's grandest old hotel; overlooking Inner Harbour, Parliament Buildings. Across from Royal BC Museum and US Ferries. Family Plan. Wheelchair access. Small pets. Expensive.

Strathcona Hotel, 919 Douglas Street, Victoria V8W 2C2. Tel: 383-7137. Older hotel but recently redecorated. British pub and restaurant; Near tourist attractions. Reasonable.

Swans Hotel, 506 Pandora Avenue, Victoria V8W 1N6. Tel: 361-3310. Located in heritage building on Inner Harbour. Spacious suites; Continental breakfast. Moderate.

Sooke Harbour House, 1528 Whiffen Spit Rd, RR#4, Sooke VOS 1NO. Tel: 642-3421. Well-known hotel outside town with a restaurant worth travelling for. Ocean view units. Antique furnishings. Expensive.

Olde England Inn, 429 Lampson Street, Victoria V9A 5Y9. Tel: 388-4353. A bit of Olde England. Tudor mansion in English Village; Anne Hathaway's Cottage; Shakespeare's birthplace. Units furnished with 17th- and 18th-century antiques. English dining-room. Wheelchair Access. Moderate.

Victoria Airport Travelodge, 2280 Beacon Avenue, Sidney V8L 1X1. Tel: 656-1176. Near airport and ferries. Some king-size units; pool; licensed dining and pub. Wheelchair access. Pets. Reasonable.

MOTELS

Most motels are located on Douglas Street north. For budget-minded travellers, motels are usually reasonably priced and conveniently located. Here are some in the downtown Victoria area and outside the city.

Shamrock Motel, 675 Superior Street, Victoria V8V 1V1. Tel: 385-8768. By Beacon Hill Park; family housekeeping units. Near shopping and sightseeing. Off-season rates; Reasonable.

Surf Motel, 290 Dallas Road, Victoria V8V 1A6. Tel: 386-3305. Open March to November. Oceanfront units. Wheelchair access. Reasonable.

Embassy Motor Inn, 520 Menzies Street, Victoria V8V 2H4. Tel: 382-8161. Quiet location. Sleeping and housekeeping units and suites. Sauna and pool. Close to Inner Harbour, Parliament Buildings and US ferries. Wheelchair access. Reasonable.

Mount Douglas Park Resort, 4550 Cordova Bay Road, Victoria V8X 3V5. Tel: 658-2171. Surrounded by 203 hectares (500 acres) of parkland. European style; kitchenettes, honeymoon suites; Ocean or park views. Jacuzzi, sauna, barbecue, play area. Continental breakfast. Wheelchair access. Reasonable.

BED & BREAKFAST

Ryans Bed and Breakfast, 224 Superior Street, Victoria V8V 1T3. Tel: 389-0012. Heritage home in residential area. Large lounge with piano and harp. Visa, Mastercard.

The Beaconsfield Inn, 998 Humboldt Street, Victoria V8V 2Z8. Tel: 384-4044. Heritage English mansion with elegant rooms. Near Beacon Hill Park and Inner Harbour. **Abigail's Hotel**, 906 McClure Street, Victoria V8V 3E7. Tel: 388-5363. Heritage tudor mansion. Adult oriented. Near Inner Harbour and Beacon Hill Park.

Prior House Bed and Breakfast Inn, 620 St Charles Street, Victoria V8S 3N7. Tel: 924-8847. Elegant English mansion near East Inner Harbour. Full breakfast and afternoon tea. Off-season rates, credit cards.

Joan Brown's Bed & Breakfast Inn, 729 Pemberton Road. Tel: 592-5929. An elegant mansion dating from 1883.

Crow's Nest, 71 Linden Avenue. Tel: 383-4492. Close to seafront. French spoken.

All Seasons Bed & Breakfast Agency, Box 5511, Station B, Victoria BC V8R 6S4. Tel: 595-BEDS. Recommendations for the region.

BUDGET ACCOMMODATION

Victoria Hostel, 516 Yates Street, Victoria V8W 1K8. Tel: 385-4511. The Victoria International Hostel was recently renovated and reopened. It is situated in a turn-of-the-century building accommodating up to 104 persons. Kitchen and laundry facilities, games room, TV room and family rooms. Open: daily 7.30am–midnight.

Selkirk Guest House, 934 Selkirk Avenue, Victoria BC, V9A 2V1. Tel: 389-1213; Fax: 389-1313. Beautiful historic home on Gorge Waterway. Fifteen minutes by bus to downtown Victoria. Non-smoking. Couples and families welcome.

University of Victoria, Housing and Conference Services, Sinclair at Finnerty Road, Box 1700, Victoria V8W 2Y2. Tel: 721-8396. Furnished single and twin rooms with shared baths available May–August. Breakfast included. Wheelchair access.

Victoria YM-YWCA Women's Residence, 880 Courtney Street, Victoria V8W 1C4. Tel: 386-7511. Sleeping units; shared bath. Women only. Near tourist attractions. Reasonable.

COUNTRYSIDE

ACCOMMODATION

VANCOUVER ISLAND

Chemainus: Laughing Gull Guest House, Willow Street, tel: 246-4068; Horseshoe Bay Inn, Chemainus Road, tel: 246-4525; Fuller Lake Motel, 9300 Island Highway, tel: 246-3282. *Budget lodgings:* Robert and Vi Matula, 3040 Henry Road, RR1 Chemainus BC, V0R 1K0. Tel: 246-4407. On Island Highway to Henry Road. Near village, railway and bus station. Phone for pick-up. Includes breakfast, kitchen, showers. Open: year round. No sleeping bags. Females only between 12 June and 4 July. Phone for advance bookings.

Nanaimo: Dorchester Hotel, 70 Church Street, tel: 754-6835; Westward Ho Motel, 250 Terminal Avenue, tel: 754-4202. *Budget lodgings:* Moni Murray, 65 Nicol Street, Nanaimo BC, V9R 4S7. Tel: 753-1188. Located in downtown Nanaimo on Trans-Canada Highway. Open: May–September. Ten beds available. Kitchen and laundry facilities. Bicycles for rent.

Qualicum Beach: The San Pebbles Inn, West Island Highway, tel: 752-6974; Qualicum College Inn, College Road, tel: 752-9262; Ben Bow Inn, tel: 1-800-663-7301.

Courtenay: Arbutus Hotel, 275 Eighth Street, tel: 1-800-663-2146; Westerly Hotel, 1590 Cliffe Avenue, tel: 1-800-232-7547; Washington Inn, 1001 Ryan Rd, tel: 1-800-663-0191; Sleepy Hollow Inn, 1190 Cliffe Avenue, tel: 334-4476.

Campbell River: Anchor Inn, 261 Island Highway, tel: 1-800-663-7227; The Austrian Chalet, 462 South Island Highway, tel: 1-800-232-7207; Thunderbird RV Park, Spit Road, tel: 286-6949.

Port Hardy: North Shore Inn, 7370 Market Street, tel: 949-8500; Thunderbird Inn, tel: 949-7767; Port Hardy Inn, 9040 Granville St., tel: 1-800-663-1021.

WHISTLER MOUNTAIN & THE GULF ISLANDS

The resort town of Whistler has over 60 hotels, lodges, b&bs or condominiums which guests can use. The most lavish is the beautiful **Chateau Whistler Resort**, which attracts skiiers and landscape-lovers from all over the world, at all times of the year, to its elegant surroundings. Tel: 938 8000. Bookings can be made for the Chateau Whistler and other properties around the five lakes and two ski areas by contacting the **Whistler Resort Association**, tel: 685 3650, or 1-932-4222. Alternatively, try the **Whistler Hostel**, PO Box 128, Whistler, BC, V0N 1B0. Tel: 932-5492. Reservations recommended; advance deposit required.

For accommodation on the Gulf Islands, phone the **Gulf Island Bed and Breakfast Registry**, tel: 539-5390. Accommodation on most islands is limited and reservations are needed.

CAMPING & TRAILER COURTS

SUNSHINE COAST & GREATER VICTORIA AREA

Klahanie Campground & RV Park, Box 890, Squamish V0N 3G0. Tel: 892-3435. On Highway 99. Scenic treed sites near Murrin Lake, opposite

Shannon Falls Provincial Park. Pets. Reservations accepted.

Uptown Motel & RV Park, 710 North Road, Box 425, Gibsons V0N 1V0. Tel: 886-2957. Five km (3 miles) north of Langdale ferry terminal on Highway 101. Wheelchair access. Pets on approval.

Wilson Creek Campground, 4314 Highway 101, Box 1653, Sechelt VON 3AO. Tel: 885-5937. On Highway 101, south of Sechelt on Wilson Creek. Near beach. Swimming, fishing, golf, horseback riding.

KOA Victoria East, 3000 KOA Road, Box 129, Saanichton V0S 1M0. Tel: 652-3232. Eighteen km (11 miles) north of Victoria. Ocean view, secluded. 176 sites. Water included. Pets. Visa accepted.

FOOD DIGEST

You can sample food from almost every country in Vancouver, and many of the chefs are internationally experienced. Here are a few restaurants, chosen for their popularity, reputation or interesting fare. Restaurants are rated **Expensive** (over $30); **Moderate** ($15–$30) and **Inexpensive** ($15 or less), excluding alcohol and tips. The standard tip is 10 to 15 percent. A 10 percent sales tax is added to alcohol and the GST of 7 percent is applied to the cost of meals. Most restaurants recommend reservations. As a courtesy, if you are unable to keep the reservation or will arrive late, please phone the restaurant so your table can be given to other diners. *Bon appétit.*

VANCOUVER AREA

REVOLVING RESTAURANTS OR THOSE WITH A VIEW

Cloud 9, 1400 Robson Street (42nd floor of the Sheraton Landmark Hotel). Tel: 687 0511. Moderate. All credit cards.

Top of Vancouver, 555 West Hastings Street. Tel: 669-2220. Dining atop the Harbour Centre. Seafood and Sunday buffet. All credit cards. Expensive.

Grouse Nest Dining, 6400 Nancy Greene Way, North Vancouver. Tel: 986-6378. Elegant dining atop Grouse Mountain. All credit cards. Moderate.

Horizons on Burnaby Mountain, 100 Centennial Way, Burnaby. Tel: 299-1155. Excellent seafood. Mastercard, Visa, Amex, JCB. Moderate.

The Roof Restaurant and Lounge, 900 W. Georgia Street. Tel: 684-3131. In the Hotel Vancouver. Formal dining. Ballroom dancing. All credit cards. Expensive.

OUTDOOR DINING

Aca Joe's Grill, 398 Kingsway. Tel: 876-8822 A California-style party restaurant. Informal and inexpensive. Mastercard, Visa, American Express.

Park Royal Hotel, Tudor Room, 540 Clyde Avenue, West Vancouver. Tel: 926-5511. Luxury inn. All credit cards. Expensive.

Fiesta Mexicana Restaurant, 1200 Lonsdale Avenue, North Vancouver. Tel: 985-8226. Moderate. Mastercard, Visa, Amex, Diners Club.

Athene's, 3618 W. Broadway. Tel: 731-4135. Inexpensive. Mastercard, Visa, Amex.

SEAFOOD RESTAURANTS

The Boathouse, 566 Cardero Street. Tel: 669-8851. Coal Harbour next to the Bayshore. Moderate. All credit cards.

The Cannery, 2205 Commissioner Street. Tel: 254-9606. Cosy, with a harbour view. Moderate. All credit cards.

Joe Fortes Seafood House, 777 Thurlow Street. Tel: 669-1940. San Francisco-style seafood grill. All credit cards. Moderate.

Jonathon's Seafood House, 1333 Johnston Street, Granville Island. Tel: 688-8081. Dine at the harbour and go for an after-dinner cruise. All credit cards. Moderate.

Salmon House on the Hill, 2229 Folkestone Way, West Vancouver. Tel: 926-3212. Excellent seafood; panoramic view of city. Mastercard, Visa, Amex. Moderate.

DINING IN THE PARK

The Beach House, Stanley Park (foot of Beach Avenue). Tel: 681-7275. Elegant dining in an old beach house. Moderate. Mastercard, Visa, Amex, Diners.

The Prospect Point Café, Prospect Point, Stanley Park. Tel: 669 2737. Romantic harbour view. Dine on the deck in nice weather. Moderate. Mastercard, Visa , Amex.

The Teahouse Restaurant, Ferguson Point, Stanley Park. Tel: 669-3281. Quiet dining in the park. Moderate. Mastercard, Visa, Amex.

Season's in the Park, Cambie Street at 33rd Avenue. Tel: 874-8008. Fine dining in Queen Elizabeth Park. City view. Moderate. Credit cards.

LATE NIGHT DINING

Fresgo Inn, 1138 Davie Street. Tel: 689-1332. Large servings at reasonable prices. Open: Monday–Saturday 8am–3am, Sundays and holidays 9am–midnight.

The Bread Garden, 1880 W. 1st Avenue, tel: 738-6684; 812 Bute Street, tel: 688-3213. Deli food; good breakfasts; muffins and cakes. Open: 24 hours. Inexpensive.

GASTOWN

The Landing Restaurant, 375 Water Street. Tel: 688-4800. Harbour view. European cuisine. Moderate. Mastercard, Visa, Amex, Diners.

The Old Spaghetti Factory, 53 Water Street. Tel: 684-1288. Informal, turn-of-the-century atmosphere. Family oriented. Reserve for parties over six. Inexpensive. Mastercard, Visa, Amex.

(see also listings under Asian Restaurants)

WEST END

English Bay Café, 1795 Beach Avenue. Tel: 669-2225. Dine on the Bay. Excellent food, good reputation. Moderate. All credit cards.

Hy's Mansion, 1523 Davie Street. Tel: 689-1111. Dine in an elegant old West End mansion. Expensive. All credit cards.

Fogg 'n Suds, 1215 Bidwell Street, English Bay. Tel: 683 2337. Informal pub fare. No reservations necessary. Mastercard, Visa. Inexpensive.

The Raintree, 1630 Alberni Street. Tel: 688-5570. Northwest Coast regional food. Moderate. Mastercard, Visa, Amex, Diners.

GRANVILLE ISLAND/FALSE CREEK

Mulvaney's, 9 Creek House, Johnston Street, Granville Island. Tel: 685-6571. Cajun-style food. Inexpensive. All credit cards.

Anderson's Dining on the Creek, Granville Seawalk North (under the Granville Street, Bridge). Tel: 684-8080. Waterfront view. Moderate. Mastercard, Visa, Amex, Diners.

Pelican Bay, 1253 Johnston Street, Granville Island. Tel: 683-7373. Outdoor patio. Moderate. All credit cards.

Café Splash, 1600 Howe Street (North Shore of False Creek). Tel: 682-5600. Waterfront dining. Moderate. Mastercard, Visa, Amex.

KITSILANO/FOURTH AVENUE

Angelica the Restaurant, 2611 W. 4th Avenue. Tel: 737 2611. West coast cooking. Moderate. Mastercard, Visa, Amex.

The Alma Street Café, 2505 Alma Street. Tel: 222-2244. Informal; live jazz Wednesday–Saturday evenings. Inexpensive. Mastercard, Visa, Amex.

Soft Rock Café, 1925 W. 4th Avenue. Tel: 736-8480. Dinner theatre; live jazz Sunday. Inexpensive. Mastercard, Visa, Amex.

The Rattle Snake Grill, 2340 W. 4th Avenue. Tel: 733-2911. Jazz and blues nightly. Rattlesnake actually served here. Inexpensive. All credit cards.

ASIAN RESTAURANTS

CHINESE

Pink Pearl Chinese Seafood, 1132 E. Hastings Street. Tel: 253-4316. *Dim sum*; Cantonese and Szechuan cuisine. Moderate. Mastercard, Visa, Amex, Diners.

Ming's Restaurant, 147 E. Pender Street. Tel: 683-4722. Excellent *dim sum* served 10am–2pm. Inexpensive. Credit cards.

Szechuan Chongging, 2495 Victoria Drive. Tel: 254-7434. Inexpensive Szechuan-style food.

Dynasty, 1133 W. Hastings Street (at New World Harbourside). Tel: 689-9211, ext: 288. Fine dining. Expensive. All credit cards.

JAPANESE

Kobe Japanese Steak House, 1042 Alberni Street. Tel: 684-2451. Hibachi-style cooking. Expensive. All credit cards.

Tsunami Sushi, 238-1025 Robson Street. Tel: 687-8744. Vancouver's largest sushi bar. Informal. Inexpensive. Mastercard, Visa, Amex.

Japanese Deli House, 381 Powell Street. Tel: 681-6484. Inexpensive sushi in old Japantown. No credit cards. Closed: Mondays.

THAI, VIETNAMESE, CAMBODIAN

Thai House Restaurant, 1119 Robson Street, tel: 683-3383; 1766 W. 4th Avenue, tel: 737-0088; 129-4940 No. 3 Road, Richmond, tel: 278-7373. Bangkok trained chefs. Inexpensive. Mastercard, Visa, Amex.

Phnom Penh Restaurant, 244 E. Georgia Street. Tel: 682-1090. Real Vietnamese atmosphere. Inexpensive. Closed: Tuesdays.

Malinee's Thai Food, 2153 W. 4th Avenue. Tel: 737-0097. Excellent, authentic Thai food. Moderate. Credit cards.

Seoul House, 36 E. Broadway. Tel: 874-4131. Japanese and Korean food; tatami rooms. Reserve for parties over six. Inexpensive.

Pho Hoang, 3610 Main Street. Tel: 874-0810. Authentic Cambodian food. Inexpensive. No alcohol; no credit cards. Closed: Wednesdays.

The Mongolie Grill, 467 W. Broadway. Tel: 874-6121. Mongolian barbecue; food priced by weight. Inexpensive. April–September closed for lunch.

Tea and Silk, 455 W. Broadway. Tel: 872-8866. A fusion of East/West with traditional food from Asian countries. Wheelchair access. Inexpensive. Visa. Closed: Sunday.

FRENCH

Chez Denis, 217 Carrall Street, Gastown. Tel: 685-6252. Superb cuisine and live jazz/blues. Expensive. Mastercard, Visa, Amex.

The Hermitage Restaurant, 1025 Robson Street. Tel: 689-3237. Lovely outdoor patio. Moderate. All credit cards.

The Railcar Restaurant, 106 Carrall Street, Gastown. Tel: 669-5422. Dine in an antique railcar. Moderate. Mastercard, Visa, Amex.

GREEK

Romio's Greek Taverna, 2272 West 4th Avenue. Tel: 736-2118. Excellent feta cheese omelettes. A good place to have lunch. Inexpensive. Mastercard, Visa, Amex.

Acropol, 2946 W. Broadway. Tel: 733-2412. Authentic Greek food. Full meals or appetizers. Live bouzouki music, singers and lots of dancing on the weekends. Moderate. Credit cards.

Vassilis Souvlaki Greek Taverna, 6558 Kingsway, Burnaby. Tel: 434-0626. For atmosphere this has to be one of the best Greek tavernas in town. It has an excellent selection of well prepared food. Inexpensive. Credit cards.

NATIVE INDIAN

Quilicum Westcoast Indian Restaurant, 1724 Davie Street. Tel: 681-7044. Experience a native west coast potlatch feast. Moderate. Mastercard, Visa, Amex.

The Tomahawk Barbecue, 1550 Philip Avenue, North Vancouver. Tel: 988-2612. Family restaurant. Crowded for weekend brunch. Yukon-style breakfasts in a unique native Indian setting. Inexpensive. Credit cards. No reservations.

ITALIAN

Arriva Ristorante Italiano, 1537 Commercial Drive. Tel: 251-1177. Authentic Italian food. Moderate. Mastercard, Visa, Amex.

Bacchus Bar and Ristorante, 845 Hornby Street (Wedgewood Hotel). Tel: 687-7777. Romantic European setting. Moderate. All credit cards.

Settebello Ristorante, 1131 Robson Street. Tel: 681-7377. Outdoor patio. Inexpensive. All credit cards.

La Piazza Ristorante, 3075 Slocan Street (at the Italian Cultural Centre). Tel: 430-2195. Authentic Italian cuisine. Moderate. All credit cards.

VEGETARIAN RESTAURANTS

Bodhi Vegetarian Restaurant, 337 E. Hastings. Tel: 682-2666. Casual. Buddhist vegetarian food. Inexpensive.

The Naam Restaurant, 2724 W. Fourth Avenue. Tel: 738-7151. Established popular vegetarian restaurant with a varied, inexpensive menu. Live music at lunch and dinner. Licensed. Open: 24 hours.

Greens & Gourmet, 2681 W. Broadway. Tel: 737-7373. Salad bar and hot buffet. Delicious breakfasts. International menu. Open: Monday–Friday 9am–10pm, Saturday–Sunday 8am–10pm. Live entertainment Thursday–Sunday. Inexpensive.

Woodlands & Atrium, 2582 W. Broadway (upstairs). Tel: 733-5411. Breakfast; vegetarian buffet; international cuisine. Open: daily 7am–10pm, Saturday–Sunday 8am–10pm. Inexpensive.

Capers, 2496 Marine Drive, West Vancouver. A natural food store/restaurant with organic produce and baked goods. Open: Monday–Friday 7am–7pm, Saturday–Sunday 7am–6pm.

VICTORIA

Deep Cove Chalet, 11190 Chalet, Sidney. Tel: 656-3541. Elegant country atmosphere. All credit cards. Expensive.

Barkley's Grill Room and Polo Lounge, 777 Douglas Street. Tel: 382-7111. Steak, seafood and special pastas. All credit cards. Expensive.

Chez Daniel, 2524 Estevan. Tel: 592-7424. Fine French cuisine. All credit cards. Expensive.

La Petite Colombe, 604 Broughton. Tel: 383-3234. Excellent French dining, located downtown. All credit cards. Expensive.

Parrot House, 740 Burdett. Tel: 382-9258. Panorama view from the top floor of Chateau Victoria. All credit cards. Moderate.

Japanese Village, 734 Broughton. Tel: 382-5165. Master chef prepares food at your table. Sushi bar. Credit cards. Moderate.

Metropolitan Diner, 1715 Government. Tel: 381-1512. Creative, unusual and featured on Graham Kerr's cooking show. Moderate.

Rebecca's, 1127 Wharf. Tel: 380-6999. Waterfront location. Outstanding use of herbs and excellent presentation. Moderate.

Siam, 1314 Government. Tel: 383-9911. Authentic Thai cuisine with attentive service. Credit cards. Inexpensive.

Sooke Harbour, 1528 Whiffen Spit Rd, RR#4 Sooke, VOS 1N0. Tel: 642-3421. Worth making a trip out of town for the Sooke Harbour, known for its country-fresh ingredients and innovative recipes. Expensive.

HOT, 608 Yates. Tel: 382-6468. Simply HOT! Credit cards. Inexpensive.

Great Wall, 809 Craigflower. Tel: 383-7822. Full range of Chinese cuisine. Credit cards. Inexpensive.

Pagliacci's, 1011 Broad Street. Tel: 386-1662. Great pasta and cheese cake. Trendy, youthful ambience. Live music. Inexpensive.

John's Place, 723 Pandora. Tel: 389-0711. Large servings of good food in a relaxed atmosphere. Inexpensive.

THINGS TO DO

ACTIVITIES FOR KIDS

For family fun, take the children to **Playland Family Fun Park**, located on Hastings Street between Renfrew and Casiar. Lots of rides, concessions and games. Open: 24 June–15 August, Friday and Saturday 11am–11pm; Sunday–Thursday 11am–11pm. During the Pacific National Exhibition in August, it opens daily at 10am.

Wonderland Amusement Park, Highway #1 Exit 95, Abbotsford. Tel: 850-0411. Miniature golf, indoor jungle golf, batting range, video games. Restaurant and theatre entertainment. Picnic area. Open: daily.

Maplewood Farm, 405 Seymour River Place, North Vancouver. Tel: 929-5610 for admissions and information. This is a real farm scaled down for children. Lots of baby animals in the springtime. Picnic area. Open: Tuesday–Sunday 10am–4pm. Closed: Monday except on holidays.

Vancouver Game Farm, 5048 265th Street, Aldergrove. Tel: 856-6825. Safari park and game preserve. More than 60 exotic species. Open: daily 8am–dusk. Picnic area, gift shop, concession.

Colbrook Trout Farm, 13067 Colbrook Road, Surrey. Tel: 594-1865. Small admission per family pays for bail and rods. You pay for fish according to size. Six fishing ponds for children. Open: year round on Sunday only 10am–6pm.

Richmond Go-Kart Track, 6631 Sidaway, Richmond. Tel: 278-6184. There's no minimum age to operate the go-karts but a minimum height. Open: daily noon–dusk.

Imagination Market, 528 Powell Street. Tel: 253-1033. Recycled materials for making creative art projects. Free drop-in classes on Saturday and Sunday afternoon but drop in any time for lots of fun. Open: Thursday–Sunday only.

The **Kids Only Market** on Granville Island is a two-storey building of shops and lunch spots designed for children under 14. Very busy on weekends. Open: daily in summer, Tuesday–Sunday in winter. There's also a children's **Water Park** and **Adventure Playground** near the False Creek Community Centre on Granville Island. Supervised daily from 10am–6pm.

Stanley Park Zoo. Children's petting zoo and pony rides. Miniature Railway near the petting zoo.

Chuck E. Cheese's, 9898 Government Place, Burnaby. Tel: 421-8408. A pizza/hot dog restaurant just for kids with rides, video games, clowns. Birthday parties are a speciality.

Vancouver Kidsbooks, 3083 W. Broadway. Tel: 738-5335. This is a specialty bookstore just for children.

VANCOUVER
ATTRACTIONS

For information on current events, where to go and what to see in Vancouver, tel: 439-3311. **"In Touch"** is a "press or speak" system. Simply dial the number; when instructed, enter the code 3200 or, if you are phoning from a dial phone, wait for the instructions then say the code number.

Canada Place, located at the foot of Burrard Street. Tel: 688-TOUR. This impressive complex resembling an enormous ship with billowing sails, houses the Vancouver Trade and Convention Centre, cruise ship docking, Vancouver Board of trade, World Trade Centre, restaurants, a hotel and IMAX theatre. Free tours year round pre-booked.

BC Place Stadium, on Beatty Street at the foot of Robson. Tel: 669-2300. This is the world's largest air-supported domed stadium. It hosts major sporting events, consumer shows and concerts. The new BC Sports Hall of Fame and Museum is here.

Capilano Salmon Hatchery, North Vancouver. Tel: 987-1411. Discover the marvels of the salmon's life at this hatchery, open year round.

Cleveland Dam, North Vancouver. Tel: 987-1411. Views of Capilano Canyon from the dam water-shed area.

H. R. MacMillan Planetarium, tel: 736-3656. Programs on astronomy and space science. Special children's presentations. Wheelchair access.

The Lookout at Harbour Centre, tel: 689-0421. Ride the glass elevator up for a view of the harbour. Open: daily.

Science World, tel: 681-7832. Discover the wonders of the world in this unforgettable family adventure. See the OMNIMAX film on the world's largest dome screen. Open: daily except Christmas.

Stanley Park Zoo, located in Stanley Park in a forest setting. Tel: 681-1141. Children will enjoy the petting zoo and a ride on the miniature railway.

Vancouver Aquarium, located in Stanley Park. Tel: 682-1118. In addition to an exhibit of aquatic wildlife this aquarium includes an Arctic Canada exhibit featuring Beluga whales and an Amazon jungle gallery with rare plants, birds and monkeys. Open: year round. Phone for hours and admissions.

Simon Fraser University, located on Burnaby Mountain. Tel: 291-4323. Campus tours July and August.

University of British Columbia, tel: 222-1047. Canada's third largest university, located in scenic Point Grey. There are many attractions including the Botanical and Japanese gardens, museums, theatres, galleries and aquatic centre. See the world's largest cyclotron TRIUMF. Free 90-minute tours twice daily in summer, twice weekly in winter, from Wesbrook Mall.

TOUR PACKAGES

Priority Plus Tours: (to Victoria) tel: 876-6559.
The Vancouver Trolley Company: tel: 255-2444, fax: 251-5923. Tour around Vancouver on a classic turn-of-the-century trolley.
Town Tours: tel: 733-4711 (24 hours). Victoria and Vancouver.
Vance Tours: tel: 222-1966. Three daily city tours of Vancouver.
Paddlewheel Harbour Tour: tel: 688-7246. Inner Harbour tours on a turn-of-the-century paddlewheeler.
Fridge's Early Motion Tours Ltd: tel: 687-5088. Provide a tour in a restored Ford Model A Phaeton touring car.
Black Top Cabs Ltd: tel: 731-1111 or 681-2181. Checker Cabs Limo Service.
Star Limousine: tel: 983-5577. Night club tours by Rolls Royce, Lincoln or Cadillac.

WALKS

The best way to see Vancouver is on foot. Get yourself a street map, some comfortable shoes, and start walking.

Almost any area of town is safe and enjoyable. There are few places where you cannot view the mountains or the sea, and there are a number of pleasant walks where you can do some sightseeing while you're enjoying the exercise.

Walk along **False Creek** pedestrian route to avoid the downtown traffic. It's a tranquil stroll from the **Aquatic Centre** at Burrard Street bridge to the Plaza of Nations at **BC Place** where you can stop at the Unicorn Pub for a pint and a snack.

Go along Commissioner Avenue by the waterfront on a Sunday afternoon when there is no commercial traffic. You will see the harbour close-up, cruise ships and merchant vessels and boats cruising Burrard Inlet. Walk along the sea wall from Sunset Beach to Stanley Park. This is especially rewarding just before sunset, but if you go during the day the wall goes all around the park. Another sea-wall walk is on the North Shore at Ambleside in West Vancouver.

If you prefer more organised walks, **P. J. Tours** operates historical walking tours, rain or shine, leaving from designated areas. The Downtown Tour meets at Centennial Fountain, Georgia and Hornby streets on Saturday, Sunday and holiday Mondays at 10am. The Gastown/Victory Square Tour meets at the corner of Water Street and Cordova on Saturday, Sunday and holiday Mondays at 1pm. Chinatown Tours meet at Pender and Carrall S.E. corner on Saturday, Sunday and holiday Mondays at 3pm, tel: 264-1955 for more information.

For an ingenious walking adventure, **Gumshoe** offers a cassette guided walkabout that lets you participate in a 1940s-style detective novel while you explore downtown Vancouver. Their schedule is flexible. Book anytime Monday–Friday 11am–7pm, Saturday till 6pm and Sunday till 5pm, tel: 687-3311 for information and reservations.

Free **historic tours** of Gastown are available Wednesday–Sunday from 375 Water Street at 10am–2pm and noon–4pm from the Gassy Jack statue. For information, tel: 683-5650.

Vancouver is a city of parks – there are 147 in all, ranging in size from the immense parkland of **Stanley Park** to the small oasis in **Cathedral Square** on Burrard Street. There is no better place to walk than in the parks and really to experience the West Coast you must walk in the forest. Just minutes away from the bustle of downtown Vancouver are dozens of recreational areas with quiet trails for hiking and exploring the natural beauty of British Columbia. There are remnants of the original forest in the form of old stumps and sometimes a solitary tall tree towering alone because it was not logged. Some of these trees are well over 100 years old. The parks are a haven for nature-lovers, birdwatchers and recreational hikers or families out for an afternoon picnic.

BEACHES & LAKES

Vancouver has 14km (9 miles) of beaches and most of them have picnic facilities. All are life-guard patrolled and safe for swimming. The beach temperature in Vancouver averages at 21°C (70°F) in summer. Dogs, alcohol and nudity are not allowed on the city beaches. There is only one nude-bathing beach in Vancouver, **Wreck Beach**, located in an out-of-the-way area below the cliffs of Point Grey on the western tip of the University grounds.

The other city beaches are easily accessible by car or public transit.
Second Beach, Stanley Park: A popular family beach with a large salt-water pool.
Third Beach, Stanley Park: A large stretch of sand with an ocean view.
English Bay, West End: One of the oldest and most popular West End beaches and site of the well-known New Year's Day Polar Bear Swim, and the July Sea Festival and annual fireworks displays.
Sunset Beach: in the West End close to False Creek and the Aquatic Centre. This isn't a suitable beach for swimming but it's popular for viewing the sunsets or watching the boats sail by.
Kitsilano Beach, Kitsilano: A mecca for hedonist sun-worshippers with enclosed pool, children's playground and a large beach volleyball area. A popular young adult beach.
Jericho, Locarno and Spanish Banks: This chain of beaches is over 3 km (2 miles) long and leads eventually to Wreck Beach. There are concessions and picnic sites and plenty of space but on hot days parking may be difficult.

In addition to the beaches there are several lakes. Near Commercial Drive in the Grandview district there is **Trout Lake**, with a sandy beach and picnic areas, ideal for families with small children. In Burnaby, near the Burnaby Village Museum and Burnaby Art Gallery is **Deer Lake**. This area is 5 km (3 miles) of wooded shore line and wilderness, a great place to take children for an afternoon outing or picnic. There is swimming, canoe, rowboat, pedal boat and sailboat rentals and a concession.

COUNTRYSIDE

ISLAND WALKABOUTS

If you want to see the beautiful scenery on some of the islands near Vancouver, **Hummingbird Nature Tours** has one-day walking tours with experienced guides, tel: 467-9219. To go on your own, check the BC Ferries schedules, tel: 685-1021.

TOUR PACKAGES

These tours are moderately priced and include trips to Victoria, as well as Howe Sound, Squamish, Whistler and the San Juan Islands. Some are bus tours, others include land/sea transportation such as the **Royal Hudson** Steam train from Squamish.
Gray Line Cruises & Tours, tel: 681-8687.
Landsea Tours, tel: 255-7272.
West Coast City and Nature Sightseeing Ltd, tel: 255-2444.
1st Tours (a division of Harbour Tours): tel: 688-7246.
Pacific Coach Lines: tel: 662-7575.
Canada West: tel: 279-2320. Tours arranged in French, Spanish, German, Italian, Portuguese and Chinese.
Alpine Adventure Tours: tel: 683-0209. Mountain tours.

ADVENTURE TOURS

These are more rugged tours or adventure experiences ranging from expensive to moderate. Some are not suited to children, seniors, or disabled persons. They are all out-of-town tours, including Vancouver Island.
Pacific Sunset Nature Tours: tel: 437-3150. Rugged tours around BC.
Rainforest Tours: Nanaimo BC, tel: 753-9453. Hikes in the wildwood forest.
Mountain Wilderness Tours: tel: 984-2441. Day hikes and climbs in wilderness areas.
Hummingbird Nature Tours: tel: 467-9219, fax: 467-9768. Hiking, backpacking, whale watching, walking. Natural history tours.
Kumsheen Raft Adventures: tel: 455-2296, fax: 455-2297.
Hyak Wilderness Adventures: tel: 734-8622, fax: 734-5718. White-water rafting on the Chilliwack and Thompson rivers.

Climax Snowmobile Ventures Ltd: tel: 596-TOUR or 936-SNOW.
Ryan's Rapid Rafting Inc: tel: 875-9745.
Whistler Snowmobile Guided Tours: tel: 932-4086.
Fantasy Hot Air Balloon Flights: tel: 736-1974.

BY TRAIN

VIA Rail Canada is the only rail line that crosses Canada or takes passengers out of BC. Some of the local destinations of VIA Rail are: Matsqui, Chilliwack, Hope, Boston Bar, Ashcroft, Kamloops, Clearwater, Blue River, Valemount, Prince Rupert, Terrace, Smithers, Prince George and some other waypoints. For fares and reservations, tel: (toll-free) 1-800 561-8630. The station is located at Main and Station streets in Vancouver. The trains go approximately three times a week.

For travel within BC on a more regular service, **BC Rail** has a daily service from North Vancouver to points north of Vancouver such as Squamish, Whistler, Pemberton, Lillooet and Prince George. There is service three days a week to Clinton, 100 Mile House, Quesnel, Williams Lake, Prince George and other waypoints. One of the best ways to see the scenic beauty of British Columbia is to take the train. You can make a day trip to Lillooet with a 2-hour stopover for lunch and sightseeing. The train leaves every day in summer at 7.30am for the 253-km (157-mile) journey northeast via Horseshoe Bay, Squamish and Whistler. The train arrives back in North Vancouver at 8.35pm. There is also a special sightseeing tour on the Royal Hudson steam train. (*See Boat Trips & Cruises.*) BC Rail: Tel: 984-5246.

On Vancouver Island, the **E & N (VIA Rail)** line serves Victoria, Duncan, Nanaimo, Qualicum Beach, Courtenay and other waypoints. Tel: (toll-free) 1-800 561-8630 for reservations and fares.

BY CAR

To travel north of Vancouver to Squamish, Whistler and Lillooet you take Highway 99 north. To travel along the Sunshine Coast you cross by ferry from Horseshoe Bay terminal to Gibsons and take Highway 101. The Coquihalla Highway (Highway 5) goes northeast to Kamloops on a scenic route. The Crowsnest Highway (Highway 3) takes you through the rugged mountain area of Manning Park. There are good tourism facilities on all these highways.

On Vancouver Island the main highway from Victoria to the cities and towns along the eastern coast is Highway 19. At Parksville, Highway 4 branches off leading to the west coast of the Island.

For information and assistance in planning tours of the scenic areas of the Lower Mainland, Vancouver Island and other parts of BC visit the **Tourism Association of Southwestern British Columbia**. They are located at 304-828 West 8th Avenue. Tel: 876-3088 or call (toll-free) 1-800 667-3306.

BY FERRY

There are two main ferry terminals serving the Gulf Islands and Vancouver Island traffic. One at Tsawwassen, 1-hour's drive south of downtown Vancouver. The other is at Horseshoe Bay, a 30-minute drive from downtown, north across the Upper Levels Highway.

Tsawwassen (meaning "towards the open sea") handles the traffic to the Swartz Bay terminal, which is a 30-minute drive from Victoria. The Gulf Islands ferries also leave from here and ferries to Nanaimo on Vancouver Island. The trip crossing from Tsawwassen to Swartz Bay is approximately 1 hour 35 minutes. The Gulf Islands trip is slightly less; the trip to Nanaimo is two hours.

From Vancouver bus terminal, Dunsmuir & Beatty (tel: 662-8074) buses run down to the Tsawwassen ferry at 15 minutes before the hour between 5.45am and 8.45pm. Tel: 681-1161 to make arrangements to meet the bus at one of the designated pick-up points. New catamarans operated by a Norwegian shipping company are expected to go into service shortly with four, round-trip sailings each day, each one-way journey taking 2½ hours. Tourism Victoria has instituted a 1-800 number (1-800 663-3883) through which visitors can inquire about or book accommodation from anywhere in North America.

The Horseshoe Bay ferry terminal handles traffic to Nanaimo, Bowen Island and Langdale on the mainland Sunshine Coast. This trip takes approximately 45 minutes. The trip to Nanaimo is 1 hour 35 minutes. For sailing times, tel: 685-1021 (24 hours) or turn to TV channel 4 before 9am for a continuous broadcast of ferry departure times.

There are usually hourly crossings from May–September sailing from each of the terminals from 7am–10pm. Ferry schedules are available from the Vancouver Travel InfoCentre at 1055 Dunsmuir Street or at most major hotels. *The Vancouver Sun* newspaper publishes ferry schedules on the first page of the classified section every day.

BC Ferries are among the best in the world. They are modern and comfortable, transporting 19 million people and 7.5 million vehicles annually. Five of them are the largest of their type in the world. They all have a restaurant, snack bar, newsstand and ship-to-shore telephones. No smoking is allowed on any vessels and pets must remain on the car deck. All the ferries are wheelchair accessible and have lifts for passengers who are unable to walk up the stairs.

Ferry traffic can be quite congested on holiday weekends so allow yourself plenty of time, and always double-check the schedule.

If you want to take the ferry trip from Vancouver to Victoria, you can travel all the way from the downtown bus terminal in Vancouver to the bus terminal in Victoria. Buses go every two hours during the day and the trip takes approximately three hours. Pacific Coach lines will pick up at designated stops along the way. Phone at least an hour before the bus leaves the terminal, tel: 662-8074. You don't need a reservation to ride this bus.

To go to Nanaimo by bus, call Maverick Coach lines, tel: 255-1171. These buses usually leave every two hours. Buses to the Sunshine Coast go three times daily via Horseshoe Bay. This is an excellent way to travel as the buses are the first to go on the ferry and you avoid long waits at the terminals. You get off the bus once it is on the ferry, then reboard before you reach the opposite terminal. Foot passengers can walk right on board the ferries. Public transit has bus service to both Tsawwassen and Horseshoe Bay. Tel: 261-5100.

If you have luggage the public transit will not be convenient. Foot passengers must purchase tickets 10 minutes before sailing time and can buy bus tickets on board the ferry for on-going trips from the terminals at Swartz Bay, Nanaimo or Langdale. Luggage can be checked at the ferry terminals but must be correctly tagged with your destination. You can carry on your bags, but there are no lockers on board.

For car/passenger reservations, tel: 669-1211. On holiday weekends the Tsawwassen parking lot is usually full so if you had planned to park and ride you must arrive in plenty of time. Drivers, be prepared to wait in long line-ups on holiday weekends.

For pre-recorded scheduled information on Mainland/Vancouver Island routes tel: 685-1021 (Vancouver); 656-0757 (Victoria); 753-6626 (Nanaimo).

The BC Ferries operates 38 ships on 25 routes along the coast of British Columbia. The ships carry cars, campers and RVs, trucks and buses.

There is a passenger catamaran service between Seattle and Victoria operating year-round. For information on the Victoria Clipper, tel: 382-8100 or (toll-free US and Canada) 1-800 888-2535.

Vancouver Island has ferry services to points on the west coast of the Island and also to ports in the United States.

BOAT TRIPS & CRUISES

These tours range from dinner cruises to river-boat rides and most are priced moderate to inexpensive. Many of these tours are ideal family outings, suitable for all ages.

A-Island Charters Ltd: tel: 688-6625. Sunset dinner cruise. Fishing and diving trips aboard luxury yachts.

River Tours: tel: 522-3506 or 279-8998. Departing daily from New Westminster and Bridgepoint. Trips up and down the Fraser River.

Pitt Lake Tours: tel: 522-3506, 272-9187 or 250-3485. Tours departing from New Westminster and Steveston daily.

S. S. Beaver Steamship Co.: tel: 682-7284. BC's most historic vessel. Inner-harbour and inlet cruises.

Bastion City Charters Ltd: tel: 753-2852, or

Tourism Nanaimo tel: 754-8474. Boat cruises to see sea-lions and bald eagles in the sheltered waters off Nanaimo. December–March.

Sunset Bay II: tel: 669-4604. Harbour and Salmon Barbecue cruises from the Westin Bayshore Hotel Marina.

Royal Hudson Boat Train: day trips from Vancouver to Squamish offer a choice of going by train and returning down Howe Sound by boat, making the excursion in the reverse order or going both ways by the same route. The fare is around $30 for adults. Train departs 10am daily, July and August, from BC Rail Station in North Vancouver; boat departs 9.30am daily, from Denmark Street. Other parts of the year the schedule runs Wednesday to Sunday. Optional tours from Squamish can be booked en route, like a bus trip to Shannon Falls or a Glacier Air Tour. Tel: 688-7246 for reservations.

Cruise Ship Centers: 1155 Robson Street. Tel: 684-6700. The popularity of cruises from Vancouver to Alaska has grown to such an extent that ships sometimes have to "tie-up" around the tide-swept Seymour Narrows, a congested channel near Campbell River. More than a score of cruise boats, carrying almost half a million passengers, make the north-bound trip each summer.

Cruises and bus/cruise trips to the west coast of Vancouver Island to view the **migration of whales** are available at seasonal times, usually February–April. Call Jamie's Whaling Station, tel: 715-3919 for schedules, or check with any tour agent in the Vancouver or Victoria area.

YACHT CHARTERS & BOAT RENTALS

Silver Blue Charters: tel: 689-1524 or 291-8505. Forty-one-foot luxury yacht located at Granville Island. Fishing and cruising.

Granville Island Boat Rentals Ltd: tel: 682-6287. Pleasure boats by day or hour.

Breakaway Charter Yacht Services: tel: 682-7234, fax: 682-3670. Luxury yachts, harbour tours, fishing charters.

Top Gun Yacht Charters: (Richmond) tel: 649-4473. Fish, dive or cruise. Complimentary video taping. Fishing guide and skipper.

Coal Harbour Boat Rentals: tel: 684-8811. Power-boats by day or hour rates.

NIGHTLIFE

There are several types of drinking establishments in Vancouver. If you want to enjoy live music, rock 'n' roll, blues, or country go to one of the larger beer parlours. The **Yale Hotel**, 1300 Granville Street and the **Lamplighter Lounge**, Dominion Hotel, Gastown, host nightly live shows and free Saturday and Sunday blues jams, starting at 3pm. Some smaller neighbourhood pubs also offer live music. Bistros and lounge bars often have small combos, jazz, blues or piano bars, or sing-along entertainment.

Vancouver has a wide selection of clubs and bars with a variety of entertainment from strip shows to dinner theatre. Check the local newspapers for current listings. Most night clubs have a cover charge and so do some pubs in the evening if there is special entertainment. The cover may vary according to the quality of entertainment. Some dine and dance restaurants require a minimum charge per person. Some clubs have a dress code; pubs are usually casual dress. Pub hours may vary but are usually 11am–2am, because of liquor laws no drinks can be sold after 1am. Discos are open Monday–Saturday until 2am; Sundays until midnight.

PUBS & CABARETS

George V Pub, Hotel Georgia. Tel: 682-5566.

Hollywood North Cabaret, 856 Seymour Street. Tel: 682-7722.

Crickets, Richmond Inn. Tel: 273-7878. Live country music Monday–Saturday.

Fairview Pub, Ramada Vancouver Centre. Tel: 872-1262. Local rock bands.

Jake O'Grady's, 3684 E. Hastings Street. Tel: 298-1434. Sunday night jam 7pm–midnight.

Big Bam Boo, 1236 W. Broadway. Tel: 733-2220. Live music, cover, dress code.

Club Soda, 1055 Homer. Tel: 681-8202.

Commodore Ballroom, 870 Granville Mall. Tel: 681-7838. Top music events.

Cruel Elephant, 1176 Granville Street. Tel: 688-8748. Alternative music and art.

86 Street Music Hall, 750 Pacific Boulevard. Tel: 683-8687. Top music entertainment.

Eclipse, 1369 Richards. Tel: 688-7806. After hours, Friday and Saturday 1am–5.30pm.

JAZZ CLUBS

Jazz Hotline for latest news on current events, tel: 682-0706.
Alma Street Café, 2605 Alma. Tel: 222-2244.
Basin Street, 23 W. Cordova, Gastown. Tel: 683-5351.
Café Bergman, 52 Powell Street, Gastown. Tel: 688-9668. Open stage, jazz, blues, poetry.
Café Django, 1184 Denman Street. Tel: 689-1184.
Glass Slipper, 185 E. 11th Avenue. Tel: 682-0706.
Hot Jazz Club, 2120 Main Street. Tel: 873-4131.
Cascades Lounge, Pan Pacific Hotel. Tel: 662-8111. New Orleans and classical jazz.

COMEDY CLUBS

Punchlines, 15 Water Street, Gastown. Tel: 684-3015. Amateur night Tuesday. Feature and improvisation Wednesday and Thursday. Feature acts Friday and Saturday. Show-times 9pm weekdays; 9 and 11pm Friday and Saturday.
Yuk Yuks, 750 Pacific Boulevard South. Tel: 687-5233. Shows 9pm; Friday–Saturday sometimes two shows nightly.

GAY CLUBS

Gandydancer, 1222 Hamilton Street. Tel: 684-7321. Men only Fridays.
Celebrities, 1022 Davie Street. Tel: 689-3180. Disco.
Girls Co., 1108 Hamilton Street. Tel: 684-1608. Women's bar 9pm–2am Saturdays.
Lotus Club, Heritage House Hotel. Tel: 685-7777. Country and western men and women Tuesday, Thursday and Saturday. Women's dance Fridays.
T T Country (TEESE), 339 W. Pender Street. Tel: 682-8096. Dance lessons.
Royal Hotel, Papa's Place, 1025 Granville Street. Tel: 685-5335. Live entertainment.

GAMBLING

There are several casinos in the Greater Vancouver area. These are usually located in major hotels. The proceeds of these casinos goes to local charities. Opening hours: 6pm–2am nightly.
The Great Canadian Casino, Holiday Inn, 2477 Heather Street. Tel: 872-5543.
Royal Diamond Casino, 1195 Richards Street. Tel: 685-2340.
Casino Victoria, 716 Courtenay Street, Victoria. Tel: 380-3998.
Great Canadian Casino, 91 Front Street, Nanaimo. Tel: 753-3033.
Royal Towers Casino, Royal Towers Hotel, New Westminster. Tel: 524-3777.

CULTURE PLUS

MUSEUMS

In addition to the major museums listed here, there are a number of interesting heritage sites located in the Greater Vancouver and Victoria areas. For further information on current exhibitions, admissions and times phone the museums or check the local newpapers' weekend editions.

VANCOUVER & COUNTRYSIDE

Vanier Park Museum Complex. Vanier Park is in Kitsilano at the end of the Burrard Street Bridge. It accommodates the **Vancouver Museum** which has exhibits depicting the city's history, a good selection of Pacific Northwest Indian artefacts and temporary exhibits. Open: daily, July–August 11am–9pm. Closed: Mondays and certain holidays. Tel: 736-7736.

The **Maritime Museum** is located behind the Vancouver Museum. It houses the historic *St Roch*, a two-masted ketch, the first ship to sail the Northwest Passage from west to east and the first ship to circumnavigate north America. It is a National Historic Site. Open: seven days a week 10am–5pm. Admission. Tel: 737-2211.

The **H. R. MacMillan Planetarium** is another part of the complex. Explore the universe each afternoon and evening. Open: daily in summer. Closed: Mondays in winter. The evening show is not recommended for children under eight years of age. Tel: 736-3656.

The small dome building beside the museum/planetarium complex is the **Gordon Southam Observatory**. You can gaze at the stars while an astronomer explains how the reflector telescope works. They also have a special "shoot the moon" programme for photographers. Open: every evening during summer; weekend evenings on clear nights in winter. Admission: free. Tel: 738-2855.

Behind the observatory is the **Vancouver City Archives** where you can see exhibits of Vancouver's history. Open: Monday–Friday 9.30am–5.30pm. Admission: free. Tel: 736-8561.
UBC Museum of Anthropology, located on the UBC campus. MOA is a spectacular, award-winning building overlooking English Bay. It contains excellent displays of artefacts of the Pacific Northwest Indians. The museum entrance was carved by

'Ksan master carvers. Special exhibits and public programmes. Guided walking tours, tel: 228-5087 for times. Closed: Monday. Admission: free on Tuesdays. Tel: 822-3825 for a recorded information message.

Canadian Craft Museum, Granville Island. Tel: 687-8266. Historic and contemporary costumes and jewellery.

Burnaby Village Museum is a restored heritage village depicting life at the turn of the century. It includes a miniature railway display. Restaurant and picnic facilities. At Christmas there are strolling carollers, hay-wagon rides and crafts. For hours, tel: 293-6501. You could make a day trip to this museum, include a nature walk around Deer Lake and dinner at the Hart House Restaurant or visit the Burnaby Art Gallery right across the street.

Hastings Sawmill Store Museum, located at Jericho Park. Tel: 228-1213. This museum houses a good collection of artefacts from early Vancouver. Admission: donation.

BC Transportation Museum, on #10 highway in Cloverdale. Tel: 574-4191. Has exhibits of 100 years of transportation history, including John Lennon's famous Rolls Royce. Open: daily mid-May to 1 September, 10am–5pm. Rest of the year closed Mondays.

Beatle Museum, located in the Collector's RPM Record Store, 456 Seymour Street. Tel: 685-8841. A collector's delight. Admission: free.

Vancouver Police Museum, located at Cordova and Main streets. A history of local crime and the Vancouver Police Department. Open: daily 11.30am–4.30pm. Admission: free.

Canadian Museum of Flight and Transportation, Surrey. Tel: 535-1115. Vintage aircraft.

Irving House Historic Centre, 302 Royal Avenue, New Westminster. Tel: 521-7656. A heritage house built by a pioneer riverboat captain in 1862, one of the oldest preserved homes in BC. Admission: donation.

Delta Museum and Archives, tel: 946-9322. A 1912 heritage building with exhibits of local history, agriculture and fishing. Admission: free.

Langley Centennial Museum and National Exhibition, Fort Langley. Tel: 888-3922. This is a fine little museum with an excellent heritage display of Coast Salish artefacts, crafts and furnishings. Open: daily in summer; winter Tuesday–Sunday. Admission: donation.

Fort Langley National Historic Park, tel: 888-4424. This is a Hudson's Bay Trading Post built in 1839. Original and reconstructed buildings with displays and demonstrations hosted by costumed staff. You can make a day trip to Fort Langley and go on walking tours around the town to see many interesting heritage homes and churches. Good restaurants in heritage buildings.

Museum of the Royal Westminster Regiment, 530 Queens Avenue, New Westminster. Tel: 526-5116 for hours. A collection of photos and memorabilia depicting the history of the oldest military unit in the Lower Mainland. Admission: donation.

S. S. Samson V Maritime Museum, tel: 521-1425. A floating museum on a retired paddlewheeler in New Westminster. Open: year round, weekends and holidays noon–5pm. Admission: donation.

Simon Fraser University Museum of Archaeology and Ethnology, on the campus of SFU, Burnaby. Tel: 291-3325. Artefacts from Pacific Northwest Coast Indian cultures. Admission: donation.

Surrey Museum and Archives, located in the Surrey Fairgrounds, Cloverdale. Native Indian basketry and pioneer displays. Open: year round, Tuesday–Friday 10am–4pm, Saturday and Sunday noon–4pm. Closed: Monday and holidays. Admission: donation.

Agassiz Harrison Museum, tel: 796-3545. Housed in the 1893 Agassiz CP Rail Station and displays historical items of local interest. Open: daily May–September.

BC Museum of Mining, located at Britannia Beach on Highway 99 north on the way to Whistler. Tel: 688-8735. Guided tours into the mountain with working displays, gold panning.

Kilby General Store Museum, in Harrison Mills, take Highway 7 from Vancouver. Tel: 796-9576. A BC historical site, an authentic old general store. Open: daily in summer; reduced hours in winter. Admission: donation.

If you are driving up the Fraser Canyon visit the **Yale Museum**, a BC historical site with some heritage buildings and displays of Indian artefacts. Tel: 863-2324.

VICTORIA

The Royal BC Museum, next to the Parliament Buildings, across from the bus depot and Empress Hotel. Tel: 387-3701. An outstanding museum with life-like displays of early life in BC. Travel to the bottom of the ocean, stroll through a coastal rain forest, or walk down a street of the 1920s. This museum collects, researches, preserves, stores and exhibits objects of human and natural history. A magnificent display of work by BC's native people. Open: daily.

Royal London Wax Museum, 470 Belleville Street. Tel: 388-4461. Has a collection of life-sized wax figures of royalty, rulers and rogues. Open: daily, hours vary.

Royal Roads Military College, Sooke Road. Tel: 380-4634. Gardens and grounds are open to the public. Open: daily.

Carr House, 207 Government Street. Tel: 387-4697. Birthplace of Emily Carr. Open: daily in summer 10am–5pm; reduced hours in winter.

Craigflower Farmhouse and Schoolhouse, at Admirals and Craigflower roads. Tel: 387-4697. Heritage buildings. Open: daily in summer.

Helmcken House, beside the Royal BC Museum. Tel:

387-4697. Heritage house. Open: daily in summer; reduced hours in winter.

Point Ellice House and Gardens, tel: 387-4697 for hours and admission. An Italianate Victorian residence from 1861. One of the most complete collections of Victoriana in its original setting in Western Canada.

Craigdarroch Castle, 1050 Joan Crescent. Tel: 592-5323. Built as an opulent residence for Robert Dunsmuir and his family. A fine collection of stained glass; period furnishings. Open: year round.

Fable Cottage Estate, 5187 Cordova Bay Road. Theme gardens, creative displays of outdoor animation. Guided tours. Gift shop and tea pavilion. Open: early March–late October daily from 9am.

Government House, 1401 Rockland Avenue. Tel: 387-2080. The official residence of the Lieutenant-Governor, the Queen's representative in BC. Walk in the gardens. Open: year round, dawn–dusk. Free.

Maritime Museum of British Columbia, 28 Bastion Square. Tel: 385-4222. This museum has one of the largest model ship collections in Canada. Open: year round. Closed: Christmas, New Year and Easter.

Miniature World, 649 Humboldt Street. Tel: 385-9731. Displays depicting historic scenes in miniature.

Olde England Inn and Anne Hathaway's Cottage, 429 Lampson Street. Tel: 388-4353. A trip into Olde England with authentic reproductions of Shakespeare's home and Anne Hathaway's cottage. The Inn has a notable collection of antiques. (*See Hotels, Victoria.*) Guided tours and tea parties.

Parliament Buildings, tel: 387-3046 for information. Designed by Rattenbury in 1897 commemorating Queen Victoria's Diamond Jubilee. Tours on weekdays except when house is sitting. Illuminated at night by 3,000 lights.

VANCOUVER ISLAND

BC Forest Museum, just north of Duncan on the Trans-Canada Highway. Tel: 748-9389. Open: daily May–September.

See the unique murals in the little town of **Chemainus**. Festival of Murals every July. Chemainus is on the Trans-Canada Highway between Nanaimo and Victoria. It is a historical lumber-shipping town.

The Native Heritage Centre, 200 Cowichan Way, Duncan. Tel: 746-8119. Has a Native American theatre, totem carving, canoe carving and other native arts and crafts.

THEATRE

The **Arts Hotline** (tel: 684-ARTS) provides information on music, dance, theatre, visual arts and museums. Phone Monday–Saturday 9am–5.30pm. Their office is at 884 Granville (in the Granville entrance of the Orpheum Theatre). This is also a Ticketmaster outlet where you can buy tickets for most major events. To reserve tickets, tel: 280-4444.

They take Mastercard, Visa or American Express.

The entertainment sections of both newpapers, *The Vancouver Magazine* and the *West Ender* community newspaper have all the listings for theatre events. Vancouver has a wide variety of theatre with quality productions. For theatre in natural settings **Bard on the Beach** at Vanier Park is held in a festival-sized tent and during the summer presents plays by Shakespeare. **Theatre Under the Stars** at Malkin Bowl, Stanley Park, presents popular musicals during July and August. Shows are nightly, weather permitting, except Sunday. Curtain time is 8.30pm. Dress warmly. Tel: 687-0174.

The most famous theatre in Vancouver is the **Orpheum**, home of the Vancouver Symphony Orchestra. This grand old theatre was built in 1927 at the height of vaudeville. It was later converted into a movie house and in the 1970s a campaign to "Save the Orpheum" ended with the city purchasing the building and renovating it. Tours of the building are conducted twice a week. Tel: 665-3050. The Orpheum is located on Granville Street near Smithe.

Here is a list of some of the theatres in Vancouver where you can attend small productions, musicals, theatre sports, improvisational theatre, dance events and concerts:

Arts Club Theatre, Granville Island. Tel: 687-1644.

Back Alley Theatre, 751 Thurlow Street. Tel: 688-7013.

Firehall Arts Centre, 280 E. Cordova Street. Tel: 689-0926.

Presentation House, 333 Chesterfield Street, North Vancouver. Tel: 986-1351.

Queen Elizabeth Theatre and Playhouse, Georgia and Hamilton Street. Tel: 665-3050.

Vancouver East Cultural Centre, 1895 Venables Street. Tel: 254-9578.

Waterfront Theatre, Granville Island. Tel: 685-6217.

The Fringe Festival, which consists of theatre and performance art at venues throughout the city, is held in September each year. Tel: 873-3646 for information.

DANCE

The Dance Centre is a non-profit organisation that provides information on dance activities in Vancouver. Tel: 872-0432. The Thursday *Vancouver Sun* and the Friday *Province* as well as the *West Ender* and *Vancouver Magazine* also provide listings.

Ballet British Columbia stages performances at the Queen Elizabeth Theatre and throughout Canada. The repertoire ranges from classical to contemporary. Tel: 669-5954 for information about the Company.

The Anna Wyman Dance Theatre, tel: 662-8846, is the best known of Vancouver's dance companies. Their popular performances are colourful and energetic. This was the first modern dance company to perform in China.

EDAM, is an Experimental Dance and Music collective. They also teach dance and composition, tour nationally and perform for children. Tel: 876-9559.

The **Karen Jamieson Dance Company**, tel: 872-5658, features Canadian composers, designers and artists.

MUSIC

There are a number of music societies, choirs and instrumental groups in Vancouver. The **Festival Concert Society** presents Coffee Concerts every Sunday morning from September to June at the Queen Elizabeth Playhouse. This is an inexpensive way to spend your Sunday morning, before you go for brunch. Concerts start at 11am. Tel: 736-3737. The **Vancouver Symphony Orchestra** performs at the Orpheum and in summer the VSO performs free outdoor concerts. Tel: 684-9100.

The **Vancouver New Music Society** has seven concerts annually promoting 12th-century music. Concerts are held at the Vancouver East Cultural Centre. Tel: 874-6200 for information.

Early Music Vancouver promotes medieval, Renaissance and baroque music using authentic instruments. Tel: 732-1610 for information.

The summer **Chamber Music Festival** is held at St George's School, presented by the **Vancouver Recital Society**. They also have performances by international performers at The Playhouse. Tel: 736-6034 for information.

MOVIES

Two blocks of Granville Street from Robson to Nelson are known as Theatre Row. All the downtown movie theatres except Cineplex are along this area. Cineplex, a complex of 10 small theatres, is located in the Royal Centre, lower level, Georgia and Burrard streets. If you like first-run contemporary films, art films or foreign films, **The Ridge** at 3131 Arbutus Street (tel: 738-6311) and the **Park Theatre**, 3440 Cambie (tel: 876-2747) have special rates Tuesdays and discounts for seniors, disabled and children. For reruns and double bills at bargain prices, go to the **Hollywood**, 3123 W. Broadway (tel: 738-3211) and the **Starlight Cinema**, 935 Denman Street (tel: 689-0096). See the newspapers for films and times.

If you enjoy art and experimental films, **Pacific Cinematheque**, 1131 Howe (tel: 688-FILM) is a non-profit society with an annual membership which is still a bargain to visitors because of the low price and excellent quality of the films shown. The IMAX Theatre at Canada Place has a giant screen and 3D adventure movies. For information, tel: 682-4629. At Science World, the OMNIMAX Theatre has the world's largest dome screen and wrap-around sound.

Tickets include Science World admission. Tel: 875-6664. There are several theatres in Vancouver that show Chinese or East Indian films. The **Golden Princess** is a new Chinese theatre at Broadway and Commercial Drive. It's popular enough to always have queues.

The **Vancouver International Film Festival** is held September–October. Tel: 685-0260 for further information.

SHOPPING

Prices can be high in Vancouver especially because of the General Services Tax and the added provincial Sales Tax. Some shops will include the GST in their retail price but if they don't, visitors from outside Canada can apply for a rebate. You can get forms from any Tourist InfoCentre. The **Army and Navy** department store on Hastings near Abbott Street is the place to shop if you are on a budget. It sells everything from camping equipment to clothing at very low prices.

SHOPPING MALLS

A number of excellent shopping malls in Vancouver sell good-quality, general merchandise. Some of these are new, modern complexes where you can browse for most of the day, stop for lunch or dinner and even stay for a movie in the evening. All of them are accessible by public transit.

Royal Centre Mall, 1055 West Georgia at Burrard Street. Open: Monday–Thursday 9.30am–5pm, Friday 9.30am–7pm, Saturday 9.30am–5.30pm. This mall includes theatres, the Royal Bank Foreign Exchange and 10 Cineplex Odeon cinemas which are open weekdays, weekends and holidays. Walking distance from the Cruise Ship terminal at Canada Place.

Pacific Centre, located right in the centre of the city with entrances off Dunsmuir, Howe and Robson Streets. There are almost 200 stores set underground with a three-storey waterfall and glass skylights. Open seven days a week.

Sinclair Centre, located at 757 W. Hastings Street near Canada Place and the Waterfront SeaBus terminal. Heritage buildings transformed into a beautiful mall with boutiques and restaurants. There are some government offices, Immigration and Canada Manpower and the Passport Office are also located in this complex, as well as a post office.

Metrotown, BC's largest shopping complex, is located in Burnaby on Kingsway between Willingdon and Nelson streets. You can get there by taking the SkyTrain to Metrotown Station. There are over 380 shops and services including Eaton's, Sears, Woodwards and The Bay department stores. It is composed of Metrotown Centre, Eaton Centre, Station Square and includes Holiday Inn Hotel. At Station Square there are 12 Cineplex Odeon and Famous Players theatres, a games arcade, recording studio and many restaurants. There is an underground car-park and some street parking lots. It's a 15-minute SkyTrain ride from downtown Vancouver.

Store hours: Monday, Tuesday, Saturday 9.30am–5.30pm; Wednesday, Thursday, Friday 9.30am–9pm; Sunday noon–5pm.

PUBLIC MARKETS

False Creek used to be a smoke-belching industrial area. **Granville Island** was dredged out of the mud flats, and until 1973 consisted of only factories and industries. Then the federal government decided to renovate the old buildings and turned the area into this very successful public market, one of the most popular places in town to shop and browse. To find your way around the market area you can obtain maps and brochures from the **Granville Island Information Centre**, tel: 666-5784. The market is open 9am to 6pm every day in the summer, closed Mondays in winter. There are boat marinas and rentals, a houseboat community; a waterpark and playground areas; a hotel, theatres, restaurants, a brewery, the **Emily Carr College of Art and Design** and several excellent galleries. To get there

By Bus: take a #51 Granville Island bus at Broadway and Granville (till 6.30pm).

By Car: There's lots of traffic on the weekends with limited parking. It's best to park outside the island area and walk in.

By Boat: **Granville Island Ferries** run from Thurlow Street behind the Vancouver Aquatic Centre to Granville Island daily 7.30 am–10pm in the summer and to 8pm in the winter.

Take the SeaBus across to North Vancouver to **Lonsdale Quay**, a scenically beautiful shopping area. It's open every day including holidays. You can buy seafood right off the boat, fresh flowers and produce, gourmet selections and crafts. There's lots to see and do in the plaza and there's also a spectacular view of the Vancouver Harbour. To get there, take the SeaBus from the Waterfront Station or drive across the Lions Gate or Second Narrows Bridge along Marine Drive to Lonsdale and south to Esplanade.

Robson Public Market is a small area located on Robson Street at Cardero in the West End. Its specialty shops are noted for food and general merchandise. It's a good place to buy snacks and requisites for a picnic in the park. Close to English Bay and Stanley Park. Take the SkyTrain to New Westminster station just across the road by the Fraser River for **New Westminster Public Market**, where you'll find fresh produce, general merchandise, and excellent seafood restaurants.

SPORTS

SPECTATOR

The **Vancouver Canucks** are not always a winning team, but they have enthusiastic supporters. They play in the National Hockey League. For information on the Canucks, tel: 254-5141.

The **BC Lions** football team play all their games at the BC Place Stadium. Their season is from June to late October. For information, tel: 681-5466.

If you enjoy baseball, the **Vancouver Canadians**, of the Pacific Coast League, play at the Nat Bailey Stadium from April to September on Sunday afternoons and weekday evenings. Tel: 872-5232 for information or check the newspapers.

Tickets for professional football, hockey and other sports events can be purchased from any Ticketmaster outlet. There are branches at major department stores and information booths in the malls, or tel: 280-4444. They accept phone reservations and credit cards.

PARTICIPANT

GOLF

This is one of the most popular year-round sports in Vancouver. Every year the BC Open is held in June. The BC Golf Association can supply information, tel: 294-1818. There are several golf courses close to the city centre, and about 20 public courses in the metropolitan area. Some of the private clubs accept guests if you accompany a member and if you are a member of another *bona fide* club. Bring your membership card and/or a letter from your club pro and phone for confirmation.

These are some of the popular courses:

Fraserview Golf Course, 61st and Wales. Tel: 327-3717. Par 71, 6,165 yards.

University Golf Club, University Boulevard. Tel: 224-1818. Par 72, 6,147 yards.

McCleery Golf Course, 7170 MacDonald. Tel: 261-4522. Par 72, 6,168 yards.

Langara Golf Course, 290 W. 49th. Tel: 327-4423. Par 71, 6,103 yards.

BICYCLING

Vancouver has few actual bike paths, but there are interesting routes to cycle along around False Creek and the beach areas. It is illegal to cycle on the sidewalks and police will ticket cyclists for traffic violations. Helmets are not mandatory but suggested as a safety precaution, especially when riding in the city. Bicycles are allowed on the SeaBus on Saturdays, Sundays and holidays. They are not allowed on the buses or SkyTrain. From June–September there is a shuttle service for bikes through the George Massey Tunnel on Highway 99. Tel: 271-0337 for information on times.

The **Vancouver Bicycle Club** meets Sunday mornings at 10am at Broadway and Granville for a half-day trip around the city. Beginners are welcome as well as serious cyclists, but no children. The **Bicycling Association of BC** has an information hotline listing current and upcoming bicycling events. Tel: 731-7433.

The main cycling event of the year is the **Gastown Grand Prix** held in July. The race starts in the morning with all categories and makes a 900-metre (1,000-yard) circuit around the city streets for a total of 60 km (37 miles) equalling 65 laps.

BOATING

The **Royal Vancouver Yacht Club** has docks located at Coal Harbour in Stanley Park, tel: 688-4578 and at Jericho, tel: 224-1033. The Clubhouse is located at 3811 Point Grey Road, tel: 224-1344.

If you are an experienced sailor you can rent sailboats for part-days or longer. Sails are prohibited in False Creek and the maximum speed is 5 knots. Charters can be arranged with or without a skipper. There are also sailing schools offering cruise-and-learn vacations. Contact **Westcoast School of Seamanship**, 1618 Duranleau, Granville Island, tel: 684-9440.

(*For a list of boat rentals see Things to Do.*)

SEA KAYAKING

The West Coast is one of the most fascinating maritime areas in the world and sea kayaking has become a popular sport for exploring the coastal areas. **Ecomarine Ocean Kayak Centre**, tel: 689-7575, rents kayaks and provides instruction.

DIVING

Most diving around Vancouver is done in Howe Sound and Indian Arm. To dive in the outer harbour, permission is necessary. Contact the Vancouver Port Corporation, tel: 666-2405. The most popular diving areas for scuba and snorkelling are Whytecliff Park, Lighthouse Park, Porteau Cove, Tuwanek Point, Cates Park, Howe Sound and the Gulf Islands. Wet suits are needed in BC waters, especially off the west coast of Vancouver Island. There are several stores in Vancouver that will rent diving equipment:

Diver's World, 1523 W. 3rd Avenue. Tel: 732-1344.
Diving Locker, 2745 W. 4th Avenue. Tel: 736-2681.
Adrenalin Sports, 1512 Duranleau, Granville Island. Tel: 682-2881.

WINDSURFING

There are windsurfing schools at several beaches in Vancouver. They supply boards, wet suits and life jackets as well as instructions. The rental-instruction packages are from one to six hours. There are windsurfing schools at English Bay and Jericho Beaches. **Windmaster**, English Bay Beach House, tel: 685-7245; and **Windsure Windsurfing School**, 1300 Discovery, tel: 224-0615.

TENNIS

The tennis season is from March–October but sometimes you can even play during the winter. There are 180 public courts, some of them outdoors and free. You'll find courts at: Stanley Park, Queen Elizabeth Park, Kitsilano Beach Park, Jericho Beach Park and at most community centres around the city. The only night-lit public courts are on the Langara College Campus, on 49th Avenue, between Cambie and Maia. Indoor courts at UB, tel: 228-2505; and the Delta Airport Inn, tel: 276-1140. **Goro's Sports Shop**, located at 1678 Robson Street, near Stanley Park, rents racquets by the day, tel: 682-7640.

SKIING

BC's Coastal Range provides year-round skiing. There is snow on the mountains of the North Shore from November–March and summer skiing at Whistler and Mount Baker, Washington. Closest skiing areas to Vancouver, only a ½-hour drive from downtown, are at **Grouse**, **Seymour** and **Cypress mountains**. World-class skiing in the **Whistler-Blackcomb** area is about a 2-hour drive. **Mount Baker** is 120km (75 miles) south of Vancouver.

For information on local skiing, tel: 922-0176. For Whistler snow and ski reports, tel: 687-7507 or Whistler 1-932-4211; Mount Baker, tel: 688-1595.

There is cross-country skiing from December–March at **Cypress**. Hollyburn Lodge has food service. It's usually busy on weekends. There are cross-country ski trails at Whistler in the Lost Lake and Cheakamus Lake areas. The best cross-country skiing is at **Manning Park**, a 3-hour drive from Vancouver.

HORSEBACK RIDING

Vancouver has several riding stables where you can hire horses by the hour or all day. Most of the stables are outside the city, but the **Southlands Riding Club**,

7025 Macdonald, has indoor and outdoor riding areas. They don't rent horses but you can call them about equestrian events. Tel: 263-4817.

Stables outside the city area include:

Alpine Riding Academy, near Buntzen Lake. Tel: 469-1111. Trail rides. Reservations.

Tall Mountain Riding Stables, 1301 Lilloett, North Van. Tel: 980-0299. Rides in Mount Seymour Park. Lunch provided. Overnight trips. Ponies for kids.

FISHING

There are several places in the Vancouver area where you can fish, in addition to the numerous lakes and streams in the Greater Vancouver area where you can spend the day or go on an overnight fishing/ camping trip. You can either rent a small power boat, go on a Charter, or fish from one of the wharves, piers or sea-wall areas where you can catch rock cod, ling cod, sole, flounder, red snapper, halibut and perch. In some areas you can catch crab.

Call the Department of Fisheries 24-hour toll-free info line, tel: 1-800 663-9333; or in Vancouver tel: 666-2268 for recorded information on where and when to fish, restrictions, bait and other information. You can buy tackle and obtain licences at the **Army and Navy**, 27 W. Hastings Street; **West Coast Fishing Tackle**, 2147 E Hastings Street; **Hunter's Sporting Goods**, 2140 Kingsway; or the **Three Vets**, 2200 Yukon.

FURTHER READING

HISTORY

Barkerville Days, by Fred W. Luddith. Mitchell Press, 1969.

Beyond the Island: An Illustrated History of Victoria, by Peter A. Baskerville. Windsor Publications, 1986.

British Columbia: A Centennial Anthology, ed. by Reginald Eyre Watts. McClelland & Stewart, 1958.

British Columbia, a History, by Margaret Ormsby. Macmillan, 1958.

British Columbia's Logging History, by Ed Gould. Hancock House Publishers, 1975.

Canada, the Story of British Columbia, by the Rev. F. A. Peake. McGraw Hill Co. of Canada, 1966.

Distant Neighbors: A Comparative History of Seattle and Vancouver, by Norbert MacDonald. University of Nebraska Press, 1987.

Early Vancouver, seven vols. self-published by Major J. S. Matthews, 1933–59.

Heritage Vancouver, by Richard Edward Allen. Josten's Publications, Winnipeg, 1983.

Island in the Creek: The Granville Island Story. Harbour Publications, 1988.

The Journals of George M. Dawson: British Columbia, 1875–78, ed. by Douglas Cole & Bradley Lockner. University of BC Press, 1989.

Malaspina and Galiano, Spanish Voyages on the Northwest Coast, by Donald C. Cutter. Douglas & McIntyre, 1991.

The New El Dorado or British Columbia, by Kinahan Cornwallis. Thomas Cautley, London, 1858.

The Pacific Coast Scenic Tour, by Henry T. Finck. Charles Scribners & Sons, 1907.

The Pacific Northwest: Its discovery and early exploration by sea, land and river, by Edward W. Neiffield. Hancock House Publishing, 1990.

Understanding Vancouver. City Planning Dept., 1970.

GENERAL

Banners and Bands: A Guide to the Festivals of the Pacific Northwest, by Eileen Marrett. Upper Case Publishing, 1991.

British Columbia: Visions of the Promised Land, by Brand Lee White. Flight Press, 1986.

Guide to Western Canada, by Frederick Pratson. Globe Pequot Press, 1987.

Guidebook to Ethnic Vancouver, by Ann Petrie. Hancock House, 1982.

Insight Guide: Canada. Apa Publications, 1991.

Raincoast Chronicles, by Edward Howard White. Harbour Publications, 1983.

Sunshine and Salt Air. Harbour Publications, 1987.

The National Dream, by Pierre Berton. McClelland Stewart.

Vancouver, ed. by Chuck Davis & Shirley Mooney. Vancouver Board of Trade, 1986.

Vancouver: Sights & Insights, by Donald Stainsby, drawings by George Kuthan. Macmillan of Canada, 1962.

Vancouver, by Eric Nicol. Doubleday, 1978.

The Vancouver Trivia Book, by Craig O. Henderson. Polestar Press, 1985.

PEOPLE

The Canadians, by Andrew H. Malcolm. Times Books, 1985.

Hundreds and Thousands: The Journals of Emily Carr. Clarke, Irvin & Co., 1966.

Saltwater City, An Illustrated History of the Chinese in Vancouver, by Paul Yee. Douglas & McIntyre, 1988.

THE OUTDOOR LIFE

Bicycling Greater Vancouver and the Gulf Islands, by Maggie Burtinshaw and Mary Ellen Bradshaw. Gordon Soules Publishing, 1990.

Easy Hiking Around Vancouver, by Jean Cousins and Heather Robinson. Douglas & McIntyre, 1990.

Horse Trail Guide, Southwest BC. H. T. Publications, Cloverdale, 1990.

109 Walks in British Columbia's Lower Mainland, by Mary and David Macaree. Douglas & McIntyre, 1990

Salmon Fishing British Columbia, by Mike Cramond. Heritage House, 1990.

West Coast River Angling, by Eric Carlisle. Hancock House, 1990.

SPECIAL INFORMATION

GAY

For entertainment in Vancouver see the gay clubs listed under *Nightlife*. For further information contact: The **Gay and Lesbian Centre**, Bute Street, tel: 684-6869. For information on events, tel: 684-0444. This organisation promotes events for lesbians and gay men including the annual Stonewall Festival commemorating police persecution of gays in Greenwich Village, NY. There are also several theatre groups, choirs and sports events for gay people. Annually in August there is the Gay and Lesbian Pride Festival at Sunset Beach.

DISABLED

New building codes in Canada are addressing the needs of people with disabilities, providing accessible parking, entrances, interiors and washrooms of public buildings. The BC Transit is attempting to make the bus system in Vancouver fully accessible to people with disabilities. There are some transit buses in Vancouver and Victoria that are equipped with lifts for wheelchairs and all vehicles have reserved seating for the disabled and elderly. The SkyTrain and SeaBus services, except for the Granville Street station, are fully accessible and there is a HandyDart bus service available for seniors and disabled persons. Call HandyDart at least 48 hours ahead to book door-to-door service, tel: 430-2692. For information on bus routes that provide wheelchair-access coaches, tel: 265-5000.

For a complete guide to Vancouver for people with disabilities, the **BC Coalition of People with Disabilities** has produced an excellent book. *Accessible Vancouver* can be obtained from their office at 204-456 W. Broadway, Vancouver V5Y 1R3. Tel:

875-0188; fax: 875-9227. Some other service agencies for persons with disabilities are:

Message Relay Centre for the Deaf, tel: 681-2913 or (toll-free) 1-800 972-6503. Persons who use a Telecommunication Device for the Deaf (TDD) are requested to telephone 681-1932 or (toll-free) 1-800 972-6509.

Western Institute for the Deaf and Hard of Hearing, tel: 736-2527.

Telecom Centre for Special Needs (Disabilities), tel: 430-6378 or (toll-free) 1-800 242-8643.

Canadian National Institute for the Blind, tel: 321-2311.

BC Paraplegic Association, tel: 324-3611.

USEFUL ADDRESSES

INFORMATION CENTRES

Travel information centres will book accommodation, make tour reservations, advise you with your tour plans, make car rentals and restaurant reservations for you. You can get maps, brochures, BC Transit tickets and schedules from the InfoCentres. Summer hours: 8am–6pm May–September seven days a week; Winter hours: Monday–Saturday 9am–5pm. There are also tourist information booths on the main floors of Eaton's and The Bay department stores in Vancouver.

Vancouver Travel InfoCentre, 1055 Dunsmuir Street. Tel: 683-2000.

White Rock Travel InfoCentre, 1554 Foster. Tel: 536-6844.

Richmond Travel InfoCentre, Highway 99 at the George Massey Tunnel. Tel: 271-5323.

North Vancouver Travel InfoCentre, 131 E. 2nd Street. Tel: 987-448.8

New Westminster Travel InfoCentre, New Westminster Quay Public Market, 810 Front Street. Tel: 526-1905.

Tsawwassen InfoCentre, Ferry Terminal Causeway. Tel: 943-3388. (Seasonal openings.)

Delta InfoCentre, Highway 10 at Highway 99. Tel: 590-3666. (Seasonal openings.)

Tourism Victoria, 6th Floor, 612 View Street, Victoria BC. Tel: 382-2160.

Travel InfoCentres are operated by the provincial government. There are 140 of them throughout the province of BC.

CONSULATES

There are 40 consulates in Vancouver, but no embassies. If you need to contact your country's consulate, the *Yellow Pages* directory lists consulate and foreign representatives. Here are a few:

Australia, tel: 684-2191.
Britain, tel: 683-4421.
France, tel: 681-2301.
Germany, tel: 684-8377.
Greece, tel: 681-1381.
Hong Kong, Hong Kong Trade and Development Council, tel: 685-0883.
India, tel: 662-3894.
Italy, tel: 684-7288.
Japan, tel: 684-5868.
Philippines, tel: 685-7645.
Singapore, Singapore Trade Development Board, tel: 662-7055.
United States, tel: 685-4311.

ART/PHOTO CREDITS

INDEX